"With searing honesty, Donna Keel Armer sweeps us along on a sun-kissed, soul-stretching journey of discovery. Her lyrical descriptions, as vibrant as postcards, capture the beauty and spirit of the ancient village in Salento that healed her heart. A life-affirming vicarious voyage that captures the magic of Italy and the joys of coming into one's true self."

— **DIANNE HALES,** author *La Bella Lingua, Mona Lisa: A Life Discovered, La Passione: How Italy Seduced the World,* Knight of the Order of the Star of Italian Solidarity

"A captivating joy for armchair travelers and a balm for wounded souls, Donna Keel Armer's empowering memoir transports us into the wonders of southern Italy on a pilgrimage of healing and self-discovery. Armer writes with the spirit of a born storyteller, inviting readers to linger in her language and champion her voyage inward. Robust with artfully presented metaphors, intoxicating in sensual details of adventures abroad, and courageously forthright in chronicling the reclamation of a sense of self from the fragments of a damaged life, *Solo in Salento* is a heartfelt and venturesome triumph."

— **JONATHAN HAUPT,** co-editor of *Our Prince of Scribes: Writers Remember Pat Conroy*

"A sassy and sacred memoir for those sorting out what's most valuable in life."
— **CASSANDRA KING CONROY,** author of *TELL ME A STORY: My life with Pat Conroy*

"Donna Keel Armer's gorgeous memoir is an invitation to explore Italy with an artist's eye, a sommelier's palate, and a mystic's heart. Her story—reflective and riotous, intimate and illuminating—bares a bold and vulnerable personal journey of loss, discovery, and epiphany. Don't miss this book!"

— **REBECCA BRUFF,** author of *Trouble the Water*

"*Solo in Salento* is a mosaic—a rich tour of Italy, an art history lesson, a culinary adventure, a primer on trash, a tale of self-discovery, a love story, and so much more. Donna Keel Armer assembles the pieces with the flair of an artist and the care of an artisan. This book is for anyone who has ever felt the pull of wanderlust or the desire for some time alone."

—**TIFFANY QUAY TYSON**, author of *Three Rivers* and *The Past is Never*, winner of the 2018 Willie Morris Prize for Southern Fiction

"Donna Keel Armer . . . traveled to Otranto, Italy, to find beauty in a broken world, and to rediscover value in the fragmented pieces of her life. The lessons she learned . . . enhanced her own personal healing from abuse and rejection. Even the village's rituals surrounding the organization and removal of trash mirrored her own process of sorting the obligations, schedules, and social engagements that littered her life. Part personal memoir and part travelogue, *Solo in Salento* is the story of one woman's journey of magic, mystery, and music on the way to finding her heart place. A work of colorful literary prose, this is a book for everyone looking for strength, courage, and joy in their life."

—**SUSAN CUSHMAN**, author of *Friends of the Library* and *Cherry Bomb*, and editor of *Southern Writers on Writing* and *A Second Blooming: Becoming the Women We Are Meant to Be*

"This book is so much more than a book about travel. It's a touching memoir of self-discovery and renewal. The stunning prose will transport you to the Puglia region of Italy, where you'll see masterful mosaics and taste Italian delicacies, and be moved by Donna's personal journey."

—**CELE SELDON**, travel journalist, Seldon Ink

"Armer sets off on her solo journey to rediscover the self she has forgotten, to step into her power, to heal, and we eagerly read on to discover what she learns about her life so that we, in turn, can learn about ourselves."

—**JOAN DEMPSEY**, author of *This Is How It Begins*

"In the words of Donna Keel Armer, 'Enchantment comes to those who open their hearts, minds and souls to its possibilities.' *Solo in Salento* is an enchanting story of her time in a small village in Italy. In inviting us to share a journey to rediscover herself, Donna opens up with vulnerability, honesty, and, yes, enchantment. She is so masterful with descriptions, we walk alongside her, seeing the village, tasting the food, dancing with new friends. This is not a book to race through. It's a book to savor, to linger over each dinner, to enjoy outings and new people, to struggle with language, to feel the cramping of hands creating mosaics, and to take in the gems of insight she weaves seamlessly through the story. You will feel you've been to Salento and met a new friend."

—**DONNA BEARDEN**, Author of *Finding More Me: Journaling to Go Soul Deep*

"*Solo in Salento* is a journey of self-discovery amid the white-washed town of Otranto. There's sumptuous seafood, delicious wine and local hospitality like no other! *Solo in Salento* will woo you completely and make you dream of visiting the boot of Italy . . . to experience it all yourself."

—**ISHITA SOOD**, India's only blogger on Italy, *Italophilia* www.ishitasood.com

"Donna gives each reader permission to follow her playful lead . . . diving into their own hearts, cleaning off who they aren't, and snuggling up, ever so gracefully, to who they really are."

—**SALLY VEILLETTE**, author of *Coming to Your Senses: Soaring With Your Soul* and *Sicilian Roots*

"As both an avid reader and a worldwide traveler, I enjoyed *Solo in Salento* immensely. Donna brought to life the magic of this lesser-known region of Italy, and I could relive my past visits through her eyes. It was also a story of a women coming to terms with her life and the meaningful relationships she found along the way. I highly recommend it to anyone looking to immerse themselves in a beautiful story about love and friendship."

—**PANDA RICHIE**, owner, Windows of the World Travel LLC

Solo in Salento

by Donna Keel Armer

Published by

 köehlerbooks™

3705 Shore Drive
Virginia Beach, VA 23455
800-435-4811
www.koehlerbooks.com

Solo in Salento

a memoir

Donna Keel Armer

VIRGINIA BEACH
CAPE CHARLES

To Ray, *l'uomo del mio cuore*

Table of Contents

Prologue: Once Upon a Time—*C'era Una Volta* 1

I—INCEPTION

1. The Lie—*La Bugia* 9
2. The Book—*Il Libro* 15
3. Fragmented Faith—*Fede Frammentata* 18
4. First Steps—*Primi Passi* 23

II—MOSAICS

5. Arrival—*Arrivo* 33
6. Paul and the Cathedral—*Paolo e La Cattedrale* 39
7. The Apartment—*L'appartamento* 49
8. I Am Strong—*Io Sono Forte* 58
9. Mosaic Magic—*La Magia dei Mosaici* 65
10. Emerging Patterns—*Modelli Emergenti* 77
11. Accidental Americans—*Gli Americani Accidentali* 84
12. Mosaics and Storms—*Mosaici e Tempeste* 88
13. Passing Through Life—*Passando Attraverso La Vita* 95
14. Strangers in the Night—*Stranieri Nella Notte* 101
15. More Than Spiders in My Hair—
    Più di Ragni nei Miei Capelli 106

16. The Song of Songs—*Il Cantico dei Cantici* 114
17. Tourist Information Italian Style—
    Informazioni Turistiche Stile Italiano 121
18. My Sunshine—*O Sole Mio* 126
19. Mosaic Lessons—*Le Lezioni di Mosaici* 136

III—TRASH

20. The Importance of Trash—
    L'importanza della Spazzatura 145
21. Night Music—*La Musica della Notte* 154
22. More Trash—*Più Spazzatura* 161
23. Flip-Flops—*Infradito* 166
24. Welcome to the Table—*Benventi al Tavola* 174
25. Fredrika 181
26. Did They Ever Return?—*Sono Mai Tornati?* 189
27. The Salento Sun—*Il Sole del Salento* 199
28. The Last Train to Otranto—
    L'ultimo Treno per Otranto 203
29. Give Me the Simple Life—*Dammi La Vita Semplice* . . 212
30. It's Greek to Me—*Per Me È Greco* 221
31. Pants Down—*Pantaloni Giù* 226
32. Food, the Bread of Life—*Cibo, Il Pane della Vita* 232
33. Sicilians, Beware—*I Siciliani Guardano* 240
34. Refocus—*Rifocalizzare* 244

IV—JOY

35. Madonna of the High Sea—*Madonna Dell'Altomare* . . 251
36. Gifts—*I Regali* 255
37. The Hill of the Martyrs—*La Collina dei Martiri* 259
38. The Chef—*Il Cuoco* 263
39. Misguided Rain Tour—*Tour della Pioggia Fuorviato* . . . 271

40. All Souls and All Saints—

  Tutte Le Anime e Tutti I Santi. 276

41. I Hope You Dance—*Spero Che Balli* 280

42. Transportation—*Trasporti* 287

43. Broken Beauty—*Bellezza Spezzata* 291

44. The Sorrow of Parting—

  Il Dolore della Separazione 297

45. The Last Supper—*L'ultima Cena*. 301

V—REENTRY

46. Leaving—*In Partenza* 311

47. Traveling—*In Viaggio* 316

48. This Isn't the Ritz—*Questo Non È Il Ritz* 324

49. Going Home—*Andare a Casa* .329

50. Home—*A Casa* 333

EPILOGUE 335

ACKNOWLEDGEMENTS. 342

AUTHOR'S NOTES 346

RECOMMENDED READING. 347

Once Upon A Time

C'era Una Volta

C'ERA UNA VOLTA—Once upon a time, a girl raised by protective, turn-of-the-twentieth-century parents came into the world. I was the fourth and final daughter born into this family. My three siblings and I were loved, totally and completely. We were sheltered from most outside influences. Our environment was safe, calm, religious, and full of rules tempered with love.

Mother raised us to be respectful and obedient ladies suitable for marriage. According to her upbringing, she was to provide us with skills to create a loving home for our husbands and children. We each absorbed our upbringing differently.

My sexual education was repressive, filled with what young ladies were not allowed to do. Along with the "thou shalt nots," Mother's rules provided me with a list of sins that I wouldn't have time to commit in a lifetime—even if I tried. Many centered around sexual activity. It was drummed into my head that no boy or man shall lay hands on any part of me until the *I do*'s had been vowed.

Consequences for not following the rules were dire. There would be condemnation to an afterlife in hell where the devil would continuously prick me with his fork. I would be shamed and found wanting. Guilt was the mainstay of my growing up. If a boy grabbed my hand or stole a kiss, I froze, knowing I had just slid further down the ladder to fire and brimstone.

I never thought to ask my older sisters or friends for their perspective on these rules as I was sure Mother had a direct line to God. I was obedient to the point of stupidity.

My marriage at nineteen to a nice young man failed. Before the marriage, intimacy was limited to hugs and kisses. I arrived at the altar a virgin, only to live in a marriage that would never be consummated. After two years of painful attempts, tears, a humiliating surgery, and a husband who wasn't interested in sexual intimacy, I was vulnerable— an easy target. A married man recognized my neediness for love. I fell for his lines.

My world shattered from the lies, the guilt, and the disappointment of failure. My family offered no direction, guidance, or help. I was too ashamed to discuss it with my friends. I had violated every rule I was raised by. My pretend marriage was over. I went home in disgrace.

With a new job and an apartment with my oldest sister, I was introduced to an older crowd, a group of people much worldlier. I felt unworthy to seek out people my own age—even my high school friends. Most of them were still single, in college, or planning their weddings. My innocence and self-worth had vanished.

The older crowd I had fallen in with sailed on yachts, flew private planes, and traveled to far-off places for drunken weekends. I tagged along, not able to pull away from the excitement, the risk, and their acceptance of me. Believing I was damaged and not worthy to seek out better, I allowed myself to enter a world foreign to my upbringing.

Eventually, I stumbled into yet another marriage, this time with an older man from this new social group. We had a quick civil service without benefit of family or friends. My assumption that I could fix myself with another marriage proved pitifully wrong.

The man was brilliant, moving gracefully into positions of power. I cringed in his shadow, humiliated by his frequent affairs, his excessive drinking, and the casual way he enjoyed bringing me to tears. His demoralizing words of *stupid, worthless,* and *immature* infused fear into my already damaged self. I couldn't divorce him. The fragile, misguided person I had become couldn't afford another mistake, or acknowledge it. Twice divorced would implicate me as a total failure. I teetered on the edge.

As his career soared, I learned to hold a perpetual frozen smile. We entertained lavishly, rubbed shoulders at the country club with the movers and shakers of each community we lived in. I played the "Stepford wife" role perfectly, taking lessons in tennis, piano, golf, and bridge, along with entertaining the appropriate wives with elegant lunches in our large, loveless house.

He made every decision regarding my life, my clothes, my hair, my conversations—all with contempt. He hammered me with my inabilities, my failures, my incompetence. He limited my contact with people to only those he selected. He made sure I formed no close relationships.

Fear kept me rooted in place, fear of not being able to survive on my own without a college education, and religious fear, which locked me in a lifetime commitment.

I realized I couldn't survive without some personal freedom. I begged my husband to allow me to attend religious services. He agreed, but only if I joined the Episcopal Church. Believing we would attend together and our marriage would improve, I became an Episcopalian. But he never entered the church. I went alone in faith. I found my niche in the openness offered, so unlike my evangelical upbringing. It also brought some small measure of importance to my husband to have a wife active in the most prestigious church in the community.

As I became more involved, my strength and faith in myself was bolstered. People welcomed me, asked my opinion, asked me to join, to become, to be included. The priest found ways to visit when my husband was at home, and he spoke about my dedication and the church's need to have me in a leadership role. The battle began in earnest when the priest requested that we both attend Cursillo, a religious retreat founded in 1944 in Spain. The retreat required couples go together to strengthen their faith and marriage.

My husband refused. The priest was persistent, but my husband wouldn't relent. The priest finally suggested I be allowed to go on the retreat alone, and my husband said he didn't care. At the retreat, like-minded people gathered me in their arms, restoring some of my worth.

The act of violence that occurred on my return home launched me on the path to a new life. The drive home had been full of hope and joy.

I stopped at the kennel to retrieve my Irish setter, Bull, and my Siamese cat, Suzy Wong. They had been forced into the shelter because my husband refused to take care of them while I was away. Overjoyed by the reunion, I overlooked my husband's house rule pronouncing the upstairs off-limits to my pets. Bull and I were romping while Suzy watched with indignation, perched on my husband's favorite chair in the master suite.

My husband appeared out of nowhere, kicking Bull down the steps, hurling Suzy over his head, slamming her against the wall. He flung obscenities in my face as he pushed past me and my furry children who lay subdued, cringing on the floor.

I waited until he returned to work. Packing my bags, I gathered Suzy and Bull into the car and left.

Darkness filled every moment of my life. Survival became my daily mantra. For five years, I sacrificed all to become a new and improved version of my younger, worthless self. I entered college as a freshman at thirty-three and graduated in three years. During those years, I worked, commuted to school, stayed active in the church, and stumbled blindly through a divorce trial that lasted five days. I added to my workload a four-year course in education for ministry from the University of the South. Graduating *cum laude* with a double major in psychology and social sciences, I interned in nursing homes, summer camps for children in need, halfway houses, crisis and hospice centers. I entered graduate school as a seminarian.

Although I had received counseling, it was the kind that didn't encourage me to repair my damaged self. Instead, I was told to be strong and move on with my life. I didn't tend to my own wounds. I became a wounded healer.

On the other side of five years, I had a promising, fast-track management job in the insurance industry. I had a house, a nice car, a good salary, a closet full of clothes and shoes, and no debt. I was single and reasonably happy.

Then Ray walked into my life. Or, rather, we bumped into each other; both rushing late to church, our hands simultaneously reached for the door handle, creating a collision.

Twenty-seven years have come and gone. As the years spun by, our comfortable, long-term relationship made me lazy. All my energy went toward my career and later the business we started together. Working on myself took a backseat to simply surviving.

Along the way, I forgot to tend to my own wounds, the ones that were only partially healed. I forgot about my own personal freedom, my need for solitude and creativity. I forgot to work on becoming myself.

PART I

INCEPTION

Would you please tell me, please, which way I ought to go from here?

That depends a good deal on where you want to get to, said the Cat.

I don't much care where—said Alice.

Then it doesn't matter which way you go, said the Cat.

~LEWIS CARROLL, *ALICE IN WONDERLAND*

The Lie

LA BUGIA

I LIED. IT WASN'T intentional. It just happened.

For me, there are degrees of lying. Growing up Southern requires a finely tuned ability to do so. Early on I learned the subtle nuances. If my friend Elizabeth asked me what I thought about her less-than-attractive, orange polka-dotted outfit, I would respond, "Elizabeth, you are stunning."

It wasn't really a lie because Elizabeth was stunning; clearly the dress was not. But my friend was ready to face the world in that dress, and who was I to tell her differently? Is that a lie? Or is that simply a shade of gray? In my experience, it's not so much what I say but how I say it that's allowed me to get by in this crazy world of innuendoes.

Actually, much of what I said on the occasion of my lie was truthful. It's just that I didn't reveal everything. You know, that sin-of-omission lie.

My husband, Ray, and I have been together many years. We laugh and cry through all the challenges a long-term relationship throws at us. It's not a first marriage for him either, but ours has lasted. We jokingly say it's because we only stay married one year at a time.

Based on our previous marriage experiences, we created a personal marriage contract. Every year since 1983, we set time aside to discuss the pros and cons of our agreement: what went right, what needs improvement, and whether or not we are willing to recommit for another twelve months. This short-term commitment makes it possible for us to stay in the long-term one.

During the lean years of our marriage, those years when we wondered who in their right mind would want to be married, the contract keeps us together. It brings us back to the table, even during those unhappy, pain-in-the-butt years.

It helps that we're compatible, each other's best companion. He's the person I most want to be with when traveling, cooking, searching out great wines, entertaining friends and family, and volunteering for causes we're passionate about.

Throughout our contract negotiations we rely heavily on the positives of the preceding year. Honesty is a big part of our contract—well, usually. There are two years when the contract talks present opportunities for me to tell Ray about *the lie*. Each time, I fail to mention it. By the time the next contract session rolls around, I convince myself I'm not lying.

My pale shade of gray story begins with scheduled trips to Europe. It would be the first time we'd ever had the luxury of two trips in one year. It was one of those big birthdays, and it turned into a major celebratory year.

We retired early and were healthy, physically active, and worked hard all year long at putting funds into our travel account, doubling the amount in the years we didn't travel.

In the spring, we flew to France, spending a wonderful week in Paris before taking the train to Carcassonne to meet our best friends, Kathy and Bob. Together the four of us challenged ourselves to a hilarious week self-piloting a boat down the Canal du Midi.

Ray and I spent the last two weeks of the trip deliciously alone in Provence. We sampled the food, sipped the wine, tasted the chocolates, and visited every small village within a two-hour drive. It was blissful.

In between our spring and autumn vacations, my annual sisters' week was scheduled. These gatherings had begun shortly after April 1996 when my mother suffered a massive aneurysm. My sisters and I found ourselves together for the first time in years. In the midst of our fears and tears, we planned a week's vacation together, an event that became a yearly occurrence.

On the anniversary of our thirteenth year, I vacationed with my sisters in Beaufort, South Carolina, but without our oldest sister Jean. Her husband was terminally ill. In the evening while sitting at the pool, sipping wine, we would call her to chat about our day and offer support from a distance. At the time it didn't register that this thirteenth year of our gathering was the beginning of a long, dark period in our lives.

Our sister Claudia flew home to Milwaukee where she was met at the airport by her son instead of her husband. While she was in flight, her husband had been involved in a freak accident. He was hospitalized with life-threatening injuries. There were ongoing phone conferences. Ray and I discussed canceling our trip.

Surgery was pending and Claudia was hopeful. There was nothing we could do and she insisted we go ahead with our plans to Italy.

It was a tumultuous trip of highs and lows, beginning in Lazio and moving to Umbria in the footsteps of St. Francis. We were joined by our friends, Carl and Sandy. Within a few days our trip deviated from a glorious journey to a weeping pilgrimage.

Our first week we visited many of the monasteries where St. Francis sheltered when the outside world overwhelmed his spiritual capacity. We walked in his footsteps, in awe of this small-in-stature but giant of a man. Leaving the beautiful village of Greccio, the place where St. Francis created the first live nativity, we drove to Assisi where we'd booked an apartment for a week.

During our travels, my brother-in-law Art died. I wasn't there for my sister. She said she'd be angry if I flew home. She said my coming back wouldn't change things.

Since I decide not to return home, Assisi is the best possible place I could be to honor my brother-in-law's life.

Up early one morning, I gaze out the open window into the first streaks of dawn. When Ray joins me I tell him through tears this is the day to pay homage to Art. There's an old monastery high in the hills above the town, a place where St. Francis retreated when he'd grown weary of the world. My plan is to make the pilgrimage alone, but my loving partner won't hear of it.

Once outside the gates of Assisi, the road rises straight up. The steep, narrow, winding way to the hermitage is several kilometers, normally a short walk for us. But this twisting, ladder-to-heaven road is exhausting. No public transportation is available to take us to the top. I'm glad, because Art's memory demands that I walk. He was a true outdoorsman and a lover of God's creation and creatures.

It would be a difficult walk if I were in good spirits. But crying the ugly cry, blowing my nose continuously, and stumbling along the steep, unending road leaves me weak with sadness for a life cut short, and for my sister Claudia and her family.

Ray keeps me steady. We stop often while he points out the panoramic views of the Umbrian countryside, the Basilica of St. Francis, Santa Chiara, and St. Ruffino. During those pauses, he holds me in his arms, his strength pulsating through my body. These brief interludes grant me time to regroup.

Eventually, we crest the hill where sculptures of peace beckon us to enter the monastery.

Fortunately, we both fail to see the sign warning of adders in the woods. If we had noticed it, our pilgrimage would have ended. A bite from one of these nasty snakes can be deadly if not immediately treated.

We shuffle along the dirt path, descending into the monastery complex. The primitive rooms and surroundings with stone beds give credence to St. Francis's life of poverty. We walk through the *Capella di San Bernardino*. It leads to the chapel of *Santa Maria delle Carceri*, translated as Our Lady of the Prisons, its name signifying the solitary nature of this place. We walk out of St. Francis's roughly hewn stone bedchamber through a narrow, arched opening, down stone steps marked with the footprints of time. A dusty path leads past two statues, *Francis Freeing the Doves*, and *Ecstasy of Francis*.

Deeper into the wooded area we stumble upon the stone altar St. Francis used when he offered communion to all who sought shelter. As I kneel to pray, a flock of doves burst from the trees circling overhead, cooing their soulful message of love and peace.

My brother-in-law died trying to save a dog. This is a fitting place to honor him. The *Canticle of the Creatures*, written by St. Francis in 1224, resonates as I kneel surrounded by the soft murmur of doves, the rustle of the breeze, and the sun's rays shooting daggers of light through the autumn-tipped leaves. Creation cloaks me with comfort as Art's spirit soars with the doves.

We solemnly retrace our steps, leaving Umbria a few days later. Our friends return to the States. We drive on to Puglia, a southern province of Italy. Our small villa in Castro Marina sits high on a rocky hill overlooking the Adriatic Sea. It's here on this rocky soil that *the lie* sprouts from its seed.

With the death of my brother-in-law, it's necessary for my life's journey to turn in another direction. A need for meditation, contemplation, and reflection awakens in me. Past hurts, injustices, and unworthy feelings crowd in. Fragility invades me as my old wounds tear open.

The day we arrive in Castro Marina a fierce storm sweeps in from the sea. The caretaker brings us a supply of wood, taking time to start the fire and to ensure we have all we need.

Sipping a glass of the intense Salento wine, Ray lounges beside the luminous flames. He pats the seat, inviting me to join him, but the storm lures me outside.

Its ferocity propels me to the edge of the terrace. Hypnotized by the waves churning in dark protest against the rocks, I lean into the storm. Sheets of dripping mist roll from the sea onto the terrace, wrapping me in fog and secrecy. In that instant, I visualize what it would be like to be here alone—just me, shrouded in mist. My subdued and domesticated spirit calls out for it.

Longing permeates my body. It grips my heart—an emotion so strong I cannot shake it or push it back down. I yearn to be alone—to have time to reexamine my life and allow myself to heal from pain buried, but not forgotten. I need to stretch out and move in another direction. I need to free the banked fires of my writing self and rekindle the flame. A desire to temporarily leave the world I was inhabiting and listen again to my inner spirit cloaks me with a heavy mantle.

In that moment, *the lie* is born.

The Book

IL LIBRO

THE WILD AND STORMY region of Puglia beckons me. The memory of the stone villa, the crashing seas, and the belligerent, stormy days dare me to plan this much-longed-for journey. My personal baggage brimming with trash needs sorting. It's long overdue— something I owe myself and Ray. The possibility of going absorbs my every waking moment.

Every day I revisit scenes from our earlier stay, remembering the beauty of the undulating countryside of olive trees and vineyards. The neighboring villages of Ostuni, Alberobello, Tricase, Marina di Leuca, Gallipolli, Lecce and Otranto consume my thoughts. Each memory adds to my growing pile of reasons to return.

Cautiously, I reveal my lie to Ray. He listens quietly, unaware he is hearing only a half-truth. Despite the strength of our relationship, I cannot confide in him. Fear stands in my way—fear of hurting his feelings, fear he wouldn't approve, fear I really didn't have the courage to follow through, fear that women of my generation don't travel alone without their husbands. So many fears.

The lie I reveal comes naturally and with a cover. I have always wanted to write a book. To do that I need a large stretch of time alone. Ray knows how much I love to write. When we retired I'd started scribing articles for local magazines. A book would be a natural next step.

I thought back to our conversation in Puglia when *the lie* was planted. We had been sitting on the terrace, watching the sun plunge into the sea. We had sipped wine while listening to Andrea Bocelli.

Without thinking I said, "It would take place in Puglia."

"What would take place in Puglia?" His face revealed confusion when I switched topics in midstream, which I often do.

Before answering, I breathed deeply, my eyes searching out the lone tree, the one positioned on the furthest jut of land rolling into the sea. Its gnarled trunk was contorted from years of bending with the wind, yet its branches still stretched regally into the heavens. It was a solitary figure languishing between earth, sea, and sky. It had become my focal point each evening—the co-conspirator in my lie.

"*The book*," I said.

"Why Puglia?" he asked. "Why not Umbria? We have friends who could help you or keep you company. You wouldn't feel so alone, and I'd know you were safe."

"No," I said. "It's Puglia. There's a mystery about this place. It's begging me to tell a story. Do you remember the village of Otranto, the one with the amazing wall encircling it? It had that endless piazza surrounded by the sea, and the warrior woman standing guard overlooking the harbor."

He nodded so I continued. "That's the place. The book is meant to be written there. I'm sure it's the right place. Do you remember it? When I saw that warrior woman standing guard, I couldn't move. I stood at her feet so long that you asked what was wrong. Her strong gaze held me, refusing to let me leave. She has a story to tell. I want to hear her story, the one she whispered to me. She insisted I write *the book* in Otranto.

I paused. He didn't respond, so I kept talking. "Otranto, the name is right—loud and strong—just like the warrior woman. This is my heart place—you know, one of those places that instantly claims you. I'm sure of it. It's where I'm meant to write *the book.*"

I looked at his scrunched-up face, knowing he didn't understand. Yet he had to—at least a little. He understood the need for solitude—the long walks he often took in the woods on a bad Vietnam day told me he sought aloneness sometimes, but maybe just not as much as I did. He simply didn't verbalize his needs—nor did I.

But this time was different. This time I was articulating my longing into action. Over the years we had learned the ebb and flow of each other's nonverbal communication. But this time we were out of sync.

How does one describe a heart place? I mused. For me, it's the color of the water, rising and falling, shifting from mood to mood, or the wind—balmy one minute, biting the next. Add to that the simplicity of the agricultural area, the vibrant colors, the bold patterns in the artwork, the music, and the sacred places. Then there's the warrior woman. She had the courage to see my lie as truth. She understood my desire, so strong, so unwavering, that my only thought was to return there. But it was more than all these things. It was a longing to stay, to discover a place where I could thrive, where I could find personal freedom and risk resetting boundaries. It was a place where I could recognize and honor my spirit's voice, the one telling me that four years ago I had relocated to a place that was draining instead of nurturing. But it was also a place where Ray seemed content.

I glanced up, but Ray was staring off across the sea, not noticing the solitary tree. He turned to me, nodded thoughtfully, then poured more wine into our glasses.

Fragmented Faith

FEDE FRAMMENTATA

BACK IN SOUTH CAROLINA, my dream of returning to Otranto grows. Friends and family listen patiently while I ramble endlessly about our trip, about the book I'm going to write when I return to Italy. I don't mention I'll be going alone.

That is, if Ray is okay with my solo trip. But if he doesn't endorse my decision wholeheartedly, I won't. Maybe he's my safety net—an excuse for not going. To listen and follow my heart is a scary proposition—a break with tradition—a step out alone after so many years together. The longer I'm home, the weaker my conviction to return.

The holidays descend, bringing another year to an end. In January, my oldest sister's husband loses his battle with cancer. My sister Sue and I shuttle back and forth to Virginia, helping Jean sort through the remnants of Charlie's life—endless piles of paper and things—a reminder that time is running out for me to sort my own trash.

Spring comes early as Ray and I plan a short road trip marking our twenty-eighth anniversary. After Easter Sunday church service and on our way to coffee hour, our close friends stop us.

"Would you have time to come by the house this evening or tomorrow?" Sandy asked.

There's a quiet desperation in our friends I had failed to observe. I was too busy—Easter dinner with my family, plus putting the final touches on our road trip so we could leave early the next morning.

"Can it wait?" I asked, quickly hugging Sandy and Carl as I rushed toward the parish house.

"Yes, I suppose it can," Sandy said so quietly I turned back.

"Is everything okay? If it's important, we can talk now. I don't have to leave immediately," I offered as my excuse for being abrupt.

"No, no, go on. It will wait until you return. Would next Saturday evening work? Will you be back then? Come for dinner if you are," Sandy offered.

"Yes, we'll be back. Would around six be okay?"

"Sure, have a safe trip and Happy Easter," she said, embracing me tightly.

Later, on the drive home, Ray and I discuss the unfamiliar behavior exhibited by Sandy and Carl. Our friends are sweet, vibrant people, actively participating in the life of our church community. Today they were subdued, withdrawn, and tense.

When we returned from our trip, their story unfolded from their tightly clenched lips. They told us the church and its representatives had decided Carl had overstepped Christian boundaries and should be punished for his rash behavior. He was removed from all his functions and responsibilities. They were many: vestry member, teacher, mentor, lay person, chalice bearer. He'd been given no recourse—no road to redemption. The rest of the year we spent in fruitless attempts to sort through and assist Carl and Sandy as they navigated, almost entirely alone, through dark days.

We petitioned the parish priest, the vestry, and the bishop. We requested meetings between Carl and those who had found fault with him. Everyone turned away.

"It's the climate," they said. "It detracts from the church's image. We simply can't condone the activities that have been reported to us."

"Did he molest a child? Did he rape someone or have an underage sexual encounter?" I blurted out, knowing he hadn't.

"No," I was told. "But we can't have people in his position inserting themselves in a manner that isn't welcome."

"What does that mean?" I asked.

"Oh, we're not allowed to talk about it."

"But isn't Carl allowed to speak to those who said he offended them? Doesn't the church believe he is innocent until proven guilty? Isn't there a protocol, procedure, something, anything in place for mediation and reconciliation? Isn't that what we believe in? Christ is the great communicator. He offers forgiveness, reconciliation, fairness to all, doesn't he? Isn't that what we believe?"

I was born in the church—dedicated, baptized, and confirmed. All the graces bestowed on a churchgoing person were mine. Through the years, I was president of the women's group, sang in the choir, worked at the state level, was a lay reader, a committee person, a worker bee, a volunteer for cleanup after Hurricane Katrina. I even completed four years of education for ministry (EFM) from the University of the South, and enrolled in graduate studies at seminary. I moved easily in the sacred environment, one I had treasured all my life. Now it peeled away from me, my faith scattering into tiny fragments.

Anger, then sadness, conspired as Ray and I comforted our friends. After months of attempting to work with the church, the end of the year arrived without resolution as to why our friend had been ostracized. Together, the four of us walked away from the church—a church without reconciliation is a church without love, without hope, without peace. Christ cannot be found there.

Sunday without church left us isolated from the circle of friends we'd made in Columbia. And our intention to spend time with family after years of living far away didn't materialize either. Their lives and friendships were established, so Sunday salons, cooking family meals together, shopping expeditions and sisterly giggles, all things I had envisioned, were met with little success and interest. We found ourselves adrift and without community.

Ray continued to enjoy his part-time job as a crew member on a party boat on Lake Murray. I continued to publish magazine articles; my life on hold.

The annual mid-summer family beach trip was rocky from the start. Nerves were frayed by endless traffic and a rental that turned out smaller than expected. Overheard but misunderstood conversations were repeated and feelings were raw. Unanticipated angry words were thrown around without thought. Emotions became tattered. Lines were drawn in the sand. We left each other without forgiveness or reconciliation. The realization that we had relocated to a place that didn't nourish us begin to seep through the cracks of my soul.

Now the trip to Puglia wasn't simply a dream to be alone—it had become a necessity. My personal trash pile seemed insurmountable. For me, the trip was the only way to examine all the excess baggage of my past and present, the only way to find healing for my weary, fragmented spirit. If the only way I could go was to lie about writing a book, then I would do so. *The lie* became my story.

I wondered if I could even write a book. The thought left my head swirling, leaving a vague, unbalanced look on my face with each question I received about going without Ray.

I cranked up my petition for the solo trip. One of my biggest issues is always needing approval for everything I do. Maybe it's because I was the youngest child and had to try extra hard to gain attention or approval, or because I'd failed so many times in the past.

But this time, I no longer cared who thought I was crazy, who thought I was going to Italy to have an affair, or who thought it wasn't what a married person should do. Ray's feelings were all that mattered to me. And he, over time, came to accept my need to write a book without interference. With his endorsement, I continued with my plans.

He embraced *the lie.*

First Steps

PRIMI PASSI

THE DAYS LEADING TO my departure pass quickly. I Google to find the perfect apartment with a view of the sea. Topics surface for my book as I study the significance of Otranto. I read about the massacre of 1480 and the enlightened life of Pantaleone, the creator of the mosaic floor in the town's cathedral.

With help from Italian friends, I discover a guide well-versed in art history. Our back and forth emails reveal Paolo's knowledge of the village and the mosaics. We are magnets drawn together across the miles.

Although Ray is supporting my month alone, he is adamant about coming with me at the beginning to ensure I'd be in a safe place, and to meet Paolo. He says it's a necessary requirement. It's a small price for a month of freedom.

While I consider ways the mosaic floor and the massacre might be woven into a story, words from Terry Tempest Williams's chronicle, *Finding Beauty in a Broken World*, come back to me. In her soul-searching work, Williams looks for beauty and hope amid fragmented environmental issues and political upheaval. She had traveled to Ravenna, Italy, and learned a new language with her hands—mosaics.

Mosaics are tiny fragments of stone, glass, or pottery. If these bits and pieces are creatively placed with precision and care, they are transformed into works of art. My life has fragmented into tiny pieces. Perhaps a mosaic class could be a way to discover healing patterns—patterns to completeness.

Otranto, much to my amazement, has a language school. But even more amazing is the class in mosaics I find buried in the curriculum. The gods smile. Trembling with excitement, I sign up. Another piece of the puzzle slips into place.

When friends and family realize I'm serious about the trip, they ask the "Why Otranto?" and "Why alone?" questions. With my research and resolve firmly in place, I roll out my response:

"I'm choosing Otranto because of its location and historical significance. My research will focus on two aspects of Otranto's past: the massacre of 1480 and the life of Pantaleone. He designed the mosaic floor (1163–1165) in the cathedral. I won't know until I have a chance to research these topics which I'll write about. But I do know Otranto is the perfect location *for the book.*"

I always hope they'll forget the "Why alone?" question. When they don't, I respond. "Well, it's what writers need, alone time. Writing requires solitude. A writer writes when the words flow. Often that's three in the morning. I won't eat at normal times. I'm not going to sightsee. I'll be working the entire time. Ray would be bored and irritated to have to tiptoe around me when I'm in the throes of creativity. Writing is a solitary art form. It'll require all my concentration to make this a productive time."

My audience listens intently. Some suggest, since I'd already been to Otranto, that perhaps I can write *the book* from my memory of the place.

"No," I say, "it won't work. Being present in a place is necessary for me."

They contemplate my response, then walk away, frowning. Even my best friend says she couldn't leave her husband for a month. "Won't you feel miserable and guilty leaving Ray alone for a month?"

Yes. No. Maybe. All the guilt I had discarded over the years crept back. Why was it that one word from a friend could fill me with self-doubt?

When Ray and I first met, we were both independent and self-reliant. We each had a house, a car, a good job, and a circle of friends. Ray could whip up a gourmet meal, iron his own shirts, plant a garden, change a flat tire, wire an entire house, and show up in a tuxedo to whisk me off to a gala. I wouldn't be leaving some helpless creature behind, someone not able to fend for himself. I would be leaving a man who's perfectly capable of living a full life with or without me. A month apart will be good for both of us.

Almost two years to the day when *the lie* first took flight, I return to Otranto.

Otranto, (*OH* tron toe) with the emphasis on the *O*, is a historic seaside town within the province of Lecce. It's the easternmost point of Italy within an area known as Salento. On a clear day it's possible to see across the Strait of Otranto to Albania.

While mystics, mosaics, and martyrs abound in its history, Otranto is rarely on the list of places tourists clamor to see. Of course, it's their loss. In my journal after our first trip to Otranto, I wrote:

> *If you are lucky enough to have a chance encounter with Otranto, you would congratulate yourself on such a discovery. The Adriatic Sea invites your toes into its multicolored layers; the sunbaked rocks beckon you to sit a spell and soak up the warmth of the Salento sun; the cafes and restaurants tantalize you with aromatic whiffs of grilled seafood and freshly baked*

breads. Your parched throat is refreshed with cooling sips of a spritz made with fresh oranges, prosecco, and Aperol. Strands of Moorish music drift with you as you embrace the hidden treasures of this obscure village. Your heart is filled with lyrical notes that can be stored away to be withdrawn on a rain-filled day full of meaningless responsibilities. If you come to Otranto, you will linger in its mysterious, narrow streets. You will promise yourself to return to this land of the intense Salento sun—to return to this place that once graced your days and filled your heart with abundant joy.

As early as 191 BC, conquerors were crossing the strait, landing on the shores of Otranto, an area of rich, fertile land. Its history is interwoven with Greek, Roman, Norman, Spanish, Ottoman, French, and other invaders over the centuries. Those numerous conquests created a colorful and mixed past, spilling over into the present. But Greek influences dominate the town, stacking it with whitewashed, square buildings and vestiges of Greek language and customs.

The city was originally called *Hydrus* by the Greeks before changing to the Latin, *Hydruntum*, by the Romans. Speculation says the name was changed to *Terra d'Otranto* by Emperor Frederick II in the twelfth century. Over time, that name was shortened to Otranto.

During these tumultuous times, Otranto became an important seaport and a stopping place for pilgrims on their way to Jerusalem. This influx of pilgrims created a need for a significant cathedral, providing Pantaleone with the opportunity to give birth to the magnificent mosaic floor.

In 1480, the town was invaded by the Ottomans. The cathedral played an important role as the women, children, and the village priest hid inside while the battle outside the sanctuary raged for days. As the story is told, 800 male villagers were executed for refusing to convert to Islam. Most of the bones and skulls of the martyrs of Otranto were stacked behind glass in the same cathedral, giving some credence to Horace Walpole's Gothic, spooky novel, *The Castle of Otranto*.

After centuries of occupation by other nations, Otranto is recognized more as an ideal beach spot for Italian vacationers than for its blood-curdling history. A population of 600 spills over its old fortified walls into a sprawling post-World War II town of approximately 5,000. Otranto has been inhabited for centuries by those who fish the sea (*il mare)* and farm the land (*la terra*) for their livelihood. The inhabitants live in harmony with the seasons, immersing themselves in *il mare* and *la terra*.

I stand alone on the terrace of my temporary home in Otranto. It's a brilliant fall day. A tender breeze dances lazily through my hair. Looking toward Albania, I watch its shining white Ceraunian mountain range emerge from the sea. It shifts back and forth in my vision, creating optical illusions.

It's a mythical image for me to consider as I stretch into my new world and consider my weary spirit. My wish for the month of solitude shrouds me in reality. It looms in my face, a large question mark challenging me to rediscover value in my life, to remember what it's like to be only myself—not someone's wife, daughter, sister, aunt, friend—just me.

And because I'm still living the self-imposed life of not letting anyone down, I plan to study the ancient art of mosaics, scrutinize the cathedral floor, and learn about the massacre; and maybe, just maybe, write a book.

Writing is something I've done since my mother gave me my first diary. I was seven. It was red imitation leather and came with a lock and key. *Dear Diary*, each passage started—all my dreams, fears, and secrets were transcribed from my heart to its pages.

My first published piece was a poem I submitted to *The Statesman* magazine at George Wythe High School. I was sixteen. Later, journals replaced my diaries. All my travel experiences, thoughts, musings, and longings were captured and relegated to paper until the day came when there wasn't any time for such frivolous activity in my busy life.

Two failed marriages, entering college as a freshman in my thirties, and then a corporate career filled up the years until I met Ray. After many years in corporate America, we ventured out on our own into the world of hospitality—a restaurant, a catering service, and a bed-and-breakfast created a 24/7 work environment. Those were fulfilling but stressful years, leaving me exhausted and disoriented without freedom or solitude. Somehow, in the wee hours of the morning I found my way back to journaling—a grown-up *Dear Diary.*

It was only after we sold the business that breathing room came back into my life, and writing with conviction became a possibility. The first time I had a travel article published by a local magazine, my spirit lifted and moved toward transformation.

As I stand on the terrace of my temporary home in Otranto, my heart beats faster. This place, this tiny walled village, has called me to tend to myself, to start the process of healing old wounds. Perhaps part of this process will stoke the languishing fires of my writing spirit. My book begins.

PART II
MOSAICS

Our lives are unique stones in the mosaic of human experience—

priceless and irreplaceable.

-HENRI NOUWEN, *THE WOUNDED HEALER*

Arrival

IF NOT FOR PAOLO, the trip might have ended before it began.

One of our Italian friends, a property attorney in Lecce, recommended Paolo as a guide. There was an instant liking and trust as Paolo and I corresponded across the miles. The only problem was that Paolo had already booked his vacation to the United States. He would be leaving a couple of days after I arrived in Otranto. He was astoundingly generous to give me a day and a half before he left on his long-awaited vacation. It would have been infinitely better if I could have had an expert on hand my entire stay, but I was lucky to snag time with him.

Paolo has a degree in art history. He's been in the tourist business since 2000, forming his own company in 2006. During the summer he works in tourism, but during the rest of the year he manages a traveling theatre company. As a personal favor to our mutual friend, Paolo will be spending time with me instead of tackling all the last-minute things he needs to do before he departs for the States.

While I was making arrangements with Paolo, I was simultaneously scouting the area for a place to rent. Eventually the perfect one surfaced with only one large obstacle—the owner didn't speak English. Our correspondence was awkward and unsettling with huge gaps in time.

Once Paolo said he would work with me, I asked if he'd speak to the apartment owner. Things moved rapidly after that. Paolo was told that the owner's wife would meet us at the Aragonese castle, right next to the apartment. We only had to text when we arrived.

Ray and I departed for Italy, spending three weeks with our friends Angelica and Stefano at Agriturismo Faena outside Fratta Todina. After leaving Umbria, we spent another week slowly driving down the east coast to Puglia and then across to Matera to meet Paolo. From there we traveled to Otranto following Paolo. We'd arrived in Otranto with plenty of time to check into the apartment and spend the afternoon touring the village. As it turned out, we spent most of the day trying to check into the apartment.

The confusion was intense, and without Paolo's assistance I fear I would have been out on the street. Paolo somehow managed to understand the owner's wife, who spoke haltingly in a guttural dialect while jiggling a screaming baby on her hip.

We form a disjointed circle in front of the *castello*. Paolo translates: "The apartment was rented unexpectedly before your arrival. The cleaning is only now taking place."

With considerable effort, Paolo persuades the young woman to give us a set of keys.

"We'll be back at four o'clock," he informs her. "Please have the apartment ready."

She nods, shifting the still-screaming infant to her other hip while a steady stream of words flow from her mouth.

"Don't let this upset you," Paolo says in a gentle voice. "She doesn't mean to be unkind. She says you can leave your luggage in the apartment. Before we leave she wants to show us how the elevator works. After that, we'll have a nice lunch with cool drinks. Then I'll show you Otranto."

Although we are hot and tired and had hoped to rest before starting our exploration, we don't want to squander the small amount of time available with Paolo. The woman indicates we're to follow her. The elevator is at the other end of the courtyard. As she speaks, Paolo explains to us that the only way to reach the apartment from the front entrance is to take the miniature glass-enclosed elevator. A private elevator housed inside a courtyard in Otranto, Italy, is both unusual and daunting.

I had expected the front door to the apartment to be right off the courtyard, but it's on an upper level. The lady and squalling baby move toward the tiny elevator. I reluctantly follow. The closer we get the smaller it becomes and the more obvious the corrosion.

Continuing to speak while bouncing the screaming baby on her hip, she motions all of us into the elevator. Clearly it's not big enough for four adults and a baby. I cram myself along with Ray and Paolo into the death capsule. During the ride, I learn it's mandatory to stand in the middle to ensure weight is evenly distributed. If this isn't done, the elevator might get stuck between floors. I learn the big red button has to be pushed and held continuously during movement. If you remove your finger too soon the elevator gets stuck between floors. The woman says not to worry if the elevator bumps around a bit because it's old and needs some adjusting, which may or may not be done anytime soon. I picture myself stranded in the elevator between floors, slowly starving to death.

Instant relief floods my sweating, exhausted body when the elevator shudders to a stop.

We spill onto the small landing. To the right there are more stairs, leading to a door lodged into a concrete wall. While Ray and Paolo explore the apartment, I inspect the back door. It has a sturdy deadbolt lock and is solid, although it's seen much wear and tear. There are large cracks, and a coat or two of paint is desperately needed.

I gingerly push the door open exposing a small, narrow cobbled path extending onto the upper part of *via Castello*. Glancing around, I'm confronted with an explosion of graffiti sprawling across whitewashed walls. This leaves me to speculate how safe this entrance might be.

Empty food containers, cigarette butts, and miscellaneous debris randomly lie along the narrow, vine-choked lane. Quickly closing the door, I call up the steps saying all is in order. In the confusion with the cleaning people, the heavy dialect and the screaming baby, no one else checks the back entrance.

In our brief viewing of the apartment, Ray is satisfied I'll be safe. He declares the apartment a perfect fortress with its heavy wooden doors, surrounding walls, and solid stone structure.

When I look at the same thick walls, my eyes envision the coolness they will provide during the hot, tropical days; the strength they'll offer when storms hurl off the sea; and the warmth they'll capture as the last vestiges of fall's heat flows into winter's start.

Ray and Paolo are ready to leave all the confusion behind. I stall, explaining I need a few minutes to visit the terrace. And what a surprise it is when I open the door and three tiers rise to greet me. The first terrace is partially covered. It's a cozy, welcoming area where I can spend time with my computer and music; the second terrace is straight out of an *Arabian Nights* scene. It will be my spot to sip wine and dream; the third terrace gives me the gift of the sea, a prerequisite when I looked for a place to stay. This will be my sanctuary, the place where I'll begin each day with beauty and reflection.

Ray calls from below asking if I'm ready to leave. I place my dreams on pause, knowing they'll remain here on the terrace waiting for me. We cram back in the elevator, making a slow, tortuous descent to the courtyard. We follow Paolo out the door, leaving the young woman and the fussy baby behind.

Our exhaustion flees as Paolo's stories turn every corner of the old village into an adventure. The hours waiting for the apartment ease into an afternoon of entertainment. After a grand lunch and a cooling Aperol spritz, Paolo escorts us through the town while he dispenses history and stories, keeping us intrigued and laughing.

In late afternoon I receive a text, saying the apartment is ready. We return to find the front door encased in a steel shutter. During our earlier visit, the metal shutter had been raised. Now we stand before it looking for a solution to open it. It takes all three of us searching before we discover a small crevice with buttons. Ray is thrilled with this added layer of protection.

As we open the door, I tell Paolo I haven't paid anyone for my stay. He says not to worry. I promise myself I won't, but that would be a drastic change for me. Before leaving us for the evening, Paolo swiftly walks us through the apartment, explaining how everything works. We droop, half-heartedly following, without paying much attention to the details.

Paolo understands our weariness and our need for privacy. He says his goodbyes and promises to return in the morning when we'll continue our tour of the town and the cathedral.

After Paolo leaves, our first action is to search for wineglasses. Ray opens a bottle of Agriturismo Faena's red wine that we brought with us from our friends' vineyard in Umbria. Climbing to the top terrace, we savor our wine and witness our first resplendent sunset in Otranto.

I linger on the terrace in the evening breeze while Ray changes for dinner. My senses are filled with new smells, new noises, and new sights. On Sunday Ray will leave for home. My spine shivers with anticipation and delight. Soon my journey alone will begin.

Our tiredness propels us to arrive early at a local restaurant. The evening meal in Southern Italy doesn't usually begin before nine. Normally we adhere to the local practice, but tonight we are exhausted, requiring sleep more than food. The restaurant owner welcomes us. We're the only people on the small patio as the red-streaked sky shades into mauve. Our meal is scrumptious and the service delightful. Arm in arm we amble back to the apartment under the star-bright night.

Standing on the terrace, we absorb the atmosphere: waves cresting against the black horizon, wind chimes tingling in the sea breeze, voices murmuring. Our arms are entwined. Our thoughts are private.

We crash into sun-kissed sheets without unpacking or familiarizing ourselves with the apartment.

Paul and the Cathedral

PAOLO E LA CATTEDRALE

THE NIGHT PASSES PEACEFULLY. We awake invigorated. Paolo arrives early, suggesting we have cappuccino before we begin a more thorough tour of Otranto. As we leave the apartment, Paolo directs us to a bar around the corner. Inside, Paolo introduces us to the owner. He tells him I'm a writer from America, and I'll be staying in town for a month. The owner doesn't speak English, but I can tell from his lukewarm greeting he isn't impressed.

Paolo's English is excellent, interspersed with pleasing Italian idioms and phrases. When we leave the bar, he says, "Donna, you must find a special place to have cappuccino each morning. It's the Italian way. Do not be satisfied with this place or any other. You will know when you find the right place, the place that is just for you."

His words ease me back into the Italian way of life, where the bar you frequent for *un cappuccino* is as important as choosing your stockbroker or your primary care physician.

Paolo leads us on an extensive tour of the old walled town through narrow streets and alleyways. We marvel at the well-designed maze of confusing twists and turns. White mice in a long-ago psych lab dash through my mind. I wish I had been more empathetic to their wild-eyed, frantic attempts to find their way. Their bewilderment and frantic scrambling repeating over and over, echo through the narrow, twisted alleyways. I wonder how long I will anxiously ramble before I learn the intricacies of this place.

We tour the town inside and outside the old walled village as Paolo points out the *castello*, the hill of the martyrs, grocery stores, pharmacies, and the train station. He knows Otranto, its back alleyways, its seaside, its churches and its history. He regales us with stories both old and new. We return to the piazza and stand by the warrior woman as she gazes out to sea. Paolo tells us his heart belongs to Puglia.

"I am not myself when I am away from this place. The sea gives me all I need to regroup before returning to life's responsibilities. I cannot be away too long," he exhales, letting the sea breeze renew his spirit.

I gaze across the water, my eyes feasting on the colors flowing from emerald to cobalt in the intense morning sun. My need to be near water matches Paolo's. Its restorative powers have soothed me through many of the unasked-for-challenges life has thrown my way. The three of us stand united but lost in our separate thoughts before turning from the sea to stroll through the village.

Paolo is knowledgeable, quick-witted and easy to be with. He fills my head with interesting tidbits I'll soon forget. But I'll remember the pure pleasure of listening to his rich, warm storytelling voice.

My camera, notebook, and recorder are left behind. I don't wish to be distracted, even if it means I'll forget most of what I see and hear today. This time is for me solely to listen to Paolo's old way of storytelling, to hear the stories of Otranto over and over until they become my stories and my truth.

Gradually we make our way to the cathedral and stand in the piazza. Its massive doors beckon me, but Paolo touches my arm indicating to wait before entering.

In his best theatrical voice he begins, "*Questa cattedrale* was built to be the most outstanding church in Puglia. It symbolizes the gateway between the East and the West. Many pilgrims on their way to and from Jerusalem stopped in Otranto. The cathedral was built when the town fathers decided it was necessary to have an important church to minister to the sojourners.

"The *Basilica Cattedrale di Santa Maria Annunziata* was erected on the remains of a Roman *domus*, a Messapian village and an early Christian church. All of this was discovered during excavations carried out from 1986 to 1990 when the ancient mosaic floor was being cleaned for the first time. The foundation of the church was laid in 1080, under Papa Gregorio VII, and was completed in 1088 and consecrated under Papa Urbano II. Those were years of splendor for Otranto." Paolo pauses.

Out of the corner of my eye I notice a few tourists lingering outside the church, inching their way toward us. Once within range of Paolo's magnificent voice, they pretend indifference or busy themselves with inspecting the cobbled street or an architectural aspect on a nearby building. Paolo's voice and regal composure are what attract them to cluster within hearing distance.

Paolo is impressive. It's not just his towering height of six-four, but also his entire demeanor. His glossy black hair parts in the middle and hangs naturally below his ears. A day-old dark stubble and light-colored eyes attract attention before he speaks. His stage-trained voice projects. Emotion rolls off his tongue. His voice modulates according to the story he weaves. His theatrics endear him to those within his voice range. His warm, golden tones resonate across the cobbled street, bouncing back at me from antiquity. Sonnets roll from his lips as he grows into a character from long ago.

More people congregate. Irritation causes my attention to wander as I think angry thoughts. *This is my guide. I'm not sharing.* But then I look at the faces spellbound by his storytelling. I can't blame them for wanting to eavesdrop. I'd do the same.

When I tune back in, Paolo is describing the different periods of church history and how the architectural aspects of the church, both inside and out, were perfectly blended from early Christian, Byzantine, and Romanesque styles. He doesn't notice the gathering crowd as he says, "But, what truly makes this cathedral unique is the magnificent mosaic floor."

He turns, leading the way. We trail after him through the doors of the cathedral. Paolo waits until the small crowd of tourists disperses before continuing his Broadway performance.

"Molti anni fa," he begins.

His rhythmic voice of *once upon a time* casts a spell. I fall into its current, drifting with the musical notes accompanying the ancient story.

"There was a time when the people of the land could not read or write. During this time, pictures were used to explain the past, the present, and the future. The people were poor, living off the land or the sea, so the priests used symbols the people could easily recognize. The early church understood how instructing people would ensure not only loyal to the church but it would also ensure payments to its coffers. As with everything, there are good or enlightened instructions as well as evil or dark aspects to teaching.

"This mosaic floor was created by the great monk Pantaleone around 1163. The church's goal was to teach the uneducated people through the mosaic pictures and patterns. However, the church perhaps didn't recognize how enlightened Pantaleone was, or that he had his own ideas to express in this grand mosaic floor."

Paolo pauses as we make our way from the main entrance through the smaller door into the narthex.

He stops, turns to us. "We'll start here at the beginning with the tree of life. You will notice that it's a rootless tree standing on the backs of elephants from India. Pantaleone begins the mosaic with inclusion: Christian, pre-Christian, and non-Christian scenes coexist along with all the monsters and heroes. There are Biblical characters as well as those from literature, history, and mythology.

"This floor represents judgment and redemption—evil and good. The people were taught good things about how to live in community and harmony. Through the pictures they learned how to support one another, how to obey the law, and how to uphold justice and fairness.

"The dark or evil side is how the church sought to control the thoughts of uneducated people. The church limited what the citizens could learn and imposed guilt as the main lesson to the faithful believers. They judged the people harshly, insinuating that the expedient way to salvation was through monetary donations—a sure path to forgiveness."

Paolo pauses. "It's a sad religion that tells its followers salvation comes with a price tag, instead of freely through the Son of God."

Distant voices rumble through my thoughts. Carl's anguish and Sandy's pain reawaken in me along with angry words from family members. The sadness living in my soul from these events loosens its grip a little as I consider the troubling role religion has played in my own life.

We move forward and stand at the base of the mosaic. Paolo continues.

"The highly complicated payment of the day was extolled as indulgences consisting of contrition, confession and satisfaction. Of course, if you were rich you were indulgenced far more than if you were poor. Donations had a way of easing full remission of sin."

"Paolo," I interrupt, "who could read and write during this period?"

"Only the enlightened monks and popes—sometimes bishops and priests could read and write, but not always. And sometimes the very rich could read and write, although the universities were not yet established. The University of Bologna was founded around the same time this mosaic was being created, so it's still many years before opportunities for education became available to anyone who was not from a very wealthy family. Often rich people purchased books to show others how wealthy they were. For most people, the only way of getting information or education was through the teachings of the church. But the price was high. Judgment was abundant."

My throat closes around the word *judgment*—a dark word, one that limits and taunts people into believing they are not worthy. The puritanical teachings of my childhood religion cluster into my thoughts. I remember Mother telling me the story of how I, at three years old, asked her why God was so mean. She used the story as an example of how my question was sinful. For me, it was the innocence of a child hearing and understanding a tone of condemnation instead of love. Mom and I were never on the same page with our spiritual lives. She chose to dwell in the shadow of the fundamentalist past. I raced ahead to a more expansive view of spiritualism. But our differences never broke the love between us.

Paolo points out Pantaleone's signature and moves ahead. I linger, marveling at the work and the sheer immensity of the mosaic. Kneeling on the floor by Pantaleone's bold mosaic signature, I study the tiny bits of dark brown marble spelling out the Latin *Pantaleonis*. My fingers tingle as they trace the mosaics, the ones that formed his name almost 900 years ago. I recognize myself in this time and place. Whispers encourage me to be open to the journey. Pain, sadness, and fear accompany me as I examine the fragmented pieces of my life, but on the other side joy waits for reclamation. A puff of air touches my cheek, sending chills across the back of my neck. A presence hovers in this place. I stand, thinking it's my vivid imagination, and scurry to catch up with Paolo and Ray.

"Pantaleone started this 800-square-meter masterpiece with these two grand elephants," Paolo continues. "For me, the tree of life symbolizes the humanity of us all. This mosaic gives us lessons to follow for all times, for all ages, and for all people. It tells us that every day we choose between light and dark. It's always our choices that determine our journey."

Paolo touches my shoulder and points midway up the aisle. "Look further up and you will see how the trunk splits into two paths. The split in the tree shows us we can choose either *sinistra*, which here represents the left, the dark, the evil; or we can choose *destra*, the right, the light, the good. Sometimes we choose dark over light. But it's important to remember that at any moment we can change our life and move out of darkness to choose the path of light."

My thoughts weave in and out of his words. The story intertwines with my decision to be here on my own. I want to walk on the path of light again, reigniting and reclaiming joy as my own.

Paolo's voice beckons me back to the mosaic floor. "Now I must tell you about Pantaleone and the marvelous imagination he had. He was a very unusual monk for the twelfth century. He was headmaster of the school of painting in Otranto. He was an expert in philosophy and theology, Hindu hermeticism, mythology, and mystical interpretations. He excelled in Jewish, Arabic, and Oriental metaphysics and mysticism. He belonged to an order of both Greek and Italian monks. Above all, he was a creative and amusing monk. He included humor throughout his design.

"Pantaleone mixed all the religions of his time, plus politics and ideological thoughts, to convey that we are one large world of many cultures, religions, and values. He believed living together in harmony is life's most important journey. I often think the church hierarchy did not fully understand Pantaleone's intention when he was commissioned to do this work. Some say the church fathers were not culturally knowledgeable. Perhaps Pantaleone was aware of this."

It's as if Paolo is speaking only to me, offering a hand to guide me. My choices have led me to this time and place. The recent buildup of grief and pain blinded me to this known wisdom. My eyes and ears open to the story of this place until a door slams, diverting our attention.

More tourists enter the church, chatting like magpies. We move to the side aisle where Paolo continues without disruption. I move in close so he doesn't have to raise his voice.

Paolo's voice reverberates in the cathedral. "Right above the elephants is a naked male and female symbolizing Adam and Eve, with a little son who is portrayed as Jesus, the Son of Mankind. God is far away at the altar. Can you see the elaborate silver frontal?"

As I view the ornately carved silver altar, I think, *Wow, am I ever happy not to be on the altar guild. It would take hours or even days to keep this large silver structure polished.*

"Look at these pictures," Paolo says. "They tell us what we must do to reach God. Here at the beginning, Adam and Eve are naked and have hearts of light. Soon their hearts turn dark because they make choices the church says are evil. For me, it's hard to understand why Adam and Eve finally arrive at the altar fully clothed, which you will see when we reach that point in the mosaic.

"According to the church, reaching the altar is called *enlightenment.* But don't you think it would be better to arrive at the altar naked as the day we are born? Wouldn't that indicate we are as pure of heart as the day we arrived in the world? I think it's the laws and judgment of the church that required the human race to cover everything up. Without knowledge, we are held captive in the dark."

Paolo leans into the roped area, pointing out the strange combination of symbols and scenes depicted in the Old Testament, in mythology, in the zodiac, along with monsters and strange animals. "Look at this—a donkey playing the harp; and this—a monkey playing cymbals. Over there is Alexander the Great, born before Christianity was even a thought."

Paolo's eyes smile when he speaks. "Pantaleone placed many characters and symbols in his creation that are not biblical in nature. This one has griffins from long ago when they pulled Apollo's chariot. Do you remember the griffins from the Harry Potter books?"

"Of course," I respond, loving the connection with my favorite young adult books.

"Allora," says Paolo, "I think Pantaleone believed the church fathers wanted the mosaic to only reflect sin and judgment. But this

did not suit his temperament, so along with the Bible stories, he added humor, history, literature, and mythology."

The shuffle of tourists being herded out of the church signals it's late, and we must move on quickly.

Paolo turns to me and says, "You will come back often to study this floor. You must pay attention to the symbolism. When you do, you will begin to see many different patterns. Imagine yourself in that time, on the day the floor was unveiled. Think about all the people who have stood here where we are standing. Interpret the mosaic for yourself.

"I think it was Pantaleone's intention to unite us across the centuries. Even today, we are still faced with the same choices between good and evil. Pantaleone tells us it doesn't matter if we are pagan or religious, because all of us still have to make these choices. Today, if anything, the choices are harder."

My mind spirals to the left, to the right, to choices I've made. Sacredness is seeded within me. Sometimes the seeds land on fertile soil and receive nourishment. At other times the seeds have landed in the swamp, decaying unless I find my way again.

Left or right? I contemplate, gazing at Pantaleone's creation. I will either water and nourish the seed or I will grind it under my foot. It is my choice. *Sacredness is within me. I am sacred.*

While I've been far away in my private thoughts, Paolo has moved on. I scurry to catch up as he continues. "We work less, we worship many things other than God. We think we are enlightened by our modern technology. Here is one last thought about the mosaic before we leave," he says.

"It is not necessary to understand this mosaic in the context of today's environment. It's an icon. It's over 900 years old. Think about the Facebook icon in 900 years. It will be discovered by people who will not understand what the symbol represents. Another generation will try to guess the Facebook meaning just as we do with this mosaic floor. It's a great mystery that perhaps we are not meant to understand. Although we try to move the ancient meaning into the modern circumstances, it's not possible. We were not there. We do not know Pantaleone's mind. So we must leave the ancient where it is. We must value it for what it represented in that long-ago time and place. What we do need to understand is that this magnificent tree of life mosaic transcends the division of paganism, Judaism, Christianity, and Islam, as well as all other religions. This gift of inclusion is the greatest gift Pantaleone has given to us."

These powerful words dwell in my thoughts as Paolo's story ends. Such a simple lesson to learn but so difficult to embrace. In the pause that follows, we observe the priest rushing tourists out of the church as the steeple bells chime out the hour.

Our time in the church with Paolo seems like minutes. We are the last ones to turn away from Pantaleone's mosaic. The priest is fussing with a large ring of keys and motions us to hurry. Because I am not Lot's wife, I turn back to feast my eyes upon the spectacular mosaic one last time before the door closes on me.

Sunlight torches the center of the tree of life, spilling brilliance onto the right side of the mosaic while obscuring the left side in darkness. Light and dark, good and evil—the choices that create the stories of our lives.

Our day with Paolo ends. The promised day and a half is now whittled down to two half days when Paolo receives a phone call as we leave the cathedral because his mother has fallen and broken her arm. With hugs and promises to stay in touch, he rushes away.

The Apartment

L'APPARTAMENTO

AT FIVE THIS MORNING sleep slips away. Moving without sound, I grope my way from the bed to the terrace. Starlight wanes. Glimmers of morning shimmer on the blue-gray horizon. Goosebump breezes stir. Migrating birds nesting in the vines tweet out agitated messages when I disrupt their sleep as I climb the stairs to the top terrace.

Light curls the sea as it advances against the inkiness of the vanishing night. Closing my eyes against the approaching dawn, I wish to suspend myself in this time between dark and light. For a moment my wish is granted—then the red and gold rays of the morning sun pry open my eyes. This day will start with or without me.

Paolo left us yesterday evening. He was my only contact in Otranto. Before leaving, he hugged me and said, *"Passo Salento."*

"Donna, when I say this to you, it means a special thing. For you, I wish a time of renewal in this land of the sun. Take your time to linger in the joy of this place. Walk through Salento slowly. You will find all your heart seeks."

In a few hours Ray will leave, returning home to South Carolina. I'll be alone—on my own for a month in this tiny walled village of Otranto. I shiver with mixed emotions of sadness, anxiety, relief, and excitement. I'm not sure which emotion is the strongest. But I'm ready to *Passo Salento*.

Later in the morning, Ray and I walk the entire village. He wants to see it all—to make sure it's a good place for me. We stop for cappuccino but don't linger as his time to leave approaches. Returning to the apartment, he rechecks the doors, windows, and locks until he's sure I'll be safe.

He packs his luggage.

Hand in hand we drift toward the car. Embracing tightly, we part. I wave, blowing kisses until the last glimmer of him moves out of sight. I stand sniffling on the corner while burning tears mingle with my mascara.

The apartment waits for me, but I don't want to go there. It will seem empty so soon after Ray's departure. Blowing my nose and wiping away tears, I walk through the village, breathing the salty air, soaking up the aloneness, believing—but not believing—I'm really on my own.

The park and promenade overflow with families. Strolling toward the main piazza, I stumble across children's rides, souvenir stalls, and food stands spilling onto the promenade. I'm too new in the village to know if this is a festival or a normal Sunday afternoon.

People cluster as carousel music accompanies children's laughter. On this sunlit October afternoon, shops that have been closed since our arrival a few days ago are open. Restaurants have popped up as appendages to houses. The tantalizing odor of roasting nuts, garlicky, grilling bread and sizzling sausages mingle into one mouth-drooling Italian aroma.

Instead of joining the throngs, I stroll away from the center of town, stopping to buy my first treat in Otranto—*sorbetto di limone.* Deliciously sharp, tangy lemon flavors penetrate my palate, bringing delight to my spirit. I savor every bite. It lasts until I reach the back door of *via castello numero quattordici*—my home for the next month.

For a moment, pinpricks needle into my spine, reminding me I'm alone in a place where I don't know anyone. I long for Ray to be here. Visions surface of the key not fitting. *What if I'm locked out?* My heart races while I frantically search my pockets, realizing I left my cell phone on the kitchen table. Five deep yoga breaths still my trembling fingers as I pull the keys from my pocket. The first one fits—the well-worn lock clicks.

The heavy door doesn't respond when I push inward. Teetering on the top step for balance, I pull the door toward me. It doesn't budge. I jerk. It swings open into my face, nearly toppling me off the steps. I'll have to remember each time I use this door that it swings outward. It would be a grave misfortune to forget this procedure as I'm sure that I and anything I'm carrying would be sent sprawling into the alley.

My first stop is the washing machine on the terrace. I remove the towels I washed this morning, hanging them on a rack to receive the full heat of the afternoon sun. Then I retreat inside to study my new home. Although I've been here for a couple of days, I've put off exploring every corner until after Ray left.

I have an emotional attachment to places. It's important to me that a place feels its way into my life. Maybe it's because I moved so many times in my adult years. But place was significant to me, even as a child.

Back in those early growing-up years, I didn't have my own space. In our lively family of six, there were times I longed for a place of my own, an impossibility when you share a room with an older sibling in a small home with a large family. Being a determined child,

I kept my eyes open until one day I discovered a haven on the back porch of our family house. My secret hideaway was our beautiful, old, hand-hewn oak table. It had been relegated from our kitchen to the back porch to make way for the new metal, Formica-topped table, accompanied by miserable stick-to-your-butt plastic-covered chairs, symbols of progress in the 1950s.

Before being dismissed to the back porch, that oak table had been the center of our family. It held stories of the times when all of us were required to gather for the evening meal. Dad would sit at one end with Mom at the other, listening intently to us chatter about our days full of friends, school and, from my older sisters, the latest boyfriend. I have wonderful memories of times alone at the table with Mom before everyone else returned from school. She'd be preparing dinner but would always have a special treat waiting for me. The table represented good times before we scattered.

When I came across the oak table discarded on our back porch, my heart sank. But once I realized the table wasn't leaving, I pulled aside the long oilcloth cover. There was a perfect secret spot. My hideaway was particularly perfect on warm, rainy days when the back door was open. I could hear the hum of the house without being part of it. The enjoyment of my own space—a place where I could squirrel away treasures—was intensified when someone would call my name. I'd listen as their voices flowed throughout the house, signifying the search had begun. When the voices faded, I would slip quickly from under the table and run to the front porch. Settling myself in the swing, I would hum tunes under my breath until the door opened and someone would say, "Here she is."

Turning away from my memories, I survey the apartment, seeing it for the first time. I want it to be *my* place—not Ray's and mine together. *"Via Castello numero quattordici,"* I say out loud, savoring the Italian words on my tongue. My home for a month.

Standing at the front door, I pretend I've never seen the apartment before. I move quietly inside, breathing in ancient history, savoring the moment of my arrival, the moment when I claim this place for my own.

The formal living room is dark, not a place I'll spend any time. So I rush through knowing I'll only use it to recharge electronics, stack books, store research notes, and keep gifts I purchase to take home.

The next room features double archways, one a bright salmon pink and the other a burnt peach. Particles of sunlight filter through the area—a rainbow in progress. The space between the two arches is layered with hand-carved floor-to-ceiling cabinets in pale bleached wood.

Interlocking diamond-shaped designs adorn each of the four doors. Against shades of salmon and peach, the warm cabinets open. They reveal soft, sweet-from-the-sun linens, a hair dryer, an unusual metal stick that extends, an assortment of international electrical adapters, and a toolbox I hope I won't have to use.

The bathroom resides between the two arches. There's plenty of storage for stacks of lightweight Italian towels, the kind that dry quickly in the sun. The entire upper wall over the sink is mirrored, creating light and the illusion of spaciousness without windows.

Through the second archway is the kitchen-living room combination. It exudes home-away-from-home. It's the space where I'll spend most of my time, unless I'm on the terrace or exploring the village. There's a comfy leather sofa with a soft burgundy throw and pillow waiting for my first nap. There's a TV, a round kitchen table, and all the accoutrements required in a well-equipped kitchen. Two wide shuttered windows overlook the small cul-de-sac. I swing the shutters open, letting in light and salty breeze.

The front door of the house across the way is ajar. There's a white trash bin set on a ledge below the window. *Oh, gosh*, I think, *trash, I forgot to ask about trash.*

Recycling is a recent experience in Italy. We've been coming to Italy for years, but it wasn't until 2003 in Northern Italy that we encountered the astounding rules of trash. In the south, the process has been slow to catch on. I check drawers and counters but find no trash instructions. I send a quick text to the owner asking where the trash bins are.

After hitting send, I choose a seafoam colored wineglass. Opening a bottle of *primitivo*, I breathe in the lush grape flavors and pour. The rich, ripe earthiness blossoms, leaving the smooth, intense tang of the Salento sun. With glass in hand, I gaze around the color-laden kitchen.

The large round kitchen table will soon be draped with my mother-in-law's blue and white tablecloth. She was born during a time when women were not in charge of themselves. Yet she made her way in a man's world, working all her life while caring for home, husband, and children. She loved adventure and would have traveled with us if she had lived.

Each time I plan a trip, I tuck one of her beautiful linen tablecloths into my luggage, ensuring her spirit travels with us. This trip I packed the white tablecloth with blue stripes. It will meld perfectly with the colorfully dressed kitchen. I picture myself sitting at the table, writing, with breezes ruffling the tablecloth. That image turns into enchanting memories of my dad and me at the breakfast table.

When I was sixteen, Mom rebelled, declaring to the world that she would no longer rise at six each morning to prepare breakfast. She'd had enough, she said. That left Dad and me on our own. My sisters had scattered with marriage and jobs. Each morning Dad valiantly cooked for us—two fried eggs, two slices of crispy bacon, and toast—five days a week for my last two years of high school. It's reflected today in my outrageous cholesterol readings. But I would never replace my mornings at the table with Dad. This memory, along with ones of my lovely mother-in-law, wraps the warm coziness of the room around me, saying *this is your room.*

All the colors in the apartment merge in the kitchen. Pinks, peaches, blues, whites and greens join. Behind the stove top, pots and pans hang from a rack. Above the rack is a hand-carved driftwood shelf. It houses deliriously happy blue, orange, and pink fish swimming toward a large sailing vessel. The cabinets display an array of colorful dishes. I pick a large, oval blue and white bowl to place on the table. Soon it will spill over with tomatoes, eggplant, zucchini, onion, garlic, chili peppers, potatoes, carrots, and whatever else I'm enticed to buy from the local markets. This bowl, brimming with fresh produce, will rest on my mother-in-law's tablecloth. It will create a picture-perfect still life in my new home.

No matter what place or country, *la cucina* is always my favorite spot. There's a lovely phrase in Italian—*la cucina è il cuore della casa*—the kitchen is the heart of the home. And the heart beats strongly in this exotic, colorful kitchen.

Marble steps lead up to a large wooden door opening onto the terrace. As I move toward the door, I'm captivated by the floor design directly in front of the sofa. The tile is patterned to mimic an ancient Persian rug. The creamy background swirls with color. In the center of each tile are small green circles and peach-colored leaves. Around the outer edges are sheaves of wheat bound by peach twine. It's magnificent—patterns and colors I would never choose, yet they blend harmoniously adding vibrancy to the room.

The vivid scene reminds me of my visit many years ago to the Alhambra in Spain. When this thought occurs to me, I glance back through the archways and recognize the same Moorish influences in style and color. There's a clean, uncluttered yet ancient look everywhere I turn. My new home reminds me of Otranto's complex history—the lingering influence of many civilizations.

Heading up the steps, I fling open the door, embracing the sun, sea, and wind. The first terrace, the one right outside the door, has a roofed pergola to keep out the intense noonday sun and the torrential downpours. There's an unexpected outside kitchen with sink, gas burners, and a wood-burning fireplace for roasting meats or making pizzas. The washing machine hides away behind cabinet doors. There's a large wooden table bordered by an L-shaped seating area. The cushions incorporate the same peachy tones in stripes and plaids.

The terra-cotta floor has alternating tones of tan and cream, creating a warm, protected place—like my oak table hideaway.

Climbing the bright blue, railed stairway I arrive at the second terrace. I reclaim the *Arabian Nights* tale I saw the first day. The low walls are peach. Built-in seating surrounds three sides of the terrace, displaying cushions with the same pattern as on the lower terrace. Casually stacked blue-and-peach pillows nestle against colorful bolsters. Overhead a pergola opens, welcoming the light and air. Small wooden tables for candles, wineglasses, and delicate plates of figs, honey and nuts are wedged between the cushions. In the center, wrapped around the middle pole of the pergola, is a round wooden table where grand feasts will occur.

My eyes consume the grandeur of the terrace as I simultaneously gaze toward the sea. Sweeping wide of the dazzling white houses, the rolling sun bounces along the edge where sky and sea become one. Photo opportunities abound. My eyes take aim, tucking away golden memories. The morning sun will find me here every day that weather allows.

My photographic eyes drift north, framing white buildings interspersed with green sea pushing against the land. My lenses pass over the satellite dishes, chimneys smudged with firewood residue, cracked walls, and dirt-lined rooftops. Instead, I capture white, blue, and green melting into gold. I lock these glorious colors into my photo frame and click.

The third terrace is a step up from the second, but that one step up affords a grand view of *Castello Aragonese*. The castle is my neighbor and will become a designated meeting place for the next month. The view encompasses its front gates, where overhead a waving banner depicting Marilyn Monroe's face announces an Andy Warhol exhibit. My gaze settles back on this expansive third terrace with strategically placed lounging chairs.

The sun spirals high as I reluctantly leave the terraces, retracing my steps through the arches and into the narrow hall leading to the bedrooms. The first bedroom is small, containing bunk beds, a wardrobe, and a miniature writing desk. It's a snug environment for little ones. My luggage is stacked out of sight here, allowing me to pretend there is no impending departure date to consider.

On the hallway wall is a colossal painting of psychedelic fish. They dance on the bottom of the sea, moving in and out of colors so brilliant my eyes won't focus. The white walls against the terra-cotta floors of red, white, and gold present a sharp contrast. There is no end to the colors swarming in this vast aquarium of still life.

The confusion of color eases as I enter the master bedroom. It's spacious and smells of sea breezes and sunlit days. The bed is freshly made and turned down, revealing popsicle orange sheets trimmed with gold flowers and stripes. I will be tempted to tuck these linens into my luggage so I can take the Salento sun home with me. The coverlet is the same straw gold that graces the bed linens, and at the foot of the bed is a plump comforter of palest peach.

There's a cloud-puff-shaped window to ensure the sweetest dreams. It's directly above the bed, exposing perfect light, as does the large window on the side wall. Both can be shuttered at night from rain, or if the breeze turns cold. The wall across from the bed houses a built-in wardrobe that's large enough to conceal all my belongings. Small wooden night tables and good reading lamps complete this room of simple comfort.

I survey my sunlit far-away-from-home bedroom. The image of the oak table on the back porch of my family home again surfaces, wrapping me once more in childhood safety. Over the years and many moves, I've learned to live with that oak table tucked inside my mind and heart. It's always available to pull out and sink into on those days when there's no safety net. Now my heart tells me my journey to find home has brought me to this place, to this Salento sun-filled room.

I'm home.

I Am Strong

Io Sono Forte

I TUCK MY LAPTOP under my arm, refresh my glass of wine, and nestle on the cushioned bench on the terrace. Exhaling, I remind myself to relax and breathe.

The photos I took during the first three weeks of travel ease the tenseness in my shoulders: photos of Ray and me with our friends Clara and Gaetano at Pian del Rocchio; Angelica and Stefano at Agriturismo Faena; and Laura at her restaurant in Bastardo. The next batch contains the strange and unsettling photos of Matera. I'm lost in the spooky cave dwellings of Matera when a sudden gush of wind gallops across the terrace, slamming the door shut.

My peaceful silence is shattered. My runaway imagination freezes me in place. I'm trapped on the terrace. There's no one to rescue me. And once again, I've left my phone inside the apartment.

Thankfully, I'm spared a slow, miserable death because the slammed door didn't lock me out. After this incident I determine it's best to prop the door open using two bottles of water. They are perfect as a makeshift doorstop.

Back on my cushioned bench, the Matera photos are still there, gazing back at me in twisted agony—the gapping cave openings, the burial grounds on top of rock formations, and the somber grays shading into darkness and despair. A shiver runs down my spine as a small thud brings me straight up out of my seat with a racing heart.

This time a gentle breeze has pushed over the rack holding the freshly washed towels. They're almost dry so I shake them out and move them to the upper terrace. As I rearrange the rack and towels, I breathe in the phenomenal view of sea and castle. I set the rack next to the wall because I'm too new to my environment to anticipate the fickle wind of the sea.

Later, before my evening walk, I climb the stairs to retrieve the towels. An empty rack gawks back at me. Traipsing from terrace to terrace, I hunt for the towels, but they have vanished.

Deep breathing to steady my nerves is becoming my constant companion. I talk myself into calmness and survey over the wall of the top terrace. There, suspended on the miniature awning over the front door, the towels lie in a clump. Without a plan, I race down the stairs, grab a chair from the kitchen table, and head out the front door.

I anchor the chair firmly on the three-meter-square landing. There's nothing to lean on or hold onto for balance. My knees tremble as I gingerly rise into an upright position, while letting go of the back of the chair. My fingers reach up, but the awning is miles away. Bending my shaky knees, I step off the chair. Back inside, I begin a frenzied search for something that might create a reunion between the towels and me.

Rushing from room to room, I peer in each closet, thinking a clothes hanger or a broom might do the trick. Then I remember the peculiar long metal stick in the cabinet. Checking it out, I pull on the lower end and it extends into a long retrieving mechanism. It has a clasping part on the end that has probably seen many a towel rescue. Back outside, I scale the chair, thrusting my towel stick into the air. Teetering back and forth, I finally snag one towel. The others follow.

Bundling them in my arms, I sink into a squatting position, letting the soft, warm smell of sun and sea ease the tight knots in my neck. I've been so busy with my towel search and rescue mission that I forgot to focus on being alone. Instead, I sigh with contentment, thinking I'm exactly where I'm supposed to be. It's just me I have to take care of, just me to make decisions, just me to recognize and listen to myself. *I'm going to be okay.*

As evening gathers, I push myself to face the outside world with a *passeggiata,* a mandatory evening walk that's part of Italian culture. On my first day alone I want to be in tune with life in this small village.

After leaving my cell phone in the apartment twice today, I write out a long list and tape it to the front door. It reminds me to take keys, cell phone, and money; to lock the front door; to push and hold the button to lower the metal security shutter; and to make sure the back door is locked.

I double-check each step until I arrive in the narrow alley outside the back door. The opening to via Castello is very small. Paolo told me earlier I could gauge whether I had gained weight by how easily I can pass through the narrow passageways all over town. This early in my stay I'm able to pass through.

I join the crowds that have swelled into the walled city. Young and old clog the narrow shop-lined way. My melancholy seeks quiet meditation, so I amble down cobbled streets that allow for only single-person passage. These tiny alleyways spiral in and out of dead ends. They are a puzzle now, but soon I will know them.

Eventually, I stumble onto the main promenade and walk away from the masses. I cross the small family-filled park and follow the path outside the walled village. The sight of the sea stops me. In the glow of early evening it undulates in partial rainbow colors—green, blue, indigo, and violet. The waves entice me to follow the seawall, which ends at the bottom of recently repaired steps leading into the newer part of town. At the top, a tiny chapel perches over the water—*Chiesa della Madonna dell'alto Mare*, the Church of the Madonna of the High Sea.

The tourist sign describes the legend of the 1480 massacre. It tells a story about beheadings, a stolen Madonna, and the miracle of her return to the church. I don't have pen or paper to take notes, so I snap a photo of the information.

After my earlier trip here, I discovered a novel called *Otranto*. The author, Maria Corti, writes a historical fiction about the massacre at Otranto. The original Italian title of the book, translated into English by Jessie Bright, is *L'ora di tutti* (*The Hour of All*). There are five narrators in the book, each speaking in the first person: Colangelo, Captain Zurlo, Nichira I, Aloes De Marco, and Idrusa.

In the preface, Ms. Bright says of Idrusa, "Idrusa is a woman, a woman of that long-ago time who may even be anachronistic in her implicit rebellion against another possible oppressor—not the Turks but a society that demeans and limits her just because she is a woman. A twentieth-century voice? Or an invitation to believe that there have always been women who saw their world this way?"

It was Idrusa's voice I heard when planning my trip here. Somehow she's wormed her way into my unconscious. Her voice is strong. She pops out when I least expect her, as she does now when I'm pondering the story of the Madonna. Idrusa presents herself as a wild warrior woman, living during an age that showed no mercy for Joan of Arc characters. Perhaps she's the one I'll write about.

In Conti's *Otranto*, Idrusa is killed. But her voice in my head tells me there's more to the story. Somehow, she lives on. She insists I listen to her. Her forcefulness propels me toward the church. I open the massive door and peek inside. I hesitate, not wanting to enter, not sure of crossing the threshold, *attraversamento la soglia*, into another world. Idrusa sweeps past me. I follow.

My eyes adjust to the dim light and land on a large mosaic star. It's in the center of the aisle below the altar. It sprawls across the chapel floor, nestling a series of smaller stars between each of its points. Maritime knots circle and secure the star clusters. The ever-present Madonna stands in a corner, conveying a beatific smile of tranquility.

My knees shake as I kneel on the hard wooden bench. Images of my fragmented faith, homelessness, and separation flood over me. I petition for Ray's safe journey home and give thanks for this first day of my sojourn. In this place, instead of loneliness I'm enveloped in solitude. It strengthens me, providing a sense of freedom, seclusion, and withdrawal from my routines at home. Here there's peace, privacy, and a world I do not have to inhabit with daily responsibilities.

Leaving the chapel with Idrusa still in my thoughts, I continue my walk around the seawall. Through her eyes I see the splendid castles, now ancient ruins, trailing into the water's edge. From this side of town, night advances, casting blue softness off the homes and churches across the water in the walled village.

Wandering back through the park, I spy a vendor by the children's rides calling out to buy his roasted almonds and pistachios that grow abundantly in this region. I ask for *due etti delle pistachio e mandorle.* The vendor smiles and nods, handing me two bags of warm nuts. My change is returned with a *"Grazie, signora."*

Just inside the walled village past the main gate, strands of opera float from a timeworn gramophone at one of the antique stalls. I linger, listening to this gift of music. I wistfully think of Ray, feeling his presence, thanking him for understanding. For so long we have been in tandem, always there for each other, never apart for too long. Now a month and an ocean will separate us.

The piazza is still crowded as I weave through the backstreets until I come upon a bookstore. Here I hope to find Maria Corti's book, *L'ora di tutti,* in Italian. Although my Italian is less than elementary, I want to read about and hear Idrusa's voice in her own language.

The bookstore is tucked away in a narrow alley off the main promenade. I peek through the window and see an older gentleman at the desk. As I enter, he looks up with a warm smile. I return his smile and in my best Italian ask for the book. He seems pleased with my attempt and says, *"si, si, abbiamo questo libro."*

He believes he has a copy and disappears. After a long stretch of silence, he shuffles back to me. Disappointment shows in his pressed lips, but his response is full of possibilities, *"Se torna domani, il libro sarà qui."* He tells me to return tomorrow, and he'll have the book for me.

The sun sinks into raspberry wine. I pick up my pace wanting to reach the apartment before darkness becomes total. Fear lurks in the deep shadows of the tiny alley outside my back door.

My phone buzzes just as I insert the key into the lock. I'm sure it's Ray calling to say he misses me. Instead, it's a text from the owner of the apartment responding with instructions for trash disposal. As a visitor to another country, I'm compelled to understand trash protocol so I don't offend my neighbors. Glancing at the lengthy text, I recognize daily obligations I thought I had left behind. I attempt to unscramble the message, but it's a mixture of Italian and English. It's long and confusing.

After a cursory glance, I decide it's more important to eat. Fresh produce and paper-thin strips of *scallopini* await.

Inside my safe fortress, I survey the stove, trying to remember the instructions Ray gave me about how the burners work. For Ray, it was an easy turning of knobs. I watched instead of trying it myself. Now I twist and turn the same knobs exactly as he demonstrated. A gaseous odor drifts into the room. I gag, but no clicking, no flame. I try for several minutes until I realize I risk blowing up myself and the apartment. Opening the door to the terrace to air out the fumes, I stand outside stretching my neck and shoulders to ease the apprehension.

My happy thoughts slide away, replaced by inadequacy. Gritting my teeth, I text Ray in Rome, where he overnights before his flight home. I had assured him repeatedly that I could take care of myself. And now the first thing I do is ask for his help. This stove problem diminishes my self-sufficiency, and it may heighten his concern about leaving me. While I wait to hear back from him, I visit the stove again, attempting to find a solution.

Perhaps when I was looking for the kitchen light, I inadvertently turned off the gas. I rotate through the switches until the hood light comes on. With a twist and a click, the flame appears. With relief and delight, I text Ray. His text back, *I knew you could do it.*

My playlist is loaded with Andrea Bocelli. I melt into the rhythm of his voice while preparing supper. The stove responds to my commands. It turns out *scaloppini* layered with prosciutto and oozing mozzarella; sautéed zucchini and onions; crispy potatoes with garlic— all complemented with a glass of the robust sun-kissed Salento wine.

My first night alone. *Io sono forte.*

I am strong in my belief that this is a magical journey. Andrea Bocelli crescendos into my thoughts, wrapping me with his passionate words, inviting me to be strong on my journey. It's been a long time since I've been on my own. But here I am. An image of the warrior woman protecting the harbor emerges. She gazes out to sea. I stand by her side.

Insieme Siamo Forti.

Together We Are Strong.

Mosaic Magic

LA MAGIA DEI MOSAICI

ON MY FIRST NIGHT alone I fell asleep on the sofa instead of under the sun-kissed sheets on the bed. I felt safe tucked away in the kitchen with fish dancing on the walls and Italian game shows fading into my sleeping dreams.

Italian game shows have been Ray's and my only foray into Italian TV. We discovered the shows on our first trip in 1995. The shows are entertaining, and they teach us a little Italian.

The game show hosts are a constant—old friends we see once a year. We've watched some of the best—Mike Bongiorno, Fabrizio Frizzi, and our favorite, Carlo Conti. His show is a mixture—part variety, part game show with a bit of erotica thrown in when skimpily clad girls jiggle their way on and off the set—enough to capture Ray's attention. I recently learned that Italian game show hosts keep their jobs until they die. Up-and-coming wannabes must find other means to support themselves while they wait for a vacancy.

When I fell asleep it was to the sound of a familiar voice lulling me into a place I know and feel safe in.

This morning I struggle awake, stiff from my night on the sofa. Climbing to the highest terrace, I marvel at the sun rising on the back of the sea. I stretch my arms into the sky to welcome this new day and my new life. I'm exhilarated and anxious—exhilarated because I'm finally alone, anxious because I'm finally alone—except in thought.

I think of Paolo's oration in Santa Maria d'Annuniziata, and how his words combined mystery and magic to usher life into Pantaleone's mosaic floor. Terry Tempest Williams's words from *Finding Beauty in a Broken World* encircled me there, making beauty out of brokenness. Mosaics celebrate brokenness and the beauty of being brought together.

I hear Paolo's voice insisting I visit the mosaic floor often to study the tree of life and all it teaches us. The symbolism of the tree is universal. It's found in all cultures, religions, philosophies, and mythologies. The tree, whose graceful branches reach into the universe, instructs us to renew ourselves, to spread our wings, to embrace physical and spiritual transformation, and to seek nourishment for our souls.

I'm eager to revisit the cathedral and the floor, but my class in mosaics at *Scuola Porta d'Oriente* starts at ten this morning. The class will chart the course of my journey. My intention is to learn this art form from antiquity while simultaneously seeking to fit the fragments of my life into a workable pattern.

Another intention for the mosaic class is to ease me into the town to meet people and to find my way around. I'm not an artistic person, so I'm edgy about my ability to produce anything remotely resembling a work of art. It's been many years since I've tried so many new things at one time.

There's plenty of time for my favorite Italian breakfast of fresh creamy yogurt and a tangy juice of carrot, orange and lemon. It's the fresh burst of citrus tempered by the natural sweetness of the carrots that pleases my palate. But breakfast doesn't blot the fearful thoughts crowding my mind. I'm alone, halfway round the world, facing a weeklong mosaic class without prior experience. I gulp in big breaths, but the *Why are you doing this?* tape plays loud and clear. Negative thoughts tumble into each other.

What if I can't communicate with anyone at the school? Barbara, the director, has corresponded with me in English, but I've learned that this doesn't indicate whether someone is versed in another language or if they are using Google Translate.

I continue with the deep yoga breaths as I leave the terrace and the view behind. At the kitchen table I pull a clean notepad in front of me, scribbling down the reasons I won't let fear interfere with living. But I'm not successful. Dark memories of my first day at school surface. That day cemented my need to be obedient, to follow the rules, and to keep quiet to avoid as much discomfort as possible.

With my hand clasped firmly in my mother's, we walked the five endless blocks to school. I didn't want to go. I was happy at home, content and safe in my small, cozy world. Each day my sisters returned from school and taught me what they had learned. I was an eager and willing student. I had no need to attend school, to leave the safety of my nest.

When Mom let go of my hand and walked away, the day turned dark and spun out of control. This is the one clear image I have of that miserable day.

The teacher handed us a piece of blue-lined paper. "Children, you will print your name and address on these lines on this piece of paper. When you are finished, please raise your hand."

Within seconds my hand shot up. Her scowling face came close to mine. She collected my work and held it up for the class to see.

"Class, pay attention! Look at what this little girl has done." I trembled with excitement, so proud of my accomplishment.

She continued. "The rules for this class are always to be followed. I will not accept anything but what I ask for. Do you understand?"

"Yes, ma'am," we whispered in unison.

"Now, little girl, you clearly did not listen to me. You did not *print* your name and address. You *wrote* it. Writing is not taught until second grade. You cannot write in my class. You have failed your first assignment."

My head bows in shame and humiliation. The other children snicker. Later, when Mother returned for me, the teacher scolded, "You must break your child of these bad habits. She is only allowed to print in this class. She must follow my instructions. She must obey me, and she must always follow the rules."

I look with expectation at Mom. I knew she would tell the teacher how proud she was of me because at five I could write. Instead, Mom's head dropped in embarrassment. "Yes, of course," she murmured.

With mounting dread, I staggered by her side on the longest walk home. When the school was no longer in view, Mom stopped and said, "It's my fault. I shouldn't have let your sisters teach you to write. From now on, you must listen carefully to your teacher. You must always do what they tell you. Your teacher is always right. You must always, always follow their instructions and rules."

For the remainder of my school years and trailing me into adulthood, I subjugated myself to everyone else's rules, believing anyone in authority knew better than I did. I excelled because I feared being wrong and being ridiculed in front of the class

Today, on another first day of school, that insanely tense feeling of impending humiliation and inadequacy tightens its grip. Each new experience, no matter my age, clogs my mind with fear and shame of not getting it right the first time.

I shake my head and start another list of things I want to see and do. The neatly written list (I never learned to print) slows the internal trembling. My breathing evens out.

The folder I'm taking to mosaic class is waiting on the table. Before leaving South Carolina, I had gathered several design options as possibilities for my mosaic project. As I glance through the folder, each design appears more complicated than the next. Fear pushes against the spongy sides of my brain.

What possessed me to select such difficult designs? What if I don't understand the instructions? I never thought to ask how many people would be in the class. I wonder if the other students will be skilled in mosaics. And most of all, I wonder if I will I have the guts to be creative, or will I be obedient and follow someone else's rules.

Then more complicated questions rumble: *Will a class provide me with the skill to complete one of my complicated designs? Will it provide me with an understanding of the intricate mosaic floor, enough for me to write about it? What if I don't understand the complexity of the art? Will the art of mosaics bring magic to my writing fingers? Will I find beauty in the broken pieces? Will I learn a new pattern for myself? Will I follow my own rules—the ones I've worked so hard to establish for myself?*

The Salento light spins my questions back into the sun-dappled sea without answers.

Noticing I still have a few minutes before I leave, I tuck the list away and position my laptop by the kitchen window. I write about Idrusa, occasionally glancing up to catch the clouds licking foam off the sea. The benign sun brings warmth to this already sacred day. *I won't waste it with negative thoughts.*

At nine forty-five I leave for school. Adrenalin rushes my feet ahead of themselves. I spiral forward, avoiding catastrophe by the slimmest margin. I'm not the most graceful person, as my daddy would say if still around.

His words evoke a smile. "Virginia, can't you teach that child to stop spilling her milk, to stop walking into things, and to stop breaking the dishes when it's her turn to help?"

"Oh, honey, she's just a child. She's a bit of a daydreamer. She'll outgrow it."

She would often quote the children's rhyme to me. I was Tuesday's child, and she would say, "Donna Lee, Tuesday's child is full of grace. You need to live up to that."

Slow down and breathe, my internal voice commands, knowing I've never outgrown my klutzy ways. Grace still eludes me. I gulp and release air like a blow toad slowly pushing out its cheeks. That image sends me into fits of giggles, forcing me to slow down and relax.

Looking at the colorful display windows, I note a few shop locations for a future visit. The rhythm of my walk changes into a soft, easy pace as I meander toward my destination.

The school is outside the walled city. An ancient wooden bridge full of gigantic holes must be crossed. It partially covers what was once the moat surrounding Castello Aragonese. It's on my list of things to explore once my week in the classroom ends. Only later do I discover the castle will close for the season before I have a chance to visit the Andy Warhol exhibit.

I march across the bridge, avoiding the holes, and stride away from the old walled village into post-WWII civilized horror. Two different worlds converge. Inside the wall is safety; outside trash gathers in front of the tired, dusty, neglected buildings. Cars, which aren't allowed inside the walls, jam into every possible space, lining the streets like silent sentries. Once on via Antonio Primaldo, I check for number 70.

There's no sign to indicate a school in these shapeless, bleached-out buildings, but soon number 70 looms over the door of a two-story, nondescript lump of cement blocks. Pushing through the gate, I notice the unusual design cut into the metal. Its circular curls and spiraling rays display an ancient symbol of the sun. My fingers lightly trace the design before closing the gate and entering the building. There's a small reception area, quiet and cool after the intense tropical sun. No one is around. Indecision hovers. Shaking it off, I climb the stairs.

Barbara, the director of the school, and I had exchanged numerous emails. Few Americans come to this region, so she had been very solicitous about answering my questions. She assured me that I would be safe, as everyone would watch out for an American woman traveling alone.

At the top of the steps, I peek in the first door. A beautiful woman looks up and says, "Ciao, Donna." Her soft, lyrical voice skims across my skin on magical dancing notes. It matches her ebony hair, sun-dazzled skin, and sea-colored eyes. It's Barbara, just as I imagined her.

She introduces me to my instructor, a young woman with many body piercings, tattoos, neon orange hair, and a cautious smile.

"Mi chiamo Francesca," she says, "non parlo inglese."

Okay, so she doesn't speak English. I only speak a little Italian. Instead of defeat, I accept this as a challenge.

She sizes me up, instinctively knowing I don't have a clue about mosaics. Through Barbara, she tells me I am her only student. She will teach me for several hours every day for one week. There is no room for questions or chitchat as she continues with her instructions. I follow her down the hallway and into a small, cluttered classroom. Barbara trails behind, stopping to chat with students scurrying to other classes.

Once in the classroom, Barbara continues to interpret. The first step is selecting a design. Francesca indicates with her hand it's to be small and simple, something the size of a coaster or trivet.

I stand firm and present my file folder with three very convoluted designs. Being prepared is high on my list of important activities. This is a trait I use often to overcome my anxiety of not knowing what's expected of me.

She nods, and opens the folder.

The first design is the coat of arms for Otranto. It's a complex lighthouse entwined with a large, menacing serpent. A crown perches on the top pinnacle as branches surround the base proclaiming *Civitas, Fidelissima, Hydrunti.*

Francesca frowns, shaking her head no.

My second choice is a series of pagan symbols taken from the roofs of ancient *trulli* in Alberobello. Again, no.

My last design swarms with masses of red starfish suspended in surf. Francesca's mouth opens in disbelief. Her face moves from astonishment into retreat mode. Her eyes say, *una pazza americana* (crazy American).

She sighs, shrugs, and says, *"Molto difficile."* Even with my limited language abilities, I understand her words—too difficult.

We stare at each other, both of us entwined in our own separate silence. Fear stands next to me. My frozen mind leaps into action, forcing my creative juices to intervene. My hands flail, pointing outside while I open and shut an imaginary gate. *"Il sole sul cancello,"* I say, smiling joyfully when I remember the words for sun and gate to indicate the primitive Salento sun on the metal gate to the school.

Barbara's been observing us, so I turn toward her and say, *"Posso?* May I be allowed to mosaic the Salento sun?"

They confer. Francesca nods and says, *"Va bene."*

She hands me a board, a pencil, and drawing paper. I rush down the steps and out the front door. She follows at a sedate pace. She points at the gate and to the drawing board. My heart does little flip-flops, shuddering with more memories of grade school disasters. My sketching ability is zero. Even attempts to draw stick people exceeded my skill set.

I explain to Francesca in a smattering of *Italish* that I have no skills in drawing or painting. She sighs, takes the board and pencil from my hands, and draws a basic outline. She hands it back to me, indicating I must flesh it out.

Once back upstairs, she hands me a heavy piece of cardboard.

She pantomimes that I'm to transfer the sun design to the board. While I complete something that comes close to resembling the sun on the gate, Francesca takes another sheet of paper and sketches a small part of my design on it. She pencils in geometric shapes to represent the mosaics. She points to my sketch, nodding that I'm to do the same.

This laborious task requires all-consuming concentration. There's much erasing by me and much guidance by Francesca.

Finally, she says, *"Bene,"* indicating I can stop.

My trembling fingers tightly grasp the pencil. A painful slouch has crept between my neck and shoulders. I fear it might be permanent. But step one is complete, and the design is my own.

Next, colors must be chosen for my Salento sun. *"Giallo,"* I say, *"o rosso."* Francesca shakes her head no. There are no yellow or red marble sticks. *"Quali colori avete?"* I ask, fully expecting unlimited choices.

"Blu, bianco, verde, rosseto, grigio, e nero," she responds.

Now it's my turn to sigh as blue, white, green, pink, gray, and black are not colors I visualize for the sun.

Contemplating my choices, I recall a painting of the Salento sun. It was blue. *"Va bene, voglio un sole blu con uno sfondo bianco,"* I respond, summoning in my mind a mosaic with blue sun and white background. Yellow and red, my preferred choices, must be the most popular colors. Since this is the end of the teaching season, the supplies must be low, I reason. So it's blue—not a blue moon sadness, but a bluebird happiness like the showy, blue hydrangeas all over the South.

Francesca finds a supply of blue and white marble pieces. She points to a chair. I sit.

From the other side of the table, she shoves one large glove toward me. My hand rambles into the empty space, coming to rest on years of grit lodged in each finger hole. Along with the glove, an ancient stone cutter slides across to my side of the table. Pantaleone must have left it on the premises, judging from the rusty, crude instrument I'm faced with using.

Francesca signals I'm to watch her before attempting the task. She maneuvers a stick of marble into the palm of her glove until only the tip peeps forlornly from her grip. She positions the ancient cutter in her right hand, enclosing its rusty mouth around the scrawny neck of the protrusion. Her tattooed arm bulges. There's a crisp snap. A perfectly shaped piece of marble lands in front of me. She continues to snip, scattering precisely cut stones across my board.

"*Ora è il tuo turno,*" she says, indicating it's my turn. I slip the marble stick into the palm of my gritty glove and grip the cutter with all my strength. I squeeze. Nothing happens.

"*Più forte,*" she encourages.

I try harder. Still nothing. I ease off the cutter, making minor adjustments. My teeth are clenched, my tummy sucked in. My grip pulsates a wimpy muscle along my forearm. Holding my breath, I squeeze. The crack of marble boomerangs against the stone walls. The tiny piece flies across the room, ricocheting from the wall to the table to the floor, rolling in some unknown dark corner of the room. Silence follows as we both peek under the table. Then Francesca throws back her head and howls out laugher. I join in. My anxiety flees as we both wipe laughing tears away and refocus on our task.

Francesca points at the stack of marble sticks. She draws squares and rectangles on the paper, pointing at the shapes I need to cut. I understand my instructions and begin. The task requires all my focus. My hand soon throbs. Heat from the exertion radiates into my face, but I continue to cut until my hand locks up.

Francesca observes this and says, "*Fermati,*" letting me know I can stop.

Next, she demonstrates how each piece is cut into various shapes to fit the design. I glance at the clock and realize with a huge relief that class time is over. I stand, preparing to put away my mess and bolt out the door.

"*Ma, no,*" Francesca says, "You must stay to complete at least one ray of sun."

I sit and begin. When the first tiny blue ray of sun comes to life, the magic of mosaics seeps under my skin. She nods, and then shows me how to place some of the stones in blue and white concentric circles. These reveal a pattern from which the sun's eight blue rays will radiate. Under her tutelage, I visualize my blue Salento sun bursting from the marble stones.

As I place the last blue stone into the first ray of sun, Francesca taps my shoulder and says to stop. She looks at my swollen hand and indicates she will clean up. I painfully push myself away from the table. Fatigue and gritty marble dust cling to every pore. It irritates my skin, clogs my nose, scattering from my hair onto my shirt and jeans. Shaking off as best I can, I mumble, *"Grazie mille, arrivederci,"* leaving everything on the table.

Trudging back to the walled village, I hold my throbbing hand high to prevent swelling. As I drift along, I consider heading to the apartment. I'm desperate for a shower, I need ice on my hand, and I need to become familiar with trash instructions, as soon as possible. I have a growing stack of garbage in the kitchen container. But I'm exhausted and hungry, so I turn toward the Blu Bar for sorely needed refreshment.

Paolo introduced me to it on my first day in Otranto. When we lunched here previously, he'd taught me the best, and least expensive, way to eat is to order the *aperitivo,* a plate of appetizers and a drink.

With false bravado, I ask to be seated outside. I order the *aperitivo con spritz,* just as Paolo advised. While I wait, the breeze from the sea flows through the ruins, sweeping marble dust from my hair.

The spritz arrives, bursting with fresh orange slices mingled with fizzy prosecco, burnt orange Aperol, and a splash of soda. The knots in my shoulders and neck ease up a bit, but my hand stares back at me in swollen insolence.

A large platter of appetizers arrives, overflowing with morsels of prosciutto and burrata; miniature *taralli* jeweled with cherry tomatoes and arugula; a triangle of *salumi* and tomato; tiny meatballs; *bruschetta* with roasted peppers and eggplant; baby shrimp delicately sauced; *focaccia* slathered with spicy tomatoes, rosemary, and garlic; fresh tiny balls of mozzarella; and local greens fragrant with garlic and pepper flakes on crusty brown bread.

I sip the revitalizing spritz, letting the fragmented pieces of marble and my life merge.

Both blend into my first steps toward wholeness. Completion of one blue ray of sun was a magical gift—one that adds a smile and eases the pain in my swollen hand.

It's a grand celebration of life. I sip the sparkling spritz and bite into the delectable Italian nibbles. It's my first day alone. My first day in class. The warm Salento sun casts blue rays across the corner of my table.

Emerging Patterns

Modelli Emergenti

AFTER MY SHOWER, I ice my hand and take a long nap on the Arabian Nights cushions on the upper terrace. I dream of mosaic fragments, serpents, and blue suns.

A text startles me awake. The owner is responding to my questions about the trash. This text is as long and confusing as the first one. I force myself to read through the entire message.

My interpretation of the text goes something like this: The trash containers are located in the courtyard. There are three containers in different colors designating the varieties of recyclable trash. Trash is collected six days a week. There is no pickup on Sunday. The correct container and trash must be placed outside the front door on the ledge every evening except Saturday night.

The owner lists the trash rules, emphasizing they must be followed: On Tuesday, Thursday, and Sunday evenings, food scraps are packaged in plastic bags and placed in the white container. The bin is moved outside the front door onto the ledge for pickup the next morning. On Monday and Friday evenings, the yellow container is to be filled with plastic, paper, and aluminum and placed on the same ledge after bringing in the emptied container from the previous pickup. Wednesday evening the black container with glass goes out.

It's disconcerting to think I will have to attend to trash six days a week. I reread the message, trying to clarify what day, what container, and what type of trash is the correct combination. I write down all the possibilities, knowing I should study them, but the evening *passeggiata* beckons me. Trash can't be that difficult. I'll address it *domani.*

I charge out the door, making brief stops at the vegetable stand and the butcher shop.

With my shopping bags full, I return to the apartment and deposit my treasures. My *passeggiata* is short this evening. I only have time to skirt the edges of the wall and discover a few more entrances and exits within the maze of tiny, winding streets.

Later, when I'm safely ensconced in the apartment, I prepare a scrumptious meal of pan-fried potatoes with plump veal sausages, complemented by fresh, ripe tomatoes and sweet red peppers. The TV game show entertains me throughout supper and into the evening as I sip a smooth Salice Salentino wine. When drowsiness blankets me, I switch off the TV and slip between the cool, sun-kissed sheets.

Early this morning before taking my sunrise walk, I start a load of laundry. It takes about three hours to get a small load washed because of the constraints required to conserve electricity. It's a way of life in Italy and makes me ashamed of how wasteful I am with water, electricity, food, and other commodities back home. So many things that I take for granted are considered luxuries in many parts of the world.

Here laundry is a daily activity, yet it doesn't impose on my time. I leave the door to the terrace open. As day awakens, sunlight splashes into the kitchen, stirring glitter dust up into the air.

Arriving for class, I find Francesca waiting. She guides me through more design work on my mosaic. Today I'm creating the center circle of the sun using white and blue marble. It's tedious work and requires my full concentration.

Francesca and I attempt to converse, but it's difficult as I struggle with her dialect. Our conversation is either pantomiming or conferring with our English/Italian dictionaries. She tells me she's from Maglie. The name is familiar. I recall Paolo telling me Maglie is where all the trains in this region connect to the rest of Italy.

As our class time ends, I find I'm not close to a stopping point. There are seven more rays of sun to complete along with all the background pattern. I fear my progress indicates I will never complete the mosaic.

"*Ho bisogno di più tempo*," I tell Francesca, indicating I need more time.

Francesca nods and leaves the classroom. She returns with Barbara, who says it's okay for me to stay each day after the class ends. She tells me the last language class ends between twelve-thirty and one.

"If you would like to stay after the language classes are over," Barbara says, "I will lock you in as I leave. When you leave, the door will automatically lock behind you."

This solution works for me.

Before Francesca leaves, she shows me how to select the stones to fit into the background. From the limited colors of marble left, I select creams, taupes, and beiges. Francesca demonstrates how each stone must fit into the next for the pattern to emerge. This requires a good eye plus a huge amount of precision and balance. As quickly as I place one stone on the design, I knock three others over.

The premise is that a small patch of stones is placed on the design. These same stones must be removed from the board while maintaining the same pattern. Then these same pieces must be individually glued back into their intended place in the design.

I work on one small area. Once the design emerges, I gingerly move it off the board, piece by piece. Francesca tells me to put a dab of glue on the bottom of each piece of marble, then place each stone back in the same spot on the board. That's how it's supposed to work.

The first bit of glue I squirt out gets stuck everywhere and on everything. The stones stick to my fingers instead of the pattern. My fingers stick to each other and to the board. Francesca giggles as I wildly attempt to shake the stones off my fingertips.

The trick, she shows me, is to spread a bit of glue on a piece of paper. Then dab the bottom of the marble, one piece at a time, into the glue. Next, I'm to position the piece back in its proper place without getting residual glue anywhere on the design. Francesca tells me the glue will ruin the pattern if it's left on the surface of the mosaic.

Before she leaves, I complete two large blue rays of sun at the top and bottom of the design and two smaller rays on the left and right. I'm thrilled, thinking this is enough for today. But Francesca insists I complete two more small rays at the bottom and the two large rays on the sides. She says the background will take the longest because it covers more space than the sun. If I don't get all the rays completed today, she says there won't be time to finish the mosaic. That thought spurs me.

Once she leaves, I immerse myself. When the pain becomes greater than the joy of creating, I stop. My back won't straighten. My right hand, which was already red and swollen, is intermingled with purple and black streaks from the continual cutting of stones that don't want to be cut.

While I fully appreciate art and the genius of great artists, I didn't have a clue about the intricacies, the backbreak, and the mundane day-in, day-out responsibility of creating art. My mind wraps around those mosaic artists who didn't have a table or chair while creating the mosaic floor in the cathedral. Instead, they squatted or knelt on the floor for as long as there was enough daylight to see. This craft is far more difficult and complicated than I anticipated. My appreciation of artists has increased beyond measure.

Before Francesca left, she drew a design between two of the blue sun rays. This design will eventually become the background. While she was here, I could see the design's intention. Now that she's gone, I struggle to figure out exactly how to create the pattern. The image in my head and the lines she drew have no connection.

Considering that there are only three more days of class left, I continue despite my pain and confusion. I poke pieces here and there, but the pattern escapes me. I don't dare glue the pieces in place because I'm sure it isn't right. There could be mosaic police lurking close by, checking to see if I'm following the rules.

I'm frustrated when I leave the school, wishing I had taken Italian language classes instead.

My plan for the week that I'm in class is to buy fresh vegetables on the way home each day. There's a small produce stand between the school and my apartment. On Monday my plan works well because I leave school at noon. Today it's after two o'clock when the school door locks behind me. All the shops are closed.

My choices are to eat out or see what's left in the fridge from yesterday's bounty.

Happily, I find enough goodies to quickly throw together a salad with canned Italian tuna, a boiled egg, tomatoes, and olives. Not beautiful enough to photograph, but certainly viable as a weight-loss program.

After lunch I take a long stroll by the sea, feeling like a grand alligator regulating my body temperature as I bathe myself in the warm Mediterranean sun. The sea walk meanders in both directions. I saunter around the point, choosing the path to the left. I snap photos of bright blue gates stenciled with Salento suns.

They're draped in yellow, red, and purple bursts of flowers alongside crumbling walls and WWII gun fortifications leaning into ancient ruins—beauty and the beast.

An elderly man sits on the seawall that follows the road around. His alert eyes follow my movements. As I walk past, he smiles, points at my camera and asks if I'm a photographer. I'm happy to practice my memorized paragraph about who I am and what I'm doing here. Thanks to Manuela Bower, my Italian teacher, the words flow so easily that no one hears the part that says I only speak a little Italian. Instead, people hear me rattle off my speech in nearly perfect Italian with a Southern drawl and decide I'm lying about not speaking the language. This gentleman is no exception.

What little I do understand of our conversation is informative and sincere. He learns I'm American and I'm writing about Otranto and gestures for me to sit beside him on the wall. Next comes a history lesson.

Satisfied he's done justice to the existence of Otranto, he moves on to the American invasion of Sicily and the mainland. He stipulates how happy the Italian people were to see the Americans. This, he says, is because most Italians thought Mussolini was crazy, and they knew Hitler was. Or at least I think that's what he says.

As daylight fades into purple shadows, we shake hands saying *ciao, ciao*. He strolls back to his group of friends gathered around a game board. He's eager to share his information with them. I imagine they had a wager going, and he was chosen to sit on the wall to discover who the foreigner might be.

The weather continues to be perfect, and my early evening stroll works up an appetite. I head to the store and then home, but not to eat, as there's still work to be done.

Shortly after I arrived in Otranto, I deleted all the photos from my camera after I thought they were safely transferred to my laptop. The photos represented three weeks' worth of travels in Umbria, Basilicata, and the northern part of Puglia. The transfer was successful except a few days ago the photos disappeared. Yesterday I downloaded an app to recover them. Again I thought the problem was fixed. However, when the app recovered the photos, it put them into Finder instead of iPhoto. Now Finder refuses to give them to iPhoto. The photos are either quarantined or jailed, and I don't have the Apple smarts to get them out. I place a call to the support team and spend an hour working through the problem with a tech rep.

When the call ends, I complete moving the photos to their proper resting place and transport my laptop inside. Choosing a deep blue wine glass, I pour from the open bottle of Salice Salentino and climb to the top terrace for a photo-perfect sunset.

With mosaics, photography, and wandering the town keeping me busy, I haven't spent much time sorting through my pain and sadness. Merely being alone triggers the healing process. Exploring this ancient, sacred village fills my days with endless possibilities. No loneliness or sadness. The days flow, moving forward as I spend time recognizing myself, a person I'd forgotten about.

Accidental Americans

GLI AMERICANI ACCIDENTALI

ON DAY THREE FRANCESCA tells me we're running out of time. At least one section of the mosaic must be completed today. She points to the upper left-hand quadrant, indicating this would be the easiest place to start as it's almost finished. Tomorrow we'll make the mortar and apply it to the section I complete today. On Friday, our last day, she'll show me how to clean the completed section. After that, I'll be on my own.

"Cleaning is a slow process," she says. "It cannot be rushed. It requires a steady hand and concentration. Once I teach you the steps, you will complete the project without my help."

All day I glue bits and pieces of marble to create the background pattern in the upper left- hand quadrant. I drift, lost in thought, as I dab and glue pieces of marble into their proper position. My concentration snaps when a door slams and stomping feet leave the building. I push back from my work, noting that the creams, taupes, and beiges blend into a blob—not what I had in mind.

Morning runs into late afternoon. I stop when I can no longer focus. I find myself, as usual, covered with marble dust. It clings to my hair, gathering on my face, up my nose, and in my eyes. The gritty texture coats my teeth and tongue. Gulping a mouthful of water, I swish it around, moving my tongue over my teeth, attempting to dislodge the grit and grime. I wash my face and hands at the tiny sink in the closet. I find a scruffy sponge in the cabinet under the sink and use it to wipe down the table and chair.

As I clean up, I think about the mosaic floor in the cathedral and the people who toiled for years to complete the masterpiece. That drifts into thoughts about people working in marble quarries, coal and diamond mines. What I have touched on in this class pales in comparison. I push away these depressing thoughts, quickly finish cleaning and leave. Perhaps the fresh air will unclog my brain and airway.

After a shower to soak the marble dust out of every pore, I prepare fresh veggies for lunch and take a nap on the upper terrace, snuggled into Arabian cushions drifting on soft sea breezes. It's early evening when, refreshed, I amble down the steps and out the back door. Local wine, olive oil, and produce are on the list for the evening meal.

Leaving the walled village, I stroll across the bridge to one of the shops Paolo pointed out to me. A gentle *buona sera* from the owner's lips welcomes me. She invites me to sample olive oils and wines before making my selections. There are small plates of flatbread smeared with olive paste, basil, and hot pepper sauce. After tasting the tempting tidbits, I add several to my purchases before exiting with two heavy bags.

As I cross the small bridge leading back to the walled village, there's a commotion in the churchyard of San Antonio and San Francesco. Crowds spill out of the church doors onto the sidewalk and into the street. It must be a pilgrimage. Nuns from the convent, villagers dressed in Sunday best, and vested priests congregate in a haphazard shuffling line. Slowly they ramble toward the Hill of the Martyrs.

Stopping in the middle of the bridge, I inhale whiffs of incense. The hazy smoke drifts into my space as the censer swings in time to chanted prayers. The assemblage falls into step, creating a solemn cavalcade.

A man and woman pause in front of me, blocking my view. Then as they pass, snatches of American accent tickle my ears. They move on, then hesitate on the other side of the bridge. Their American voices reverberate in the quiet air. For a few minutes I gather information, observing their tall, willowy frames, hippie-style dress, and coastal bronzed skin.

I debate whether to approach them. If they're just passing through, a conversation with English-speaking people would be nice. If they plan on staying for any length of time, I'd prefer not to meet them. My time alone requires protection. But the chance of tourists lingering in Otranto is slim. It's a remote area of Italy. I decide if they move on before I cross the bridge I won't pursue them. But if they continue to stand and watch the procession, I'll introduce myself.

They stay in place.

"Hello, are you Americans?" I ask, wandering into their view.

"Yes," says the woman. "We're from California."

A longer-than-expected conversation ensues. They tell me where they are staying, how long they have been traveling, and how often they travel. We exchange stories on why we're in Otranto.

They retired three years ago and have spent most of those years traveling in Spain, Portugal, Belize, Mexico, and Germany. This is their first trip to Southern Italy. Their stories are wacky, colorful, and succeed in providing me with a healthy dose of laughter and a nourishing amount of English.

"What's going on at the church?" she asks.

"I believe it's a pilgrimage to the Hill of the Martyrs," I respond. "Are you familiar with the massacre that occurred here in 1480?"

"No," they respond in unison. "What's that about?"

I provide a brief history, but they don't seem interested and glance around restlessly as I'm speaking. I reduce the massacre to a thumbnail sketch, letting the story trail off into space. They fill the void by reminding me they only arrived in Otranto today and don't know anything about the area.

"Why did you choose Otranto?"

"No reason in particular. We were just moving around by train and bus. This is just another stop on our way south. We'll stay here a couple of nights and then move on."

"Oh," I say, delighted their stay will be short, "how nice."

"Where can we buy wine, food, and a few supplies to tide us over while we're here?" he asks.

"Oh, I just came from a great shop. They have wine, olive oil, and snack food. It's right over the bridge on the corner, the one with the green awning. And right past that shop is a small grocer. Then there's a veggie stand at the edge of the park. It's still open."

They thank me and we exchange email addresses. They suggest we meet for lunch or a glass of wine.

"Yes, that would be great," I smile. "When you're settled, send me an email and we'll meet."

I watch them wander off in the direction of the wine shop, realizing I don't remember their names. I dub them Priscilla for her West Coast sophistication and Bobby for his shy country-boy demeanor. Companions and English conversation for a day or two might be enjoyable.

Lingering on the bridge in the fading sunlight, I observe the procession as it continues to meander toward the Hill of the Martyrs. As I walk back to the apartment, my pace slows. I peer into shop windows brimming with exotic pieces of pottery and jewelry. I savor my evening *passeggiata,* not realizing how much this chance encounter would impact my time in Otranto.

Mosaics and Storms

MOSAICI E TEMPESTE

THE WEATHER SO FAR has been splendid. Brilliant sun-filled days have smiled on me with an occasional overnight shower to refresh and replenish the earth. Camelot comes to mind. But today storm clouds gather over the sea, haze hovers low on the waves.

Colors alternate in splashes of cobalt blue, dark gray, and brooding black as the sun and clouds smack into each other. Flicks of white foam form a chorus line, kicking up as each wave crests, rushing toward shore. The musky breath of the storm arrives on persistent breezes. The low clouds mist humidity into my already frizzy hair and add dampness to my clothes as I roam the village.

Scirocco stirs in the wind, in the dark and threatening sky as I scurry to class. There's electricity in the air. It charges through my body with restlessness and tension. My focus continues to be mosaics. My heart beats to the sound of my clippers against the marble. My right hand is forever paralyzed in pain, worthless to write with.

Mosaics—clean cuts of marble, durable, strength passing from my hand forming a Salento sun. The chaotic pattern shows no sign of meshing into a work of art. There's a desperate push to complete it, to make it whole, as if the pieces, once in place, will bring the same completion to my own life.

For the past two days I've stayed late, for two and sometimes three hours. And, I've arrived an hour earlier each morning. I'm working six to seven hours a day, yet the mosaic is unformed, a mass of tiny stones swarming randomly across the board. Today we'll pour the mortar on the one corner I completed. The mosaic must be at a stage to pass Francesca's inspection.

Bounding up the stairs, I find Francesca already there. Initially I don't see her because there's such a jumble in the classroom—tables, chairs, marble pieces, marble dust, a sink, the wall cabinets and two floor-to-ceiling windows. It's the scrounging noises I hear before I see her squatting inside one of the cabinets. She straightens up and smiles triumphantly as she holds up a plastic bag of powder, a plastic drinking cup, and a plastic spoon.

Francesca brings her treasures to the table, handing me a metal spatula and a well-used rag. She checks out the section I completed yesterday and nods. She indicates she will mix and pour the mortar. When she pours, I'm to rapidly spread the mortar on the completed section of the mosaic while wiping off any excess.

Before we begin, she says forcefully, *"Devi lavorare velocemente o il mortaio non sarà più diffuso."*

It's the first long sentence in Italian she has spoken to me. It's meaning is clear. If we don't work quickly, the mortar will be impossible to spread.

She pours powder into the cup, adds water, and vigorously stirs the mixture. Nothing happens. She adds more water, and the mixture instantly seizes up. A hint of fire flames in her eyes, creating a variance from her usual patient personality. She starts over. It takes several attempts to produce the right consistency. With each attempt, her lips flatten. She mutters under her breath. Finally it's ready and she pours. I spread and wipe, making sure we only cover the section that's glued down.

We wait. Once she's satisfied the mortar is hard enough, she hands me a slim wooden stick shaped like a cuticle instrument. It's so primitive I'm sure it's the same tool used by Pantaleone. I examine the stick, wondering what I'm supposed to do with it. Francesca takes it from my hand. She leans the flat end at a precise angle against the marble. Once the placement is to her liking, she drags it delicately across the marble pieces removing any excess mortar from the surface.

Each time I attempt to maneuver the stick, it slips from my grasp. My knuckles scrape against the uneven stones. My blood mingles with the mortar. Francesca rushes over with a wet cloth and wipes up the blood.

She takes my hand in hers and gently presses down, forcing my hand to relax into an unnatural and awkward position. She pulls back on both our hands. Bits of mortar flake away. She touches the stick down on the channels running between the pieces and says "*No*," indicating I must be careful to only clean the surface.

The goal is to remove the excess while not dislodging the mortar in the crevices or popping out the stones. She tells me I'm to let the mortar harden overnight.

The time for Francesca to leave arrives far too soon. Tomorrow is the last day of classroom instruction. At the end of the day, the mortar will be poured over the entire piece. Before I leave today, the mosaic must be completed.

"How did the last day arrive so swiftly?" I mutter to myself. "How can I possibly finish it all today?"

Francesca senses my concern. She tells me to focus only on gluing the pattern in place. She says I can work on cleaning the mosaic next week after classes are over. She reminds me that I can work in the classroom until the mosaic is complete.

She starts to leave, stops, turns around and comes back to the table. She takes the wooden stick from my hand and pries out one of the white stones. She looks among the discarded marble and picks out a pale-yellow piece. She places it in the vacant spot. Its awkward, raised edges set higher than the other pieces. I watch in horror as she glues it in place.

I wait for an explanation. Francesca briefly leaves the room and returns with Barbara. They speak rapidly, and then Barbara says, "Francesca wishes you to understand why she did this."

She explains that the stone is called the *humility stone*.

"When you look at this mosaic, I want you to recall many things—your desire to learn, your hard work, your perseverance, your eye for beauty, and your knowledge of the skill required to create art. Most of all, when you look at this raised stone, I want you to remember only God's creation is perfect. All other things we strive to do are feeble attempts toward perfection. You have done well, and the Salento sun smiles in your heart."

It's a moment of unexpected grace. I nod, acknowledging her words and whisper, *"Grazie mille."*

After Francesca leaves, I cut the remaining marble and fill in the background. The pieces ramble happily in disjointed directions until they run out. A series of open spaces stare back at me. Leaving the unfinished mosaic, I methodically check through the cabinets. There are only small pieces of marble in the colors required to complete the mosaic. I stand on tiptoe, reaching into the furthest recesses on the top shelf. My fingers wrap around a few sticks of marble. I drag them across the shelf along with dust and grit. In my grasp are two sticks of red marble.

I'm giddy with delight, or perhaps it's just the inhalation of marble dust. Triumphantly, I cut the red marble into diamonds and place them in whimsical fashion throughout my design.

This screws up the pattern even further, but there's a grand freedom in gluing outside the lines. The Salento sun smiles back, expressing gratitude for red diamonds that add fire and heat to its blueness.

It's almost four in the afternoon when I push back from the table. My attempts to add whimsy to the pattern will most likely unsettle Francesca. Fatigue has settled into bricks on my back. There's no time to remove the red diamonds, even if I wanted to—which I don't. They add depth and beauty to the mosaic, reminding me it's okay to be spontaneous. It's okay to color outside the lines. It's okay if Francesca is disappointed. It's all okay because the red diamonds reflect an inner courage I thought I had lost. The red diamonds tell me I'm still there under the layers of marble dust.

Sliding my hands over the mosaic, I touch the roughness so unlike the silky smoothness of the cathedral floor. I acknowledge my artistic bent is not in mosaics. These little marble stones need too much direction.

My reluctant heavy feet drag down the silent hallway. Fatigue trembles in my knees. Hanging onto the railing, I descend the staircase. The door snaps shut behind me. The cup of yogurt and glass of juice I had at six-thirty this morning have long faded from memory. My stomach snarls in protest.

I stop at a food stand and order a large slice of pizza with tiny cherry tomatoes, arugula, and mozzarella. The fresh, spicy greens, the sweet tangy tomatoes, and the fat-oozing cheese merge in my mouth.

In my state of exhaustion and covered with marble dust, I stumble to the sea with my slab of pizza. Sagging onto the seawall, I nestle into my favorite hideaway niche. The lunch crowd has vanished, and it's too early for the evening walk. The promenade is empty.

Seabirds dive for fish, their piercing squawks dissolve and drift on the wind. The sky swirls overlapping patterns of white, then darkens into deeper grays against the ebony sea. The sun peeks from a spot to find me. Its radiant warmth releases all my tiredness into the wildness of the approaching storm. The wind gathers strength, darting in and out of the waves. It scoops up massive gulps of water and spews out mouthfuls of foam into the vastness of the universe.

It's time to hurry home to shower, check email and settle into my PJs. The brooding storm might create electrical failures. I want to be safe and snug if it does.

The storm approaches, gathering steam as it crosses the sea from Africa. The rain falls from buckets held by giants. I fall asleep on the sofa dreaming of red diamonds that morph into ropes, ladders and trees, transporting me into survival mode.

The wind ruffles my hair. I stand on a tiny tin plate at the top of a twenty-five-foot pole, trembling yet braced to jump off. My heart gallops into my throat, my blood pressure climbs the pole with me, and my knees quiver in anticipation of the leap.

It's all part of a survival course my management team has been coerced into performing.

I'm one of only two women out of thirty participants. One member has already failed, facing humiliation and embarrassment. I have had enough of both in my life.

I begin my ascent—the trust ladder done, the rappelling done, the tightrope walking done.

But climbing this narrow, swaying pole—with spikes too far apart and legs too short to manage without great exertion—is close to breaking me. Sucking air, I force my trembling hands to grasp the last spike. I heave myself onto the thin metal plate at the top. I don't look down. If I do, I will fail.

I look up. A slight breeze parts the autumn leaves. The sun smiles warmth into my soul, steadying my shaking body. My head and heart tell me this will be the last time I'll do anything outrageous simply because someone else requires it or expects it of me.

This will be the last time someone else will dictate my destiny.

In the moment before I jump I recognize that Ray and I will move on with our lives. We will move away from the pressures of corporate oversight, away from the need to continually please others. I will divorce those monstrosities the same way I did my second husband.

With sunlight touching my spirit, I spread my arms and jump.

Passing Through Life

PASSANDO ATTRAVERSO LA VITA

I AWAKE. THE FEAR I encountered from that mandatory team-building survival course lingers in my thoughts. That fear almost swallowed me that day as I reached the top of the pole. It's a continual reminder of how swiftly life passes and how daily courage is essential to live fully.

The heart-stopping weekend changed the direction of Ray's and my life. When I returned home, we initiated an action plan. One that shifted the direction of our lives and granted us fortitude to leave corporate jobs and open our own business.

Perhaps the greatest gift I acquired that weekend was the knowledge that humiliation, failure, and even success do not define me. The day I climbed to the top of that pole and jumped was the day courage reentered my life.

The last day of mosaic class arrives, and I've long forgotten the initial reasons I signed up for the class. Was it a book about Idrusa and the mosaic floor? Was it a need for healing? Or was it to find a pattern for my fractured life? Whatever the reason, the journey has challenged me to move out of my comfort zone.

During the entire week of the class, I haven't thought too much about my fragmented life. There's been no time. The work requires all of my energy and focus. When my mind drifts, the pattern drifts. Yet restoration has taken place without my interaction or intervention. Calmness rules my thoughts, fortitude is my guide, and an abundance of energy accompanies me.

The simplicity of life brings joy to me with each new sunrise. Solitude is my delightful companion. The class, the long walks, the fresh food, and listening to my inner voice without interruption provide me with pleasure while offering healing.

There's been no time to write or to do research. Actually, I haven't thought about *the book* much.

Idrusa keeps her distance in the classroom. She shows no interest in mosaics. Occasionally she tags along on my evening walks. Her long, red hair woven with silk ribbons flows down her back, her bare feet slap against the cobbled path, and her animated gestures pull me from one place to the next.

This morning before class I lounge on my upper terrace daydreaming. Clouds blot the sun long enough for my negative tape to turn on. The warbled voice reminds me of other people's expectations. Thoughts scream in my head. *You're here to write a book. Ray thinks you're writing a book. What will you tell everyone when you return with nothing?*

I turn off the tape, reminding myself I'm strong. Courage brought me to this time and place in my life. My thoughts wander to another time and place when great courage was required to overcome an abusive marriage.

In anger, he packed my suitcase, threw it on the driveway, and took my car keys.

"Go ahead," he sneered, "you'll be back. You're too stupid to make it on your own."

Instead of cowering with obedience as I had for too many years, I booked a tour to Spain and Africa. I had summoned the courage to tell him only a few weeks before my departure. He said he wouldn't go, and he wouldn't allow me to go. I said the money for the trip was nonrefundable. He said I was stupid to spend his money so foolishly. I almost dissolved. But an epiphany struck as we glared at each other with mounting hostility.

"All the people in our circle travel," I sneered. There was silence, so I continued. "It would add to your standing in the community to be well traveled. No one in our group has been to Spain or Africa. You'd be the first."

He walked away without committing to the trip.

It was my tiny step toward freedom from a life lived in mental and emotional poverty. This act of defiance signaled to me that perhaps this was the way out. Perhaps I could walk away, removing myself from the mire.

The trip to Spain and then Africa bordered on disaster. His constant patrolling of my every movement, his uninhibited drinking, his self-importance exhibited when he endlessly threw money around in front of our traveling companions left me despondent.

But there were small moments of freedom. When he passed out, I'd sit quietly until his breathing deepened. Then I'd slip away for a few precious minutes alone. I found beauty and dignity wherever I looked. A desire for a life other than the one I was trapped in invaded me, tagged along by my side, rattled my every thought.

On one of our planned tours in Spain we visited a Damascene steel factory, where the finest handmade swords were crafted. My husband, a skilled marksman and swordsman, immersed himself in the process, running his hands across the burnished, razor-sharp steel. His knowledge drew the tour group into his realm. His moment of glory crescendoed when the factory owners asked him to participate in a thrust-and-stab pretend game.

I was forgotten.

Joyfully, I wandered away from the tour, slipping unnoticed through a side door. A small dusty path angled up a hill. As I moved away from the highway and the factory, songbirds and cicadas brought a sweet rhythm to my walk. The path crested abruptly, dropping steeply on the other side. A farmer and his mule, moving together in harmony, emerged on the far slope. The freshly turned furrows around the ancient, gnarly olive trees fashioned bold, staggered patterns of precision.

The unity and simplicity of their task flooded me with distant memories of my father and grandfather plowing the land—my grandfather's straight back, his silver hair, and his black eye patch; my father's strong, steady hand on the bridle as he guided the mule in a straight line. Peace engulfed me as the memory gathered strength.

Standing in the shimmering sunlight, I was saturated with the intense heat. As I closed my eyes, some of my pain abated. A taste of goodness crept into my life. It was a moment of such intense longing—a hungry pang so strong, calling me to create a better life for myself.

When I opened my eyes, people from all generations paraded before me. Fearing I was hallucinating, I stood without breathing. The people kept coming, moving through the landscape. Each one acknowledged me, singing out to me to join them in the journey to my own life. The scene vanished in a moment, replaced by the farmer and the mule persisting in their weary path through the olive grove.

Breath whooshed from my mouth. Tranquility doused me in creamy layers. A blanket of safety descended. I had seen and heard the call. One day, not too far off, would come a day when I would live again. The door had cracked open, yielding me a glimpse of freedom.

These distant memories shift to the present. Francesca tells me she's pleased with the amount of work I've accomplished. She spies the red diamonds I slipped into the design yesterday after she left. She likes the idea but tells me it's a bit off-center. My head and heart recognize off-center as my intention. It's too complicated to explain in another language, so I nod.

Barbara sticks her head through the door and asks about my progress. She and Francesca lean over my artwork and discuss it in Italian too rapid for me to understand. They point, nod, and smile— or maybe those are grimaces.

Barbara looks up and speaks in her magical voice, "Francesca showed me the flaws in your work, but she also pointed out your creativity. She appreciates your efforts, your intensity, and your understanding of the craft. She applauds what you've accomplished and says your heart understands mosaics."

Praise does not come easily from Francesca.

"Please thank her for me," I respond. "Tell her she has been an excellent instructor and guide in a very complicated art. We have worked in harmony without benefit of a mutual language. She has given me gifts of patience and beauty."

Satisfaction washes over me as I gaze at my still-to-be-completed mosaic. I had no expectations of excellence on my first attempt with this medium. What I wanted, worked for and obtained was the experience to better understand an ancient art. This week gave me a glimpse into the lives of real artists who toiled hours, days, weeks, months, and years to create Pantaleone's mosaic floor. But the real treasure I received from this class was learning that fragments, when properly restored, turn into wholeness.

My still-unfinished mosaic is a much larger endeavor than the four-by-four-inch coaster Francesca envisioned for me. When I return home, it will be a daily reminder of my accomplishment. It contains the story of my journey to this place. The pain and joy of cutting the marble shows in its surface. A lasting stain of blood is part of the design. Joy was experienced when a piece of marble fit into a vacant slot and when the design finally emerged. Gifts not easily forgotten. My aching, swollen hand, the permanent slouch between my shoulders, marble dust oozing from my pores—all united the fragmented pieces into a whole.

I have come on a long journey to put the fragments of my life together. This class has given me the tools to begin. Terry Tempest Williams's words have journeyed with me to this sunny Salento place: *It's mandatory that we find beauty in a broken world.*

We finish mixing and pouring the grout. There's nothing more I can do today. The mortar must dry before the cleaning process begins. Francesca's time with me is over. She hugs me with her in-the-eyes smile and gives me the traditional cheek-to-cheek kiss. We clean up the room together. She leaves, *arrivederci* lingering after her departure.

I stay behind, studying the mosaic. I consider how scraping away the mortar will be tedious yet necessary—a reminder that scraping away unnecessary stuff in our lives allows beauty to shine through.

It's only when the room grows dark that I glance out the window. The skies open, releasing pent-up tears. Trees bend to the wind's command. I gingerly place the mosaic on the shelf—the one Barbara said I could use—and leave.

The door slams behind me. I have no umbrella, but an umbrella would be useless against the storm's rage. Dodging swimming-pool-size puddles, I stop by the veggie stand to pick up fresh produce. Soup is on the menu tonight. It's Friday. School's over. My only goal this evening is to snuggle on the sofa, watching my favorite Italian game show. It's a mindless way to decompress after this week's intensity. Two days free from *mosaicing* wait.

The storm follows me home.

14

Strangers in the Night

STRANIERI NELLA NOTTE

BEFORE TAKING MY MUCH-needed shower, I check email. My Italian friend Laura has written. She lives in Bastardo, about three hours north of Rome. We've been friends since 2005 when Ray and I were invited to cook for a week at a local restaurant in Marsciano. Laura was the day chef and the only employee who spoke a few words of English. She welcomed us, showed us around, and introduced us to the kitchen staff. I immediately fell in love with her because of the many kindnesses she showered on us that week.

She's a great chef, and a few years ago opened her own restaurant. During our trips to Italy, we always stop to visit her, eat her splendid food, and help in the restaurant. I'm always happy to receive her joyful emails, but the one waiting in my inbox is totally unexpected and requires me to respond immediately.

Laura: *Dear Donna I found in this week an old friend from when I was a little baby in zurigo. . . after 41 years. . . and I never forget Him so he lives in Otranto and will know you*

*and visit you in Otranto. . . and He tells me if you need any-
thing he can help you. Say me please that you want to know
Him????? baci tell me immediately*

Donna: *Sì grazie mille. Does he speak English? baci, ciao*

Laura: *no but I think You can understand him. . . he's a very
good person and can know news of my life, probably He will
come today at 5 o clock baci*

Donna: *Today? Are you sure he's coming today? Next week
would be better.*

Laura: *His name is Marcello like "Dolce Vita" and he wait
for you near the castello. he drives a black Mercedes . . . I
write you the hour. . . probably 5 o clock*

Donna: *va bene, grazie mille. You and Marcello are troppo gentili. I will wait for him on the sidewalk in front of the
castle. Tell him I'll be wearing jeans, a red tank top, and a
red and white striped shirt. What can I say to him so we will
know we have found each other? Is this a short visit just to
introduce ourselves? I'm not sure I understand the situation.
Can you tell me more?*

Laura: *dear Donna if you can he is coming at 16.30 near
the castle. . . only for you. . . kisses laura. He dress jeans and
heavenly shirt and blue jacket he can help you for anything.
only un salute.*

It seems my quiet evening is not to be. Instead, I'm going to
meet a strange man in a Mercedes in a foreign country on the
recommendation of my dear friend Laura. I'm not sure whether to
laugh or cry. I don't want to meet a strange man. But Laura's email is
so full of joy, imagining her two friends will meet. Exhaustion layers

on my back, but I can't disappoint Laura. My nemesis is saying *yes* when I want to say *no*. I ignore my pleasing-everyone attitude and convince myself it would be a good thing to know someone local in case I need assistance. So I drag myself off the sofa.

It's a few minutes before four-thirty. Fortunately, I'm next door to the castle. The storm has abated, although brooding skies indicate it will soon return without warning, dumping gallons of water. I told Laura I would be there, and I will.

It's too late for a shower. I brush marble dust out of my hair, slip into clean jeans, red tank top and striped shirt and rush out the door to meet the mystery man—Marcello. There's no waiting. As soon as I reach the street in front of the castle, a black Mercedes pulls to the curb. The window rolls down and a man says, "Donna?"

I say, "Marcello?"

He smiles, revealing beautiful white teeth and dimples, and a heavenly shirt. His nod says he's Marcello, so I climb into the car of a total stranger—something my mom told me never to do. Maybe it's another way to color outside the lines—to write instead of printing.

We drive a short distance while I assess the situation. I glance sideways, and he appears harmless. His chiseled, sun-bronzed face and his strong, blunt fingers grasping the steering wheel don't threaten. Before we have time to exchange greetings and acclimate ourselves to the situation, he pulls off the road.

Thankfully, I don't panic. He takes out his phone and places a call. He hands me the phone. On the other end is Laura's bubbling laughter. She asks me how I like her friend. We chat a few minutes. I return the phone to Marcello. He chats a few minutes before slipping the phone back in his pocket. He tells me Laura says we must stop for a coffee or wine and become acquainted.

It's a bizarre situation. Laura speaks a bit of English, I speak a bit of Italian, and Marcello speaks only Italian. We are a loosely connected threesome.

He pulls back on the road and finds a place to park in town. We walk a short distance to a bar and sit on the crowded terrace. He orders red wine for me, coffee for himself. The waitress places our drinks on the table as the sky collapses into flood-style rain. Rolling thunder prevents any conversation, even without a language barrier. Lightning snaps and sizzles, gaining on us.

I form Italian words in my head to suggest we move inside. Focusing so intently on the correct thing to say, I don't notice the terrace is flooding—until water swirls against my shoes.

Rain advances in harsh gray walls from every direction.

We pick up our drinks and try to push our way inside. It's crammed with people spilling out the door. There's no room. Marcello motions toward a small space under the awning. We press against the wall, sheltering under the tiny overhang. It offers minimal protection from the violent gusts of wind, spraying rain into our cubbyhole.

Marcello tries to start a conversation, but my ears can't follow anything he says. The rain thunders, the thunder gallops, and the lightning dances triumphantly across the sea. My desire to collapse from exhaustion gathers strength. Add to that the immense effort required to understand Marcello. Then throw in a raging storm. My only wish is to go home. A whimper rises in my throat. I bite down hard on my lip, searching for something to say until the universal words of weather pop into my head.

"Piove, tuono, fulmine," I stammer out, teaching him the words for rain, thunder, and lightning in English. He smiles and relaxes. I smile and suggest he take me back to the *castello* as soon as the storm subsides.

As if on command, it stops as suddenly as it started. We finish our drinks. Marcello drives me back to the *castello*. I think he says if I need anything, I should let him know. He gives me his card.

"Grazie mille, hai uno spirito generoso," I say, wishing I could say so much more than just that he has a kind spirit. He smiles, shakes my hand, and wishes me *buona sera*.

Speed-walking back to the apartment, I strip off my miserably wet clothes as soon as the door closes behind me. I shower, put on my PJs and turn on my Italian game show while soup simmers on the back burner. Tiredness descends sweetly as I snuggle into the comfy spot, sipping the Salento sun wine.

It doesn't matter that the storm returns with unrelenting fury.

More Than Spiders in My Hair

Più di Ragni nei Miei Capelli

OVER THE WEEKEND I take a break from cleaning the mosaic. My fingers are raw and bleeding from slashes caused by uneven cuts of stones. Every time I scrape the mortar there's an increased likelihood of creating fresh wounds. A little Neosporin and bandages over a couple of days will hasten the healing process.

The entire weekend stretches lazily in front of me as I stroll around the walled village in the early morning light. An easy breeze tugs at my soft blue cotton skirt, ruffling it around my knees. A tune hums in my head, "I Believe I Can Fly," Etta James's version, on my playlist. I'm lost in the imagery of soaring freely above the sea when a voice breaks into my reverie.

"Hello, we've been looking everywhere for you."

Glancing back into the present, I'm surprised to see Priscilla and Bobby. It only dawns on me now that they never contacted me. I hadn't thought about them at all.

"Oh, hello. I'm surprised to see you again. When I didn't hear from you, I thought you'd moved on," I say politely.

"Oh, no," says Priscilla, "we've been trying to find you. We've looked all over the village, asking everyone if they'd seen an American woman."

"Oh, how nice, you speak Italian. I didn't think to ask you when we met," I say, positioning myself in the shade.

"Goodness, no, we don't speak Italian. But I know a little Spanish. It's the same language—well, practically the same—you know, being a Romance language. I'm sure they understand."

A warning bell dings in my head, but I continue the conversation.

"You said you'd send me an email. When I didn't get one, I was sure y'all had left town."

"Oh, no, it's just that when we met, we didn't know there wasn't an internet connection at our apartment," says Priscilla. "Can you believe that? That's why we didn't email you. We were so happy the day you spotted us and introduced yourself. Just think, another American in this part of Italy. We didn't expect that. And we certainly didn't expect to find someone who clearly knows about this area. And seeing that you're familiar with it, wouldn't it be grand if you showed us around? We've decided to stay for a while. You're the first English-speaking person we've come across since we've been in Puglia. It's a great opportunity for us—like our own personal guide."

I'm not sure how to respond as another alarm bell dings. The politeness drilled into me surfaces: *Be pleasant to everyone. Smile and provide what others request. Never be self-centered. Always put other people's desires above your own.*

Priscilla is still talking and hasn't noticed my silence. I tune back in as she says, "Since we didn't know where you were staying, we didn't know how to contact you. That's why we're wandering around—hoping maybe we'd bump into you. And, here you are. Isn't this fantastic!"

My mind stalls. Finally, I manage to say, "While I would love to show you around, it's not possible—well, actually, maybe I could spend a few hours—"

Priscilla jumps back in, "Of course, you can. What fun we'll have. We'll rent a car, visit the surrounding villages, the beaches, the festivals—"

"Oh, no, no!" I say, stammering. "No, no, I'm actually working—doing research for a book. I don't have much spare time."

Bobby has stayed in the background during this exchange. Now he speaks. "I'll rent a car. You can be the navigator. We'll tour the entire area. You decide what we should see."

I answer, thinking there's a way out. "You won't be able to rent a car. There are none as the rental agency is closed for the season. I can't even find a taxi. They don't seem to exist in this area in the off-season."

Bobby chuckles. "Oh, I'm sure I can rustle up some form of transportation for us." Priscilla interrupts, "Where's your apartment?"

"It's close by." I indicate, pointing down toward *via Castello*.

I don't really know these people. I'm alone and cautious. I don't want them having the location of my apartment—maybe if we become better acquainted, but not now.

"Gosh," says Priscilla, "you're so lucky to have found a place in the walled city. We would love to be in the middle of everything. We spend all our time here, and it's such a hassle to walk from our apartment. Can you help us find something inside the walls?"

"*No*, sorry. I wish I could, but I don't have any contacts here," I reply, making sure my *no* is emphatic. "Maybe if you ask around at the restaurants and bars someone can help you. In fact, I've been looking for the tourist information center ever since I got here. If I find it, I'll let you know. They could help you."

"Well, why don't we have a drink now? It's never too early—you know, the old 'it's five o'clock somewhere' rule," says Bobby.

Shit! I think while managing to say, "It's not convenient for me now. I'm working on some local research. But the Blu Bar is right around the corner. See those ruins, the ones at the end of the street? The bar's right there. We can use it as our rendezvous point. I walk by it several times a day. If you're there, we can plan something together—a festival would be nice."

I don't tell them it's my special place, the place Paolo said I would find. *Why did I open my mouth*? Of course, in a village this small they'd have found it without me. Saying a quick goodbye, I rush off, promising I'll see them soon. Since I told them I was looking for the tourist office, I make that my mission, as I don't want to add another lie to my growing list.

Strolling around the outside perimeter of the castle, I contemplate lies, wondering how old I was when I told my first. This is a topic I've never considered before, not until I lied about coming here. I would have told anyone who asked that I didn't lie. But when I think about it, that's not true—I'd be telling a lie if I said I'd never lied.

When I was five, I started primary school, which is what kindergarten was called all those years ago. After the writing-versus-printing disaster on the first day, I kept in the background, doing what I was told. I never offered an opinion unless I was forced to respond.

One day, a little girl in my class peed in her pants and had to be taken home by her mother for a change of clothes. Of course, she was humiliated, but the greater problem for me was she stole my yellow sweater. It was new and my pride and joy. Mother had tied a matching yellow bow in my long strawberry blonde curls, pulling them up high on my head. Although I wasn't allowed to write my name, and I was having difficulty mastering the art of printing, I still felt pretty good that day. But all the joy disappeared when the little girl stole my sweater. The teacher tried to give me the little girl's faded, pilled sweater. I was inconsolable, sobbing until Mother was called to remove me from the classroom.

Mom wasn't happy with me. She couldn't understand why I was so upset, telling me I'd get the sweater back when the little girl returned to school the next day. I don't remember getting the sweater back, but I do remember what happened when we returned home. I was given a treat and allowed to play with my dolls. Mother was very solicitous. The joyous day flew by.

The next day I was told I had to go back to school. "But I don't want to," I stormed.

"You don't have a choice," Mom admonished.

At precisely ten o'clock, I felt a stomachache emerge and asked to see the school nurse. She turned out to be a kind, gentle woman who spoke softly and stroked my hair and wiped away my tears.

Mom silently appeared at the door. She wasn't smiling. I skipped and hopped all the way home, knowing a treat and playtime awaited me. They did not. Instead, I was sent to bed. Mother said if I was too sick for school there would be no treats and no playtime. *Still better than school*, I thought.

Every morning I walked to school holding my big sister Claudia's hand. I begged her not to make me go in the classroom. Each day we cried and clung to each other as the teacher jerked our hands apart, pushing me not so gently to my desk, or to sit in some dark corner. Each morning around ten I lied, telling her I was sick and needed to see the nurse.

During the second week of my lying, a parent-teacher conference was called. Mother and Daddy were told that if I didn't attend school, the truant officer would be called, and they would be reported. Mother shaded that a bit by telling me the police would be called and that she and Daddy would be put in jail. We would have no one to take care of us. Daddy would lose his job. There would be no food, no one to tuck us in bed at night, and no one to love us. All of this would happen if I didn't go to school and stay in the classroom for the entire day.

It was the worst time in my five-year-old life. I became silent, a child who hated school, who lived in fear that my parents would be carted off to jail, and who learned that lying needs to be a well-crafted plan to succeed, not some spontaneous whim.

I'm pulled back into the present when I step off the curb into the oncoming path of a car, blaring its horn with a fist-shaking driver yelling at my stupidity.

Childhood lies fade as my thoughts wander back to Priscilla and Bobby, hoping they don't become a nuisance. It would be fun to have a car and see some of the countryside, particularly Pantaleone's monastery and the remains of the ancient lighthouse. But it would be better if I could find the tourist office. I walk around the perimeter of the town, but no tourist office.

Because of my earlier encounter with Priscilla and Bobby, I didn't stop at the Blu Bar for my morning cappuccino. Now I check the time on my cell phone and see there's still time.

In Italy, there's a cardinal rule about when you can drink cappuccino. It isn't allowed after ten-thirty in the morning. Espresso is fine anytime, but not cappuccino. I'm sure there are cappuccino police lurking in the shadowy corners.

Since I'm in the correct time parameters, I turn back, slipping cautiously inside the walled village. When I'm close to the area, I draw back into the shadows, checking out the tables at the Blu Bar. Sighing with relief when I don't see Priscilla and Bobby, I creep out of the shadow, thinking Giovanni will know where the tourist office is. In the few days I've been coming to the bar, he has become a valuable resource. Just as I reach the terrace, voices yell out to me from a small restaurant across the way, one I hadn't noticed before.

"Hey, there," Priscilla and Bobby scream out in unison. "Join us for a glass of wine."

Keeping a neutral expression, I sit in the chair they offer. For two people who claim to have traveled so much, they have very little regard for local customs. Their yelling in such a quiet village as well as drinking wine so early in the morning create an uncomfortable atmosphere. I check furtively over my shoulder to see if the wine and noise police are nearby.

"I'm headed to the Blu Bar," I say. "When I'm in a bind with my research, Giovanni helps me find what I'm looking for."

They insist I stay, which I do because it's easier than having them tag along. I decline the offer of wine. They order another. I shrink a bit more when Priscilla orders in Spanish.

"Since you know Spanish so well, it would be easy for you to learn a few Italian words. I can write some phrases for you if you'd like," I murmur.

"Oh, they get the point with Spanish. It really does sound like Italian," she responds. "They understand it. They just pretend that they don't."

Pursuing this will not be beneficial, so I change the subject. They are interested in traveling around Puglia, and ask for suggestions. I give them names of towns I've visited and enjoyed. I tell them Lecce is one of my favorites. We chat about the location of the train station and the possibility of trains being the best means of transportation.

"Oh, we'll have such fun. Let's decide where we'll go first. Why don't we head south?" Priscilla gushes.

"Oh, I'd love to, but I'm so busy with my work. I came here to write, plus I still have to finish my mosaic. So I don't have time for a trip now," I say, hoping they'll cut short their stay in Otranto—well before I feel obligated to go anywhere with them. To change the subject, I show them a decorative black, silver, and white beaded spider I bought while exploring outside the walled town.

"There are some great little shops I discovered while I was hunting for the tourist office. You might be interested. This grand spider was in the shop along with spider houses, something I've never seen before. In Puglia spiders are very significant. There's both dance and music surrounding the legends of the spider and—" I stop mid-sentence as Bobby reaches up into my hair.

"What is it?" I gasp as his hand pulls away.

"Ha-ha," he laughs, curling his fingers into a fist.

"What is it? What did you find?"

"Oh, I found a baby spider. Yours just gave birth. You've got little spiders running around in your head," he says, belting out a hearty laugh.

I turn to Priscilla. "Is it true? Are there spiders in my hair?"

They both laugh. Bobby punches me on the shoulder and says, "Hey, it's just a joke. You're so serious about that big old spider. I thought I'd lighten things up a bit."

I smile but begin to wonder how I can distance myself from these people. They're not worth the price I'm paying to hear and speak English.

Pushing back from the table, I say, "This has been fun, but I'm low on groceries and the shops will be closing soon for lunch."

I rush away waving, not giving them a chance to join me.

Song of Songs

IL CANTICO DEI CANTICI

DAILY VISITS TO THE produce stand, the bakery, and wine shops are what I love best about Italy. Mini adventures await me each time I step out my door. I practice my Italian with the vendors and sometimes find an extra tomato or pastry in my shopping bag when I unpack.

Grocery shopping falls into a different category. At home, it's on my list of least favorite things to do. Ray loves to grocery shop, which works for me, and I do the finances. We're both happy.

Today my grocery list is long. It's close to noon. I manage to get in and out of the store, only breaking one jar of something sticky. They accept my offer to pay and shoo me out of the aisle. It's another reminder that "full of grace" does not apply to every child born on Tuesday.

It's a day without relief from heat or humidity as the rain comes and goes and sweat swamps my face and drips itchy paths down my nose. A large sack tucked under each arm eliminates my ability to wipe the sweat or scratch my nose. The cobbled street meanders uphill. I huff and puff my way up, collapsing on the doorstep. I rest before hauling the sacks up the steps to the apartment.

While I'm in the process of putting the groceries away, the front doorbell buzzes. Since I have vowed not to use the elevator, I avoid answering the front door. I figure by the time I find the key to the elevator and work up enough courage to use it, whoever is there will be gone. I lean out the window and see Priscilla. I'm stunned, thinking she must have followed me. I jerk my head back in, but she's seen me.

"Hello," she yells. "We're having lunch at the Blu Bar. Bobby's already there. We want you to join us. Let's plan our trip to Lecce."

Please, I silently pray to the spider gods, *don't let my neighbors hear her shrill voice.*

Leaning out the window and praying no one will see or hear me, I whisper, "I'll meet you at the Blu Bar once I finish putting the groceries away. We can talk then."

Later, I join them explaining, "I can't eat with you today because I already have reservations for lunch at the restaurant next door. Plus," I continue, "I'm trying to arrange a visit to some of the historic sites in the countryside. The rest of my day will be taken up with that project. My research comes first, so I can't make other plans right now."

As an incredibly brainless afterthought, I ask, "Would you be interested in coming with me?"

Perhaps if they joined me, they would be content with a tour of the countryside, and I'd make progress on my research.

"What are you researching and what sites do you plan to visit?" Bobby asks.

"Well, I want to visit the original lighthouse, the site where Pope John Paul commemorated the martyrs, and the monastery where Pantaleone lived and taught."

Their blank faces indicate little interest in my research or the antiquity of the places I mentioned. I'm relieved and vow not to let my mouth get ahead of my thoughts in the future.

They discuss renting a car to drive to Santa Maria di Leuca and Gallipoli, asking me to join them. I remind them again that the one rental car agency in town is closed for the season.

"We would have to take the train or hire someone to drive us," I say. "It would take too much time away from my research. As much as I love these small towns, I've already seen most of them. But I'd be willing to go to Lecce with you. It's a beautiful city, and I would enjoy seeing it again."

They nod but don't respond. Instead, Priscilla orders antipasti and wine in Spanish. They nibble and continue to encourage me to order something.

"No," I say again. "I don't usually eat until close to two. Today I'm having lunch at *Il Cantico dei Cantici*. Giovanni recommended I eat there. His wife and son run the restaurant and he told me the food is wonderful."

Priscilla and Bobby nod. They finish their lunch, drain the last drop of wine, and tell me they're returning to their apartment for naps. I'm relieved. Gathering my belongings, I walk across the street.

I pause on the outside patio. A young man greets me graciously and seats me in a prime spot where I can view the local activities. His smile lights up the already bright, sunny day.

Instead of pointing out the specials or taking my beverage order, he says, "Signora, do you speak English?"

This hasn't been of interest to anyone in the village until now. When I say yes, the radiance of his smile spreads further.

He asks ever so politely, "May I practice my English with you?"

"Yes, of course," I respond, "But only if I can practice my Italian with you."

"*Certo. Mi chiamo Francesco.* I will take care of you today," he says.

He remembers his purpose and recommends the seafood antipasti.
"Signora, it will be enough for a meal. You do not need to order
any food but this. The fish is straight from the sea this morning. You
must try it. It's the best food you will find in our town."

It would be unkind to dispute his recommendation. The seriousness of his expression reveals his confidence comes from the
quality of the food. So I agree. To my order, I add *un bicchiere di
vino bianco e una bottiglia d'aqua naturale*—a glass of white wine
and a bottle of still water.

Francesco returns with the wine and water and a basket of the
traditional bread stuffed with black olives, including the pits. He
explains, in well-thought-out phrases, that I must remember not to
eat the pits. He stands back from my table and watches with great
care to ensure I follow his directions.

The bread is thick, crusty, and warm as I break it open. It's
studded throughout with plump, juicy black olives. Bringing a chunk
to my mouth, I'm careful not to bite into a pit. He watches closely,
nodding in approval. He moves on to the next table only when he's
sure I understand how to eat the bread without breaking my teeth.

The first sip of wine is creamy and clean with no sharp or citrusy
aftertaste. Its mellow flavors and pale straw color reflect the Salento
sun, the sea, and the brilliance of the sky.

It's close to two o'clock, and the outside dining area fills with
locals. While the restaurant name implies music, I'm not prepared
for the eerily Moorish sounds reaching my ears. The strands of
music are so ancient they must have been part of the creation story.

Settling back in my cushioned chair, I watch as life abundantly
unfolds before me. My existence in this time and place is enough.
Fragments of the past, lost faith, and broken family ties disappear as
I soak in the view, the sun, and anticipate the arrival of the best food
in town.

My gaze leisurely drifts, taking in the ruins at the end of the
street. It's hard to wrap my thoughts around this scene—sitting at

an outdoor restaurant in this ancient little village looking at ruins from the beginning of modern civilization. This amazing vista is inconceivable back home.

The antipasti platter arrives piled high with tiny red shrimp, giant steamed prawns, a sliver of seafood frittata, a purée of shrimp and potatoes spread on garlicky fried bread, grilled octopus, and thin slices of raw tuna pulled from the sea moments ago. The sea salt crystals scattered across the plate glimmer in the sunlight. Tendrils of a red thread I can't place float on musical notes, adding color and contrast to the seafood.

"What are these?" I question Francesco, pointing at the red threads.

"They are *peperoncini*," he tells me. "They are dried, then shredded to this thinness. It adds only a delicate hint of spiciness. Taste, you will like."

The first bite is exquisite. I bow my head in prayerful concentration as I demolish each morsel, one savory bite at a time. A huge sigh escapes as I finish the last mouthful and return to the present. When I do, I notice a young couple discussing the menu placed on a stand close to my table. Francesco has disappeared. The couple hesitate, unsure if they should stay or go. Their whispers are English, although I can't tell whether American or British. They shrug and start to walk away.

"Please, may I help you?" I call after them.

They turn, smile and nod. The table next to me has been cleared. I suggest they sit while I find Francesco. As I move toward the door, I spot him coming from the kitchen with a plate of food. He thanks me when I tell him about the couple. He quickly serves the plate and rushes to their table, rearranging the chairs to ensure they are comfortable and have a good view. His smile tells me he's excited to have two tables of English speakers. Beaming, he turns to the couple and begins his practice.

Our tables are close enough to make conversation without raising our voices. Francesco assists them with the menu and ordering. When he leaves, I ask them how they happen to be in Otranto. A lovely story unfolds. They are Armenian. They speak English because they have traveled widely and have lived and worked in DC and New York while expanding their knowledge of English and computers.

Their education and expertise in technology allow them to travel the world. Their customers are global. Through the internet they can maintain contact with their clients wherever they go. This freedom allows them to travel from country to country, staying as long as they wish. They tell me they've run their business this way for the past four years.

"We're gypsies," they explain.

We reflect briefly on the sadness of the genocide in Armenia between 1915 and 1922, when one and a half million people were killed and millions more displaced in the dying days of the Ottoman Empire. I share the story of the Ottoman massacre in Otranto in 1480. We discuss the possibility that those who committed the Armenian genocide were perhaps the descendants of the Ottomans who massacred the people of Otranto.

We don't dwell on the past too long as it would bring sorrow to this bright, beautiful day. We focus on the experiences they've had as they've traveled the world and observed a variety of cultures.

"We seek to understand others. It's only through understanding that we can communicate and move away from prejudice, stereotyping, and killing each other," they say.

They are wise beyond their years.

Francesco presents lunch. They nod approvingly when they taste the food. When their plates are clean, we continue our conversation. It deepens to a point rarely found with family or friends, much less total strangers.

As I listen to their lyrical voices, I'm reminded of an old Nat King Cole song about an enchanted boy who wanders the world with sadness in his heart and wisdom in his eyes. One perfect day, this young boy magically finds the singer of the song. They speak of many things— fools and kings, the weakness and greatness of humans. The song ends with the boy saying the greatest gift anyone can give or receive is to love and be loved in return.

The enchanted couple pay their bill, say their goodbyes with gentle hugs, and fade into the ancient ruins. I wonder if this place and the music have cast a spell over me. Perhaps I was in a trance during this splendid lunch. Maybe I imagined these gentle souls. I glance across to their table. I see the remains of a meal, used linen napkins, and empty wineglasses, revealing nothing.

Francesco, who vanished during this unexpected conversation, reappears with a warm, chocolate cake fresh from the oven. He tells me it's a gift from the owner to thank me for inviting the young couple to eat at the restaurant. The dense cake and the gooey chocolate interior settle on my tongue—not too sweet. I contemplate the conversation with the young couple, letting it drift in and out of my mind like musical notes as ricotta and chocolate fill my mouth.

The music rakes across my spine, reminding me that enchantment comes to those who open their hearts, minds, and souls to its possibilities.

Tourist Information Italian Style

INFORMAZIONI TURISTICHE STILE ITALIANO

MY FIRST WEEK IN Otranto is consumed by mosaics. When I'm not in class, I'm in the cathedral looking at the mosaic floor. When I'm not in the cathedral, I'm reading about mosaics. When I'm not reading about mosaics, I'm thinking about them. The only other projects consuming my time are trash and trying to find the tourist office.

Every day on my way to class I stop by a small metal shed located in the park just outside the walled village. There's a haphazard sign on the shed saying *informazioni turistiche*. Every day I stop. Every day it's closed. It must be closed for the season, like most businesses in this remote part of Italy.

One day after mosaic class I ask Barbara about it and she says, "Oh, Donna, the tourist office is open all year. Perhaps you're in the wrong location. I'll write down the address and directions for you."

This weekend I have time to follow Barbara's directions. They lead me to a part of the post-WWII town I haven't yet explored, away from the park. The big tourist office is positioned in the lower part of the sprawling town, outside the walls and certainly outside the range of my daily prowling. This office is nestled in a modern piazza among little shops and restaurants. The big international "i" for information is displayed next to a large banner that reads *ufficio del turismo*.

A flurry of activity along with *buongiorno* greets me when I step inside, but everyone continues with their work. I wait patiently, understanding Italians have a more relaxed approach to life than we Americans. Finally, a girl at the desk looks up with a smile and says, *"Posso aiutarti?"*

"Si," I respond, *"parla inglese?"*

"No, no ma aspetta." She turns her chair and calls, *"Franco, vieni qui."*

A broad-shouldered, gray-haired man comes from the back office. His expansive mustache widens harmoniously with his smile. His eyes crinkle with old-world charm as he shakes my hand and introduces himself.

"Mi chiamo Donna Armer," I say.

I rattle off my scripted story in Italian, telling him why I'm in Puglia. Then I request a car and a guide so I can spend a day exploring historical sites in the countryside. It's only then I ask if he can speak English.

Franco leans in close. I think it's to hear me better. "Donna," he says, *"non parlo inglese."*

As I consider what to do, he calls out to a woman passing by the office. She stops, and we move outside. Franco and the woman exchange pleasantries. Then she turns to me and says, *"Parla inglese un poco."*

Un poco turns out to be true as we cannot find a common thread in our attempts to converse. Franco smiles and shrugs as the woman wanders away. His brow furrows into concentration. I wait. After a few minutes, he tells me his friend Carlo speaks English. If I return in the afternoon, Carlo will be at the office.

"*Grazie mille*," I reply, "*Ritornerò questo pomeriggio.*"

In the afternoon, I return and meet Carlo. He's a delightful, well-groomed young man with close-cropped hair and just a hint of dark stubble. He speaks as much English as I do Italian. But with our bits and pieces we manage.

Carlo considers all my requests. He pauses from time to time to explain to Franco, who nods in agreement. Carlo asks if Tuesday morning is a good day for me.

"*Sì*,," I say, "*Ci vediamo martedì. Arrivederci,*" letting him I know I'll return on Tuesday morning.

We don't discuss the cost of the guided tour. I've come to understand price usually isn't discussed with Italians early on in a transaction.

On Monday morning with happy thoughts I stroll to school. There's no hurry, as the cleaning of the mosaic is on my own time. The air hums with sunshine, the kind that inspires you to raise your arms and shout for the pure pleasure of being alive. Crossing the bridge and lost in daydreams, I step from the curb. A bicycle whizzes by, almost running me down. The rider yells my name. The only yelling people I know are Priscilla and Bobby.

I wave and continue across the street. But it's too late. Bobby zips past me again waving his arms and singing, "Oh, Donna." He slams on the brakes, spins around, and comes back with a twelve-year-old's look of delight.

"Hey, hey, hey—look what I've found," he blurts out as his smile spills in every direction. "I can now get to the old city in a few minutes instead of the usual twenty-plus it takes when I walk. You won't believe where the bike shop is located. It's only a few minutes from here. Hop on and I'll take you. We'll rent bikes and that will solve our transportation problems," he says with conviction.

"Gosh, what a great discovery," I say with all the sincerity I can muster. "It's a wonderful solution for you and Priscilla, but I'm already in the old city and can walk anywhere I need to go. A bike might work for some of the closer villages. Why don't you two try it first and let me know how difficult the ride is? If it works for you and Priscilla, then I'll rent a bike."

I don't mention that I hope Priscilla isn't going to bike with flip-flops. I've never seen her wear any other footwear and have often wondered how she manages the cobbled streets. I can barely maneuver in sturdy walking shoes. I'm pretty sure flip-flops on a bicycle would be a disaster.

My flip-flop thoughts are disturbed as Bobby announces, "I'm doing the laundry today because Priscilla fell this morning."

"Oh, I'm so sorry. Did she hurt herself?" I say, although I really want to ask if she had on flip-flops.

"Not too much, just some scrapes and bruises, but enough for me to know it would be wise if I took on the task of laundry. We're not as lucky as you. We don't have a washer in our apartment. But I found this great laundromat just down the street. Do you want to see it?"

"No, no thank you," I say with astonishment. How can he possibly be so excited over finding a laundromat? Perhaps they haven't washed clothes in a while. I guess that would make a laundromat an intoxicating discovery.

We talk about finding a ride to some of the villages close by or to one of the area's many festivals. While we're talking, one of the tiny taxis that looks like a golf cart with plastic windows lumbers by, pulling into a parking area near the seawall.

"Well, I must be off to work on my mosaic," I say. "Why don't you check with the taxi driver and ask if he would consider driving us around for a day or evening?"

I could bite my tongue as the words fly out of my mouth. *Why do I continue to encourage these people?* I scurry away before he can answer.

On Monday night another fierce storm comes through. It's still raining heavily on Tuesday morning. Today is not a day for sightseeing. I contact Carlo and we reschedule for Wednesday morning. Slipping on my rain jacket, I hop across rising puddles to the classroom.

The progress of cleaning the mosaics continues to improve each day as the scraping stick becomes an extension of my hand. The wood is warm to my touch. I rip my knuckles less and the splashes of blood on the mosaic decrease. Each day I witness the fragments coming together, creating wholeness.

My Sunshine

O Sole Mio

WEDNESDAY MORNING AN EXUBERANT sunrise greets me. I check email, shower, dress, pack up my bag of essentials and head for the Blu Bar for *un cappuccino* before meeting Franco and Carlo.

Paolo's words about finding the right cafe still make me smile with delight. Owner Giovanni has become a valuable resource. He encourages me to speak Italian with him over my cup of coffee. I often prepare my sentences in the evening, memorizing the words in Italian.

Today is no different. In halting present tense, I say, *"Ho intenzione di visitare il monastero di Pantaleone e il faro originale."*

He nods in agreement with my plans, suggesting that along with the monastery where Pantaleone studied and the original lighthouse, I should add a visit to the new lighthouse. He says it's a beautiful setting.

"You'll enjoy seeing these sites. The original lighthouse is a ruin now, but it's ancient and well worth the trip. It was built before the 1480 massacre. You also need to see the red cross where Papa Giovanni

Paolo blessed the 800 martyrs of Otranto. And not to be missed is a natural lake rarely seen by tourists," he says.

Together we examine the map. He marks the places I must see. When I realize the time, I say a hasty goodbye and sprint to the tourist office. Franco and Carlo are waiting outside, eager as schoolboys participating in their first soccer match. We examine the map and Giovanni's suggestions. Franco nods. *"Andiamo."*

It's market day, which covers the entire piazza in front of the tourist office. Franco encourages me to partake and offers to accompany me.

I love local markets in small European towns. They are my favorite places to unearth local flavor, to prowl, to taste exotic foods, and to discover small treasures. The entire town crowds the narrow, crammed-full-of-goodness aisles. From years of traveling in Italy and other countries, I've found that a weekly market is the best place to buy fresh produce, meats, cheeses, breads and wine. Gradually, I've learned how to make purchases by watching locals ask for the vendor's help instead of picking up and examining the item without permission. After a few missteps, I became confident enough to buy food, shoes, scarves, jewelry, blouses, tablecloths, kitchen utensils, and even underwear.

Franco and I stroll among the stalls bustling with buyers and sellers. Voices call out to me to buy the best of this or that. I'm offered a sample of *porchetta*, fragrant with rosemary and garlic, its juices spitting in the hot oven.

Franco introduces me to the vendors. He tells them I'm a writer from the United States. Much to his dismay, I stop to take photographs of dried beans. He tries to divert my attention and camera to other views of the market. But I like the dried beans. Their jewel-toned contents spill out of burlap sacks filled to overflowing. The edges of the bags are artfully draped so that the shapes and colors of the beans are fully displayed. Red, white, green, speckled, striped, and even black *ceci* (garbanzo beans) cascade into view. My mind conjures steaming bowls of soup brimming with all these beauties.

While Franco hurries me along, I pause at a long, rambling stall containing large vats of olives. They overflow with every size, shape, color, and taste. The succulent fruit with spicy slivers of *pepperoncini* or chunks of garlic will add another dimension to my growing list of must-haves for meals.

We don't linger as Franco says it's an introductory visit and I can return on my own next week. We walk back to the car and pile in. Our first stop takes us to the cross blessed by Papa Giovanni Paolo in 1980.

Franco, as an Italian driver, has a predestined right to drive on either side of the road. He must also have the pope's blessing to drive through the roundabout in the wrong direction.

Slouching in the back seat, I clamp my eyes shut. I don't want to witness a head-on collision. Eventually, he pulls off the road just enough to pretend someone won't hit us. We hop over the road barrier and trudge through mud and weeds, the latter emitting a wild fragrance I can't place.

"*Che cos'è?*" I say, pointing to the ground as I turn to Franco.

He says the Italian name to Carlo—*menta selvatica.* Carlo looks up the word on his phone and says it's wild mint. But my cook's sense of smell tells me it's more than that. Franco grabs a handful and presses it into my hand. Aromas of mint, sage, basil, and oregano burst into my nostrils. The scent identifies the subtle but distinct flavors I've tasted but couldn't place in seafood salads and other dishes from this region. It's pungent and lightness at the same time. A heady scent lingers in the air, along with a tune Franco hums softly as we plow our way through the weed-lined lot.

Franco guides us up to the cross. Fragments of trash shuffle in the wind. Years of neglect speak of lost hope. The information board is tattered. Carlo tries but can't figure out what it says. Red paint peels off the colossal iron cross, drip by drip; the sacrificial lamb bleeds into weeds and heaved asphalt.

"Carlo," I ask, "why is this place so forlorn and neglected?"

His answer touches my heart. "The tourists are not interested in coming here so there are no funds to restore this sacred place. The cross was built specifically for Papa Giovanni Paolo when he came to Otranto in 1980 to bless the 800 martyrs who were so brutally massacred by the Ottomans. That is the only time anyone cared. It has been forgotten, abandoned, and neglected for years. No one comes here anymore."

Franco reaches into his jacket, producing a candle and matches. I'm puzzled by his actions. This site wasn't on our itinerary until after I asked about it this morning. *How did he know to have a candle and matches? How could this man be prepared for a sacred moment?* These questions dance in my head as an eerie peacefulness descends. The breeze holds its breath.

Fragments of trash lie still. Bird voices murmur in meditation. Franco kneels to light the candle. He gently places it at the base of the towering red cross. We stand in silent prayer.

It's ironic that it took 500 years for a pope to come to Otranto to bless these 800 souls who gave their lives for their faith. No memory of Pope John Paul's visit remains here, just an overwhelming sense of loss and betrayal.

Franco makes the sign of the cross. Lost in solitude, we ramble back through the perfumed grasses. Franco picks another bunch of herbs and hands them to me with his sweet smile accompanied by another song. He's a singing man, making a joyful noise as we go along. The music and words soar from his heart and give salvation to this long-neglected place.

Carlo tells me that many years ago Franco was famous for his singing. He recorded albums when he was young. Now he only sings to please himself. I congratulate myself on finding a singing guide. My body vibrates with the hum of Franco's music and past civilizations. I simultaneously hear the cries of anguish interwoven with songs of joy.

Back in the car, Franco hits the gas, spinning us into the roundabout. We leave Otranto as we plunge down a small country road. We pass barren fields with ancient *trulli* left to crumble in the wild grasses and scrubby bushes. Their broken stones slump into tangled weeds. The surrounding trees bow down to the greater power of the wind.

Our next stop involves another muddy, weedy place. We step with caution out of the car to view the ancient lighthouse called *Torre del serpente* by the locals. This place is the symbol presented on Otranto's coat of arms, the one I showed Francesca as a possible design for my mosaic—the one she shook a silent "no" to, thinking I was a crazy American.

Franco stops at a distance. We stand, taking in the antiquity of collapsing stone against the backdrop of a tranquil sea stretching into infinity. Chills scramble up my spine. Idrusa's spirit hovers. She's been silent for days. Now she's here with us, letting me know this is her place.

To break her spell, I ask Carlo, "Can you tell me the legend of the lighthouse?"

He hesitates, appearing uneasy. Finally he says, "*Molto anni fa,* a large serpent came to live at the lighthouse. Every night the serpent would slither up the tower, drinking the oil from the lamp until it ceased to burn. Without light to steer voyagers away from the boulders, the ships crashed onto the rocks, spilling lives and cargo into the murderous sea."

"What does the story mean?" I inquire, watching his jaw clench.

He pauses. "I don't know, but we don't like *il serpente*! When we were children, this was the story told to frighten us into obeying our parents."

We turn away from the ruins and cross the road. Muddy red earth clutches my shoes. It molds tightly into place, making every step forward an effort. The loud sucking sounds increase as we walk deeper into the swampy field. Franco stops before a small green pond that's surrounded by vivid red slopes. He asks me if this is what the Grand Canyon looks like. I respond "No," but the question surprises me, so I take a second look. Perhaps it does—in miniature. At times like this I long to be fluent so I could ask him about his way-off-base idea of the Grand Canyon. Instead, we stand in the muck, staring at the shimmering emerald pond.

"Carlo, tell me about this pond."

I don't understand much of what Carlo says except that it's natural water. It's green because first it's blue, but mixed with the red soil it becomes green. *Why not purple?* I wonder, but I don't say so.

Later, when I'm back at the apartment, I Google the pond and discover the green is created by bauxite, a sedimentary rock made of oxides and hydroxides of iron and aluminum. This area was an active quarry from 1940 until 1976. The bauxite was extracted and shipped to factories near Venice. Once the mining stopped, water infiltration formed the lake, creating this blood red, emerald green, alien landscape. We slog back to the car, scraping red mud off our shoes as we go.

Casole di San Nicola is next on our list. Franco turns onto a dirt road lined with what were once majestic umbrella pines. Now many are rotten, dead, or have toppled. It's another fallen-on-hard-times place of sacred antiquity. Pantaleone, designer of the mosaic floor, lived and studied here with other enlightened monks during the twelfth century.

I tap Carlo's shoulder, pointing at the rubble. He shakes his head. We pull up to a makeshift house next to the *casole.* There are snarling dogs, straining at their chains.

"Should we get out?" I ask. "Why are these ferocious animals guarding this property?"

"The government allowed someone to buy this place, so it's now private. The home of Pantaleone belongs to an individual who obviously has no funds to restore it and no concern about keeping it available for the public," Carlo says as he looks away from the disgraced property and the howling monsters.

We chance getting out of the car because I want a closer look at the monastery. The disintegrating ruin allows glimpses of its former magnificence. There's a high stone wall, barely visible ancient columns, and a barbed wire fence surrounding the entire property. I so long to prowl in the ruins, run my hands down the columns, and meditate in the place where this great man spent his life.

Franco steadies me as I climb the stone wall. He keeps his hands clasped around my ankles while I take photographs. I only have time to snap a couple before a gnarled old woman charges out of the house, shaking her fist, screaming at us to leave. Franco tells her I'm a writer from America, but she isn't interested. She yells again, inciting the dogs to make savage lunges and bare their yellow fangs. We quickly retreat, galloping to the car.

Franco speedily exits the property, then pulls off the road. He's upset and apologizes. Neither he nor Carlo can explain to me why a private citizen is allowed to own this antiquity. I try again to understand the situation.

"How can a private citizen own such an important landmark without agreeing to its upkeep and without allowing the public access?"

They shake their heads.

"There is no answer," says Carlo.

The drive to the next landmark is silent. We traverse rural emptiness. The newer lighthouse only reveals itself when we pull off the road and park on an embankment that gives way to giant boulders and scrubby grasses pitching toward the sea. The lighthouse is on the easternmost tip of Italy. Every morning, this is the place where light comes first to the Italian coast. The lighthouse was built in 1867, abandoned in the 1970s, then reopened in 2008 by environmentalists.

It's modern in comparison to the ancient stone-built lighthouse we visited earlier, the one the serpent lived in. I stare at the squares and rectangles which are out of place in this remote outpost. Thousands of years ago invaders landed on these shores. During more peaceful times, pilgrims disembarked here on their way to Jerusalem. Now tourists come to gaze at dawn's first light tipping the Italian coastline.

Standing at the edge of the cliff, I'm mesmerized by the endless swell of the sea. The white rocks spill down the cliffs, teetering on the edge. Razor-sharp sunrays shave strands of diamonds off the white lighthouse, flinging them into rainbow sparkles across the wide expanse of water. It's a golden moment to stand and watch the glory of creation.

The blues of sea and sky meld into midnight then cobalt, slipping into delicate blues and softening into aqua. The sun strokes the rocks into brilliance so fierce it penetrates my sunglasses, rendering them useless. On this easternmost point of Italy, the sun commands the universe. There is no sound where we stand high above the sea. Waves whip and whirl against the rocks in silence, sliding back into the sea before regrouping to return with increased aggression. We stand in the hush of late afternoon, watching the sea realign, flinging itself back into the bedrock.

Carlo finally says, *"Andiamo."*

Franco refuses to come further down the slope with us. He says we'll regret our decision when we have to climb back to the top. But Carlo's eyes plead to go. I nod, falling into step with him.

He pauses, helping me maneuver onto the steep pathway.

"We're walking on the same path Roman soldiers walked on," he says. "This place was and still is a strategic part of the coastline. The soldiers would have camped here many centuries before this lighthouse came into existence."

As we make our way down, sheep graze in pastoral bliss on the side of the cliff. As I turn to get closer for a photograph, the blinding sun bursts into my eyes. I can't see and hand my camera to Carlo. He tries but is also blinded. Later this evening, when I load my photos onto the laptop, the sheep appear. I gasp, awed by their bleached bodies glittering in furry whiteness, some revealing slashes of red spray paint marking which ewes have been impregnated.

We are reverent as we walk. Carlo helps me around the difficult spots. For a young man barely out of university, he's polite and interested in all my questions. He has an appreciation for the places he shows me. He tells me he wants to learn more because the questions I ask make him ashamed not to have the answers.

"This is my country," he says. "It's important for me to be able to answer your questions."

Franco is wrong about the walk back up. Carlo and I have fallen into an easy rhythm with our combined languages. Our conversation flows as we clamber up the cliff. Our topics include language, books, movies, and his favorite foods of the region.

"What is your favorite restaurant in Otranto?"

"One that belongs to my friend," he says. "You must go and order eggplant and swordfish for antipasti. Then you must try the sea urchins with pasta and the *orato* for the fish course. Dessert must always be what the chef suggests."

Our laughter rises to meet Franco, who stands at the top on the footpath. When I'm close, he reaches out his hand and pulls me up. He wants to know if I've seen enough. He needs to go back to the office before it closes.

"*Ovviamente,*" I respond, storing away all I've witnessed today. It's been a mixed day full of both beauty and destruction. There's much to consider—trash, broken and fragmented remains of antiquity, songs from the heart, candles lit in sacred silence—so many bits and pieces of lives: past, present, and future.

Franco refuses to accept money. He says it will be enough if I write a book about this place, this day, and the beauty of Salento. The hospitality and graciousness overwhelm me.

"May I take your photograph?" I ask. "I want to remember today and both of you."

After I take the photo, Carlo says, "Let me take one of you and Franco."

Franco and I walk out into the sunlight together. The vivid colors of sea, sky, flowers, and flowing grasses embrace us—warm light weaves around us, spinning me a day full of extraordinary people and places.

Franco says, "Spread your arms wide to show your friends how beautiful this place is."

We stand *insieme,* our inner arms entwined, and our outer arms stretched wide, saluting the beauty of Otranto. Franco raises his face to meet the Salento sun. His voice lifts into the warm breezes, *"O sole mio"* pours forth from his soul—my land, my sun, my Salento.

Mosaic Lessons

LE LEZIONI DI MOSAICI

TODAY IS THE FINAL cleaning of my mosaic. Taking two days off over the weekend helped my fingers heal, and today I'm aided by a pair of thin rubber gloves I purchased at the market. They're awkward to use, but my fingers are grateful, and my mosaic has been spared from more bloodshed.

Arriving early at the school, I find the building deserted. There are no classes, no instructors, no Barbara. The weekend's hush lingers in the corners, blending with dust and fledgling spiderwebs. I work until I'm satisfied with the results. Standing back, I survey the blue Salento sun nesting in the taupes of sand sprinkled with red stones. The essence of my time here is captured in the mosaic and in my heart. It will stay with me for the rest of my life.

I carefully wrap the mosaic in a towel, taking one last look at the humility stone. I clean the classroom for the final time. Terry Tempest Williams's words of finding beauty in a broken world again resonate. I consider my misplaced apprehension on the first day of class and wonder if I will ever eliminate that dread and leave that fearful, anxious little girl behind. Taking this class in mosaics has been joyous.

The broken fragments of marble will remind me every day that all is temporary, both the good and the bad of our lives. The rough patches of the mosaic taught me to open my ears, eyes, and heart—to listen, to learn, to appreciate and to be grateful for the joy I've been given.

Two years ago I listened to my voice and followed the words of my heart—the words that said I needed time alone to heal and to reflect on the rough spots so I could leave them behind.

Taking a long last look around the classroom, I close the door and slip silently down the hall to Barbara's office. She isn't in. I'm disappointed for her not to see the final masterpiece.

Barbara's absence reminds me of my first test grade in college. I was thirty-three when I entered as a freshman, coming out of a brutal divorce. The triumph of my first college *A* was wiped out when I rushed into the empty house. My accomplishment received no accolades. Standing stone-still, I took a deep breath and let my sob slip away. Then I found Scotch tape and hung my paper on the wall in the kitchen. It stayed there all through those years, reminding me I'm strong and capable, and that being proud of myself is enough.

The door to the *scuola* closes after me with a soft thud. I stride into the sunlight with the mosaic tucked under my arm, leaving the anxious child behind.

Once outside, my priority is to find bubble wrap to protect my mosaic for the trip home. Earlier in the week, I had asked Barbara where to find some. I had also asked if she would be willing to write a document on the school letterhead explaining the mosaic.

She thought my request was strange until I told her about the dreadful time I had getting through security with a Mary Magdalene statue. Every attempt was made to find the drugs I had supposedly stashed somewhere inside a solid piece of stone. The experience taught me to be more cautious. Barbara agreed to write a letter in English and Italian.

She also told me to check the tobacco shop for plastic bubble wrap and ask for *busta grande per lettere con mille bolle.* Already there's a misunderstanding as I just want plain bubble wrap, not an envelope lined with bubble wrap. It's too complicated to explain this to Barbara so I nod and thank her.

After dropping off the mosaic at the apartment, I stroll around town looking for a tobacco shop. Entering the first one I come across, I politely ask if they have an envelope lined with bubble wrapping. Clearly, I didn't get the words in the correct order as a blank look is returned. Finally, I'm told they don't stock envelopes—*stamps, yes; envelopes, no.*

Next, I stop by the Blu Bar and ask Giovanni. He tells me to go to the post office. All my previous experiences with post offices in Italy have been unsuccessful. If I follow Giovanni's suggestion, it will involve an entire day. I'll have to wait patiently in line. When I reach the head of the line, the postal employee will tell me they don't have envelopes with bubbles, or they will send me to stand in another line. The only thing I've ever accomplished in an Italian post office is paying a parking ticket. I've had far too many unusual experiences with post offices, so I scratch it off my list. I don't tell Giovanni. Instead, I thank him and wander outside the walled city to see what I can find.

I don't get far before I bump into Priscilla and Bobby. They tell me they saw a FedEx sign close to where they're staying. This sounds hopeful, and I'm thankful for their directions. It takes a while, but I find the FedEx shop. Of course, they don't have envelopes with bubble wrap or even plain bubble wrap. What they do have in abundance is hospitality. The lovely young woman comes out from behind the counter, takes my hand, and walks with me several blocks to a *cartolino* shop.

"Here," she indicates. "You'll find envelopes with bubble wrap."

She's right. It's an easy and inexpensive transaction. I leave with a large padded envelope to protect the mosaic. These wonderful chance encounters with people, who are kind enough to take me by the hand and lead me in the right direction, are what compel me to return to Italy over and over. This country deserves a hospitality award.

On my way back to the apartment, I decide this final day of working on the mosaic requires a celebration. For me, a place overlooking the sea with food and wine plus sunshine and sea equals celebration.

Sauntering through the main portal into the old city, I notice a tiny opening offset in the wall. I've not seen the door before or the small menu posted outside. I peek in. It's dark and dusty, but there are steps leading up. I wonder if this could be the entrance to the upstairs restaurant I always admire when I take my evening *passeggiata*. Up I go, then right and up again. If I wasn't already hungry, I would be after the climb. When I reach the top, there's a glass door providing a view of two women working inside.

I open the door and call out, *"Siete aperti?"*

"Si," they respond in unison. I go in, but the restaurant doesn't look open. There are no customers, and the two women are cleaning. Delicious aromas drift out of the kitchen into the dining area. My nose follows. A large glass window reveals a chef surrounded by pots and pans as steamy yumminess invades my space. She looks up, smiles, and comes to the door. One of the women explains I want lunch. The chef gestures for me to follow her.

I'm disappointed when we walk away from pristine white tablecloths set with fine silverware. The tables are adorned with red poppies in green ceramic vases. The views over the sea are spellbinding, but we don't stop. Instead, we go down another flight of stairs and out a door which opens onto the outside dining area on the lower level. The chef tells the manager to prepare a table and to take good care of me.

It's past lunchtime, but I'm not turned away. The manager seats me at a table facing the sea. Every courtesy is extended to me, starting with a complimentary glass of chilled prosecco. Lifting the bubbling liquid to my lips, I toast the completion of my mosaic and all I've reclaimed for myself during the creative process. My second toast is to the sheer joy of being in this restaurant by the sea. My third toast is for my remaining days in this magical place.

A lightly sparkling white wine arrives next, along with bottled water and my favorite bread stuffed with olives containing pits. I'm left alone to gaze across the promenade where waves rise and fall in a graceful dance. The waltzing sea tickles the sky's toes. The sun throws glitter over the dance floor. I sigh into the breeze.

This mesmerizing scene disappears when a platter of grilled peppers, zucchini, and eggplant sprinkled with coarse sea salt is placed before me. Dense golden olive oil laps at the vegetables while a scattering of parsley, just picked from the pot by the front door, is dusted across the plate by the waiter.

Slow service, slow food, and slow enjoyment express the beauty of my experience.

Appreciation of food and wine is as ancient as the village. There's always time to sip a perfectly chilled glass of wine, to savor the taste of vegetables pulled fresh from the earth, to relish seafood caught in the early morning hours, and to gaze at the brilliant sea and sky that resist boundaries.

Later, the *orechetti con cozze* arrives with fresh tomatoes, basil, a splash of wine, olive oil, and a squeeze of lemon. The mussels are succulent, their sweet juices spilling into the already delicious broth.

The promenade stretches endlessly in every direction, intermittently broken by cannonballs. It's a grim reminder to all who come here of the 1480 massacre. These cannonballs are all over town, left in the spots where they landed over 500 years ago. Some, like the ones I can see from here, are painted white and are often mistaken for decorative ornaments. Many others are scattered across the village. I have stumbled across them, cracked and slumped into the earth.

The painted cannonballs rise out of the pavers. They are majestic, appearing harmless. I first saw them before I knew about the destruction and death they brought to this peaceful village. Often, during my walks, I glide past the cannonballs without thinking about the massacre. It's only when I arrive at the feet of the statue of the warrior woman that I'm reminded to stop and recognize the significance.

The message resonates with me—to stay strong, to remember the past, to live in the present, and to move forward into the future. If I do not stand fast, if I do not guard my freedoms, and if I do not confront oppressors, I, too, can be invaded. Sitting on the sidelines, accepting what fate flings in my pathway, can no longer be the life I live. I'm learning from each of the tough lessons. I'm gluing the pieces back into wholeness.

These broken shards of history come together, breaking off into bits before coming together again. It's through the fragmented life and history of myself and others that I learn. The experience of pain and brokenness is the great teacher. As I acquire wisdom, I welcome the repair work—the work of creating mosaic masterpieces out of brokenness.

I sip the exquisite wine which captures the freshness of sea breezes. I surmise that taking a mosaic class earlier in my life would have been helpful. Still, I'm thankful for the courage and experience that comes to me now. I'm thankful for marble dust, backbreaking work, teachers who encourage, fingers that bleed, and celebrations in the Salento sun.

PART III
TRASH

What if instead of going away, our trash came back?

And, what if it came back all at once and was laid before you?

~JACQUELYN A. OTTMAN, *IF TRASH COULD TALK*

The Importance of Trash

L'IMPORTANZA DELLA SPAZZATURA

MOSAIC THOUGHTS FADE INTO the background as I turn my attention to living in Otranto. Shopping, purchasing and preparing my meals, washing clothes, and recycling trash fill my solitude with daily activities. I'm at the halfway point in my stay. My goal, vowing to live in the present, continues. I relish early morning walks, meeting shopkeepers, trying new restaurants, and avoiding Priscilla and Bobby. Idrusa often accompanies me. Her long, layered skirts swoosh when we turn corners and lift when we stick our toes in the sea.

I rejoice in the morning ritual of laundry: listening to the clunk of the machine as it whirls, transporting the damp items to the top terrace, and draping them across the rack in the morning breeze. When I return in the late afternoon, the sun has deposited its warm rays into the clothes, dusting them with the fragrance of sea breezes.

Trash is the one stumbling block in my otherwise idyllic existence. It has become a responsibility that's taken on a significance bordering on insanity.

Back home in South Carolina, trash is rather mundane. Every Monday, the small blue recycle bin with glass, newspapers, and plastic, and the big green garbage bin with wheels are moved to the curb. Once the containers are emptied by city workers, Ray returns them to their rightful place behind the house. It's a simple once-a-week-process that I never think about.

In Otranto, discarding trash, I discover, takes considerable time and effort. Recycling was introduced to Italians in the early 1990s. But the first time Ray and I encountered recycling in this country was in 2003, in Northern Italy. When we were in Puglia in 2010, recycling wasn't practiced.

When I first arrived in Otranto, I was too busy with mosaics to let trash interrupt. I was confused by which days to dump what, so I allowed the task to linger. I dump the scraps from my dinner in a plastic bag, tie it neatly, and let it sit on the kitchen counter. After a couple of days, the kitchen swarms with nasty little bugs. I don't recall the text mentioning anything about tiny flying insects accumulating in the kitchen. The microscopic creatures emit a slightly funky smell, or perhaps that's the trash.

When I finally take time to read the confusing mixture of Italian and English trash instructions provided by the landlord, I'm dismayed at the intricacies of Italian recycling.

Finding the three trash containers in the courtyard was the easy part. Figuring out which days to empty what categories of trash was calculus. Developing a grid, I list the days of the week. In the space for Sunday, Tuesday, and Thursday nights, I write OP/W for Organic Products and White trash bin. In Monday's block I add *PAP/Y* for Plastic, Aluminum and Paper with a *Y* for the Yellow bin. For Wednesday and Friday, I write a *G/B* for Glass and the Black container.

The random trips I make to empty the kitchen container have always been via the back way.

If I used the dreaded elevator, it would save time. But my fear of its jolting, sporadic ride outweighs convenience. Plus, it's a pleasant walk through the back alley and down the street to the front of the building. All I must do is unlock the door and dump the trash in one of the containers in the courtyard, or at least that's what I've done so far.

However, on the occasion of the trash bugs invading the apartment, I decide it would be unseemly to walk through the street with nasty bugs trailing behind me. I must use the elevator. I sort through the elevator rules as claustrophobic anxiety ratchets up. The corrosion along the seams from the heavy salt sea air continues to build. I fearfully remember its slow, hesitant progress during my first ride.

I review the long list of dos and don'ts about keys, buttons, and where to stand to keep it balanced. If I do not follow all the elevator rules, dreadful things can happen to me. Images of being stranded between floors swirl. *No one will know I'm stuck in the elevator. I won't be found until the end of my month-long stay.*

Standing in the kitchen, I grasp the bag that's surrounded by flying bugs. My heart thuds and sweat collects in my tightened fists as I consider the tiny rusted elevator. But trash demands a certain amount of decorum. I take a deep breath, grab the trash swarming with bugs and enter the elevator. Standing squarely in the middle, I insert the key. I push and hold the red button as we bump and grind all the way down. I'm relieved to arrive on the lower level with only shaking knees and shallow breathing.

When I reach the trash containers, my wildly beating heart increases momentum. The trash containers, which I've not looked at closely until now, are not the same colors mentioned in the text. Instead of white, yellow, and black containers, there's a murky gray (possibly white at one time), a dull orange (not close to yellow) and a dark green (possibly black at one time). The problem escalates as I realize I need to redistribute what I've already dumped into the containers. The dark green and orange containers are full, so I focus on the murky gray. If this is supposed to be the white bin, then my bug-ridden trash bag can be deposited here while I reorganize the trash in the other two containers.

Gingerly I pop open the murky gray container. In the bottom, floating in greenish slime, are two plastic bottles. The two bottles need to be removed and deposited in the yellow bin. But I refuse to touch the slime-laden bottles without something to protect my hands.

Just as I'm about to drop in my bug-laden trash, I realize Monday's organic trash has already been picked up. I missed out because I didn't put Monday's trash out on Sunday night. Now I must take the infested garbage back upstairs. The freezer seems to be the best solution for this bug-ridden bag: otherwise, the bugs will continue to populate and the odor will intensify. The freezer, when I previously checked it out, was coated with thick slabs of ice. It hasn't been defrosted in ages. But I think there might be room for a small bag of trash.

Timidly I squeeze myself back into the dreaded elevator with my garbage and trailing bugs, and repeat the elevator rules. Success. After depositing the garbage with bugs in the iced-up freezer compartment, I pick up the paper, plastic, and aluminum trash.

With great relief, I'm able to use the back door for this trash trip. Taking the long route decelerates my heart palpitations and airs out my sweaty palms. I place the trash in the orange/yellow container and wheel it outside. One of my neighbors has already put her clean, bright yellow container on the ledge. This must be the correct procedure, so I place my faded orange container next to it. I lock the door to the courtyard and stroll back to the apartment.

Later in the evening, when I'm writing at the kitchen table by the open window, my concentration is disturbed by a scraping-across-pavement sound. Peeking out, I glimpse my neighbor repositioning my trash container away from hers. Oh well, I must have put my bin in the wrong spot.

Tuesday morning I check my container. It's been emptied. I'm greatly relieved. I place the bin back inside the front door and spend a day exploring the village. Later, before dinner, I collect my garbage out of the freezer. Since the trailing bugs are frozen, I don't need to take the elevator. Sauntering out the back, I take the long way to the trash site. Placing my frozen bag into the murky gray container, I push it outside the front door.

Back in the apartment, I open my computer. I love the simplicity of my evenings at the kitchen table where I contentedly answer emails, do a little research, and consider writing possibilities while supper simmers on the stove.

As I'm sorting through email, my ears detect the same dragging-over-concrete sound I heard last night. Peering out the window, I see my neighbor relocating my trash container. I move away from the window, surmising that my trash isn't up to her standards. Before I get back to the table, I hear a different sound. I poke my head out the window again.

My neighbor has moved her pristine white container, placing it outside her front door. She has a stack of tidy little bags filled with kitchen refuse, sealed with matching blue ties. She opens her container and places each one reverently into the bin. Satisfied, she closes the lid and begins an unusual ritual, or at least that's my observation.

She marches into her house, returning with a bowl of water and a cloth. She tenderly washes the outside of her trash container, patting it on top from time to time. Perhaps this calms the trash in some manner and prevents it from jumping out. It's a step in the trash process that's open to interpretation, since it isn't in the instructions I received. My neighbor's elaborate concern for trash is puzzling. But at least I understand why her container is white and mine is murky gray.

Before I can return to my writing, she sighs and stands. She pats the top of her container and then opens it again. Her body slumps. Something must have happened since the last time she looked inside. Perhaps the bags have moved. She shakes her head and mutters.

Each neatly tied bag is taken out of the container. She rearranges them several times before she's content with her display. She closes the top. I think all is well. But to her dismay and mine the container has become dirty again.

Back inside she goes, returning with another cloth and more water. She rewashes and pats the container with great care and concern. Finally, it meets her approval. She lifts the container and gently places it on the ledge just below my window and goes inside. From my high perch, I think her efforts have made the world a safer place—or at least cleaner. But I'm too new at trash composition to understand each nuance, so I reserve judgment.

On Wednesday morning before I'm awake, the trash is whisked away. I retrieve the container, returning it to the courtyard. My busy day doesn't have time for trash. I forget about it until evening. I look at my grid and determine it's the black/green container with the glass items that must be placed on the ledge tonight.

Gathering my glass items into one small plastic bag, I bounce down the steps, out the back door, down the alley and left onto the cobbled street before turning into the courtyard. I check out my neighbor's container before I unlock the big door to the courtyard. I won't go wrong if I follow her lead. Her black container is already in place for tomorrow's pickup. I move my black/ green container outside the door.

Locking up, I return to my place at the kitchen table. But before I've had time to settle, I sense movements outside the kitchen window. My neighbor, who must be a member of the official trash police, is surveying my bin. Holding my breath, I wait to see if my trash passes inspection. It doesn't. A frown and lips pressed into a tight, straight line accompany my container as she arranges it far away from hers. I wonder if she's going to wash my container or rearrange my trash. But she stops short. She studies it for a while, then she moves her trash even farther away. Her shoulders tense in displeasure, her head shakes in disgust. Her lengthy, loud sigh travels to my perch in the window. Dark, damp disgrace settles on me. I hope she realizes that I'm still learning the importance of trash.

On Thursday night I look at the list again. It's time for garbage, so I remove all the little bags of frozen food scraps from the freezer and consolidate them into one large plastic garbage bag.

Inside the courtyard, I remember that the pesky plastic bottles are still floating in the gray mucous slush inside the murky white container. The trash collector clearly didn't want to remove them, and once again I forgot to bring anything to cover my hands. I leave them, anticipating the trash man will spirit them away for me if he sees they're still there.

Adding my frozen bag of garbage to the container, I begin to push the bin outside. The little wheels dig into the pavement, creating a dragging, scraping sound across the stones.

Freezing in place, I wait for my neighbor to confront me. No one stirs. I half lift, half push the container out the door and place it on the ledge, lining it up exactly as my neighbor does.

My neighbor is elderly. I don't wish for her to hurt herself moving my containers. Carefully I check and shift my bin until it's centered and far enough away from hers. All I can do is hope I'll pass muster when trash inspection rolls around.

Quick-stepping back to the apartment, I hover in a corner by the kitchen window and wait. Only a few moments pass before her door opens. She pauses in the doorway, contemplating my trash. Then she straightens her pristine white apron, brushing invisible strands of silvery white hair from her eyes. Her lips flatten into a tense line as she looks toward my door. Her gaze slowly moves up the building as I hastily withdraw my head from the window. I hit the chair, tipping it over as I topple onto the floor beside it. I huddle in this awkward position until I hear her door close.

On Friday morning, the rumble of trash pickup pulls me from sweet dreams. Leaving my cozy bed, I open the shutters. My first sighting of the trash truck reveals a miniature three-wheeled vehicle with a flatbed attached. It rolls to a stop at our street, and the motor is switched off. The trash collector, smartly dressed in his pressed sanitation uniform, whistles cheerfully as he leaves the cab. Leisurely he strolls up to the first trash container, opens it and pokes his head inside. He inspects the contents to see if it meets some predetermined trash rule. He must have a little checklist in his truck or perhaps his shirt pocket to record whose trash will receive a passing grade today and whose won't.

After inspecting the first container, he lifts the bags out, cradling them in his arms. He saunters back to his vehicle and deposits the bags ever so gently into their special reserved spot in the back of his truck. On his return trip he breaks into song. So far, today's work is going well for him.

There are three front doors in the cul-de-sac. The container from the first house has passed the test. My neighbor, the secret trash police person, is up next for inspection. Her reputation of perfect trash is obvious as the trash collector doesn't hesitate to remove her bags. Joy of perfection radiates on his face as he cradles and marches this crown jewel of trash to its royal resting place.

Now it's my turn. I hold my breath as the trash man surveys my container. Perhaps he's puzzled. It might be a rare occasion to see containers outside the rental property. He slips one finger under the lid and pops it open. He stares a long time. I shrink from the window, realizing a passing grade is out of the question. I close my eyes and hope. I wonder if he'll give me a grace period since I'm a guest in his country. Or will I be held accountable under the same trash rules as his regular customers?

I'm doomed. He gave me one chance to redeem myself when he didn't remove the plastic bottles from the organic trash container. It was a chance for me to right a wrong. I failed. He flips the lid back down and turns to leave. My thoughts race as I consider my alternatives: *yell out the window; run down the stairs and head him off; find a trash dump outside of town.*

Before I can decide, he stops, opens the lid, and takes my neatly tied bags to his truck. I realize too late I have broken several trash rules: first, the plastic bottles floating in slime are in the wrong container; second, my trash bags were in disarray; third, my trash container is murky gray instead of white; fourth, because my trash is trashy, I'm spoiling his pristine uniform.

The trash collector looks around. I slink back from the window until I hear the motor crank. There's much grinding of gears as the little truck moans and shuffles down the cobbled street. The rattle of my neighbor's door handle alerts me to further humiliation. Her determined footsteps move across the cobblestones. When I peek out the window, she's standing in front of my container. She lifts the lid and cautiously scrutinizes the contents. The two plastic bottles bobble up from the gray muck. Outraged, she drops the lid and moves to her container. She lifts it gently from the ledge, takes it inside and shuts her door.

I wonder how many more days before my trash learner's permit expires and I am hauled away by the trash police.

Night Music

La Musica della Notte

FRIDAY'S *PASSEGGIATA* TAKES ME rambling through the streets. The disastrous trash position I'm in pushes its way into my thoughts. This concept of salvageable trash is new to me. Through the years there have been moments of reflection and clearing out the trash, but I've never taken time to examine the fragments, to separate them, to pull out the valuable pieces, and only then destroy the bits that weigh me down.

As the sunlight packs its bags for another day, reflections on trash are replaced by Idrusa.

She skips in front of me as I return to the apartment. She smiles as I position myself at the kitchen table. She implores me to write. It's been a battle for me between writing about Idrusa or Pantaleone. But her insistent shadow, slipping in and out of my thoughts, wins her the first round. Pulling the laptop across the table, I open it. She nestles next to me. Words flow from her spirit to mine:

IDRUSA

I died August 11, 1480.

Thrusting my baby girl into someone's arms, I took the dagger straight to my heart. My last thoughts were of my precious daughter, Lucia—graceful light. I wondered who would plait and coil her hair and decorate the dark curly locks with the silk ribbons she loves so much.

Before the dagger reached my heart, my life did not pass before my eyes. But, if it had, this would have been the story of me, Idrusa.

There is no record of my birth. I have no recollection of parents or laughter. I was born without knowledge of myself or my family. I woke up one day and found myself living with a woman and man I hated. The woman says she is my sister Cornelia, and the mean-spirited man is her husband Emilio. He stares at my chest in a manner I know is wrong.

Life is hard for them because they are old and have no children of their own. They had no option but to take care of me. I do not fit into their hearts and have become an obligation. Even worse, I am a child with a fierce spirit. Every question I ask about our parents is met with silence or punishment. I am not to ask questions, I am told. This confuses me, not to know my parents.

There are still traces of my mother's smile in my heart and vague memories of my father's strong arms lifting me to the heavens.

It is too much for a child not to know her foundation, to be abandoned and left without hope. I withdraw into myself. I grow up creating make-believe stories as unwanted children must do to survive. I gave my mother beauty and strength, and to my father, a warrior's fierceness and confidence. But none of this make-believe was enough to prevent my sister Cornelia from beating me and scheming to marry me off. I was fifteen, almost too old, she said. I pleaded with her, telling her I didn't choose to marry. To be the wife of a fisherman or farmer would kill my spirit. Cornelia threatened me, telling me I would be sold into slavery if I didn't accept what she chose for me.

I was already in servitude to this sister and her husband. I was already living the harshness of slavery. I longed to break away, to be free, to run wild until I found a home in the world somewhere away from here. Marriage would break my spirit and my heart.

The cool sea breeze drifting through the window does nothing to alleviate the sweat on my brow. Heat rushes through my veins, radiating to my face, chest, and down the back of my neck. Fear of abandonment drags its nails across my heart, forcing me back to New York City. A strangled cry hisses from my lips. Intense pain invades my body.

An image of a hotel room seared in the recesses of my brain surfaces. I'm lying on the floor, blood pouring from me. I moan as the sharp edges of pain knife though my lower abdomen. His lips flatten into a thin, tight line as looks down at me, "What's all the howling about? You woke me."

"Help me," I whisper. "I'm bleeding to death."

Sometime later I was deposited, wearing a blood-soaked dress, at Metropolitan Hospital in Spanish Harlem around four in the morning. My own crying voice woke me up to gray shadows, the smell of urine, fried foods, and squalor. Images formed and disappeared as my eyes fought to find a path out of the nightmare. Darkness won.

When I awoke again, the room was crowded with Spanish-speaking people. They gathered around the bed next to mine. A nurse shooed them out. I pleaded with her to tell me where I was and what had happened. She pulled my chart off the knob at the end of the bed.

"Major surgery two days ago. You were hemorrhaging. The doc took out part of your right ovary and tried to clean out masses of cysts, but there were too many, and some on organs he didn't want to touch."

"Where's my husband?"

"That I don't know," she said as she flounced out of the room.

He never came. For the first time in my life, abandonment rested on my doorstep.

There were no phones in the room, and mobile phones didn't exist. The only phone on the floor was near the elevator. I couldn't walk. Then one night a fire broke out. Another night there was a stabbing in the next room. The janitor, a lovely man who had been stationed at Langley Field, became my caretaker when he learned I was from Virginia. He gallantly assisted me from the bed to the chair, brought me Cokes, and supported me down the long corridor to the telephone. I called my mom.

A colleague of my husband's visited. He was embarrassed when I asked him to tell my husband my release date. I was put on a plane and delivered to my parents' house where my physical wounds healed, but my broken spirit resided in abandonment.

When I cried, Mother was there. She brought me tea and toast and sat on the bed, stroking my hair. When I said I've been abandoned, she told me the story of her childhood.

When Mom was only a few months old, her mother died. Her father said he couldn't care for his three little girls—all given away—abandoned. She tells me about her struggle to return home. In silence we grieved together.

She listens in silence when I say I can't go back to him. She gently urges me to go home. She says without looking at me, "You've already been married once. Your marriage is barely six months old. You have to give it more time. He called. He's coming for you this weekend."

The front porch swing swayed in time with my tears as I waited for him. Mom and Dad's conversation from the open window drifts in and out of my sorrow. Dad fought for me to stay. Mom said I had to go. I was twenty-three and knew I was walking back into hell.

Idrusa sighs with the telling of my story, or is that *my* sigh? Abandonment crosses hundreds of years, rendering us unworthy, leaving us without love, torturing our souls, turning us into shadow people.

The computer blinks, warning me it's closing down. The comfort of my Italian home refocuses. The table covered with the blue and white cloth, the vegetables spilling out of the bowl, the warm night air hovering on the breeze all remind me: I'm no longer that fragile person.

Abandonment, rejection, desertion, neglect—all words I've tied to myself. Words I now realize I can delete from my life. I can discard them into the trash bin and replace them with words of strength, courage, and joy. I hit the restart key and continue Idrusa's story:

From morning until night, my life is filled with work—rekindling the fire before first light, heating the water for the morning's gruel, and adding fish bits left over from last night's meal.

The rest of my day is spent boiling sheets and making soap. My only freedom is when I'm allowed to hunt for marigolds, indigofera, Larkspur, and madder root used to make the dyes for clothing. This is the only thing that earns my keep. These forays into the forests and swamps are the only knowledge I have of freedom—

My concentration is interrupted, but this time by haunting vibrations drifting into my consciousness. The closeness of the sounds indicates musicians have gathered near the apartment. Singing and the trembling of musical instruments advance through the window. The wild, untamed notes rage around the corner of my building, slamming into the room.

I turn off the computer and rest my weary, burning eyes. Darkness falls gently after two nights of torrential downpours. It's a gracious respite, bringing cool sea tones and glass-tinkle laughter into the streets of the village. In the park, just outside the fortified walls, I envision families strolling arm in arm as they do every night, their faces happily buried in *gelato*. Their hands grasping newspaper cones of roasted nuts. The children squealing and tumbling in hastily formed soccer games while others twirl around on carousels.

The music rises on the night air. A spine-stirring rhythm invites me into the antiquity of its wailing voice. The ageless dance performed to this music is called *tarantella* in most regions of Italy. Here in Puglia it's called *pizzica*. The eerie sounds fill every empty space, spanning the gap between past and present. All my thoughts of abandonment dissolve as my ears tune in to the magic of night music.

Throwing open all the doors and windows, I'm graciously granted a front-row seat, but my view is of the night sky. Still, the music thumps up through the floor into my toes and up my spine, painting erotic images of frenetic passion. This ancient music whispers that it recognizes me, enticing me into its intricate web.

These same strains of music I've heard in Spanish flamenco, Tennessee bluegrass, Irish river dance and Louisiana zydeco. Its primitive nasal, guttural utterance is universal, emitting sounds sandwiched between pain and joy. The pain is agonizing. The joy is euphoric. The difference between the two blurs.

The *pizzica* is the most famous folk dance in all of Italy, regardless of what it's called in different regions. The traditional music and wild ballet dance steps are of considerable social and cultural importance. The dance had almost disappeared until a few years ago when it was rediscovered and embraced by younger generations. It's a mixture of religious belief and superstition. They've been twisted together until one becomes the other. Historians place the birth of the music around the eleventh century.

The dance is based on the bite of the tarantula spider. *Tarantismo* is the name given to the disease caused by the spider bite. These bites occurred in summer months during harvest.

Women worked more frequently in the fields, presenting opportunities for them to be bitten more often than men.

Tarantolati is the name given to the people who were bitten by the spider. The poisonous bite caused epilepsy, heart palpitations, melancholy, stupor, madness, and an uncontrollable desire to dance. It's believed those bitten were exorcised by the music and the feverish dance, which lasts until the afflicted person collapses from exhaustion. Dancing was thought to be the only cure. The dance could control the body for hours, days, or even weeks. The disease *tarantismo* no longer exists, but it gave birth to the music and to the dance called *tarantella* or *pizzica*.

Today the *pizzica* is emerging as an art form. Its roots in superstition have dissipated. The modern dance unfolds as an erotic, passionate mating ritual. A woman begins the dance. She moves in time to the frantic rhythm. When she's ready, she signals with her scarf, indicating which man she's inviting to dance with her. When she tires of him, she invites another. I wonder if the last man standing gets the woman. He would have to be a man of great endurance.

The music reaches out to me. Its dark, brooding tones come from deep within the land and the people. It weaves together beauty and a haunting sadness. It rushes up the walls, flies through the windows, wraps around the terrace. Its fast, furious sounds are all-encompassing. Its eerie taunt begs me to join in the dance.

My feet tap on the floor. I push back the chair, whirling around the room until my heart rate accelerates. I collapse, but the music goes on. In my exhausted state, freedom flows from my body. It's been years since I've danced with such wild abandon. *Abandon*—a word that can destroy or resurrect. I choose resurrection.

More Trash

Più Spazzatura

TOMORROW IS SUNDAY. THERE'S no trash pickup nor thoughts of trash on this beautiful morning. I'm trash-free until Sunday night.

After a long morning walk, I'm at my kitchen table reading Francesco Corona's book about the mosaic floor. It's a complex book, full of analysis instead of mystery. Misspellings and sentences without verbs proliferate in the translation from Italian to English. While this is a more authentic history of Pantaleone's work, this book requires more focus than I'm willing to give it this morning. I am so appreciative of how Paolo brought mosaic to life for me.

Since Idrusa is stabbed in the church, my research has taken me back to Pantaleone and the mosaic floor. I'm not sure how they will evolve. The mosaic floor and Idrusa's death are symbolic of patterns, changes, and challenges in life.

As I prod through the pages of Corona's book, my own book crosses into my thoughts. I do want to write a book. The thought has always been there, incubating, as years rushed by with *must dos* instead of *necessary for my soul to flourish dos.*

It's not too late. There are some years left—years to spend fulfilling my earth's journey, years not to waste seeking approval or trying to please, and years left to follow passions previously pushed aside.

Still, Idrusa and Pantaleone clash in my mind. Maybe the story will be intertwined with both, although Idrusa is more persuasive. My thoughts ramble down glorious avenues, testing one, then the other. Pantaleone teases me with his intellect, creative bent, and monastic life. Idrusa is an enchantress and a warrior woman. She beckons me to follow her. Whom shall I choose? Where will my words take me? I drift away on this journey of magic, mystery, and music.

Around noon, guttural voices rise in the cul-de-sac. Squinting out the sun-filled kitchen window, I spy my neighbor's ramrod back. Her starched apron, spotless housedress, sensible black shoes, and silver hair are brushstrokes waiting for a canvas. She confers with two men on bicycles. Large spray canisters are strapped across their backs. She holds court, gesturing wildly toward my apartment and then the trash container ledge.

I gasp when the two men get off their bikes and spray the ledge and around my front door. My neighbor has called in exterminators. I try to imagine my response if they ring my bell and ask to be admitted to spray my trash containers as well as my apartment. Fortunately, I'm spared this embarrassment. Instead of knocking on my door, they move inside my neighbor's house to spray for any contamination that might have migrated from my trash to hers. I'm now a contagion. I wonder if my face will be plastered on light posts all over town.

Each day I double down, striving to get the trash right. In the evening I set out the appropriate container. In the morning I put it back inside my front door. Every day my neighbor watches from inside her house. Sometimes, if I pass muster, she nods at me. To her, I always say *Buon giorno* or *Buona sera*, depending on the time of day.

Days pass and trash becomes a pleasant, if not passionate, part of my routine. If my neighbor nods, there's an extra brilliance to my day. It's like receiving a gold star. Sometimes I wonder if I'm still wanting to please, still wanting the crippling approval of others. But I don't think that's it. I came here to live in the community, to pull my weight, to learn how to be part of what makes this village a good place to live. I'm a contributor to the harmony and to the cleanliness required when living in tightly shared spaces.

Today my parcel of neatly tied trash swings by my side as I turn the corner to deposit its contents into the proper bin. My neighbor stands erect by yesterday's trash container. She's waiting for me. I'm stuck, not sure whether to proceed or retreat. My stomach quivers. I must have unknowingly committed another trash sin. She pivots toward me, speaking in heavy dialect.

"Non capisco," I murmur. She isn't interested that I don't understand. She firmly takes my arm and marches me to the trash ledge and points. I tentatively flip open the top of my container. It's still full of yesterday's trash. She guides me to her container, nodding for me to open it.

Carefully I lift the lid, revealing her cleanly stacked bags of trash. She points and nods again before we move to the third container. Yesterday's trash glares back in my face. Our eyes meet over the trash. I stand back as she closes the container. I wait for her insight and direction.

She shakes her fist, but not at me. Her deep guttural voice curses the gods or the trash man or both. The trash has not been picked up. I raise my voice to join her protest. She smiles slightly, satisfied that I'm as upset as she is. Letting go of my arm, she says for the first time, *"buongiorno, signora."*

On the inside I smile. On the outside I display no joy as that would be an inappropriate display of emotion. Later in the day, I check my neighbor's trash to determine next steps. She has added her black container next to her white container. I do the same with my green/ black container, lining it up beside my murky gray bin.

The next morning we meet at the ledge. Two days worth of trash stare back at us. The news around town establishes there is a trash strike—*sciopero dell'immondizia*. My neighbor and I stand together, strong women bonding against trash collectors who strike, these despicable people who create chaos in our lives.

Now whenever I see my neighbor, she chats away. I've told her numerous times I don't speak or understand Italian well. She's decided that I do. In a way, she's correct, because I understand her strong gestures and small nuances when discussing the trash workers, these beasties who are striking and making our lives miserable.

Wherever I walk in our tiny walled village, the trash strike is the main topic of conversation. Everyone voices an opinion.

"What a disgrace," they say. "Well, it could be worse," says someone else. "At least it isn't summer, when all the big flies and tourists are here."

In the evening I add my orange/yellow container to the growing piles. It's no longer shameful to have masses of tiny bugs circling the trash. We unite in our contempt. We hope when the strike is over the trash collectors will suffer from the mounting odor and the tiny flying bugs. We imagine the bugs in their eyes, mouths, and noses. Their discomfort brings a small pleasure to us as we meet over the trash bins. We make little *tsk-tsk* sounds and shake our heads. We look at the growing piles of trash and wonder what the next day will bring.

The fifth day of the strike arrives with no relief. Our beautiful city is drooping her head in shame. Sunday is the busiest day for tourists and we petition the gods to keep them away this weekend. This disgraceful situation is not appropriate for outsiders to view.

By seven on Monday morning, I've resigned myself to living with trash stacked up outside my front door. But I'm wrong. Around nine, an incredible racket rushes me to the window. My heart lifts with joy. Our unruly stacks of trash are being carted away by our no-longer-striking trash man.

My hands race to applaud, but I'm sure it would be breaking a trash rule. Instead, I make myself content to stand at the window and watch him hastily race our trash to his overflowing truck. A week's worth of accumulated garbage spills over the sides and into the street.

He's in a hurry. He doesn't stop to inspect the trash. He doesn't whistle or hum a tune. Instead, he grabs the bags off the top of the containers and gallops back to his little truck. He doesn't gently and lovingly place our trash into its individual space. Instead, he hurls the bags through the air. They topple in disarray onto the overflowing trash truck.

It's easy to understand why he's rushing and why he's not delighted with his work today: he's afraid of the women of Otranto. They stand in their doorways, yelling as he runs past them. Their stridency rumbles an avalanche of hard, angry words at his retreating back.

Tomorrow everyone will forget and greet him again as a friend. But today we stand united in outrage.

The moaning of the slow-to-turn-over engine signifies the show is over. Neighbors drift into homes or down the street, chatting about the strike. Turning away from the window, I'm pleased by the turn of events. Trash has risen considerably in my esteem, not so much the importance of trash as the importance of what I do with it.

Mosaics are teaching me to mend the broken pieces. Trash is teaching me to pick apart and discard those unhealthy aspects of my life as I embrace the person I am becoming on this earthly journey.

Flip-Flops

INFRADITO

I'M PAYING COINS OF gold for whatever I said or did to cause Priscilla and Bobby to put down roots in Otranto. They've become pop-up people, appearing whenever I step my foot outside my door.

Being raised in the South came with a lot of commandments. *Thou shalt* and *thou shalt not* were infused into my brain with the first change of diapers. Good manners, hospitality, and befriending those in need came with my birth certificate.

But Priscilla and Bobby challenge my Southern sensibilities. They are a persistent pair. I don't understand what keeps them here. When I ask, they say, "Oh, it's such a friendly little place. We've been traveling around so much. It feels good to settle in one place for a week or two."

Oh, horrors, I think, when I hear they're staying a week or two. When they don't see me around town, they come knocking. Initially I was involved with mosaics, making a ready excuse for not spending time with them. With the mosaic finished, I have more time. I often bump into them when I am exploring around town. They've also taken to hanging out at the Blu Bar, which irritates me, even though I'm the one who suggested it.

It's my private place . . . I found it first. Childish thoughts crowd in. I try tamping down my immature musings without much success. Fortunately, they aren't early risers, so my cappuccino time with Giovanni is spared from their takeover of my favorite cafe.

During the little bit of time I spend with them, they don't seem to have any common interests. They bicker constantly and siphon my alone time. But the worst part comes when they arrive on my doorstep. A simple knock would be suitable, but it's not their style. Instead, their lack of decorum has morphed into serenades of, "Oh, Donna. Oh, Donna." They stand outside my door laughing, yelling, and leaning on the doorbell.

Now I slip around corners when I make my way to the sea, the cathedral, food shopping, or any small task that I'd like to complete alone. They're not bad people, and sometimes they're funny and entertain me. Occasionally a brief visit would be okay, but *brief* isn't in their vocabulary. I listen to my whiney-head voice and command myself to stop. I've set parameters and most of the time I'm able to preserve my solitude. I'm so deep in thought I stumble right over them as I round the corner into the main piazza.

Priscilla yells, "Oh, you're not going to believe it, but I've fallen again."

"I'm so sorry. When did this happen?"

"This morning. I really hurt myself this time. The pain's intense."

My face, with effort, maintains blankness as she limps toward me on the cobbled streets, still wearing flip-flops. What can I say? It's her second fall. She's an adult, yet she's still wearing flip-flops. What compels her to think that cobblestones and flip-flops are compatible?

She's told me about the numerous stairs they must climb to reach their apartment. My mind flits back and forth between steps, cobbled streets, and flip-flops. This woman is a flip-flop disaster.

She shows me her bruised and bloody knees, scraped elbows, and hands as she recounts the moment of impact. In midstream she changes subjects so quickly I don't have time to sort through what she's saying.

"You must come now to see our apartment. I've been looking for you for days so I could show it to you," she gushes.

"Oh, but I'm on my way to . . . I really don't have time, I . . ."

"That can wait," she responds as she tucks her hand in my arm and tugs me along.

Priscilla has told me on several occasions what a great deal they made for their accommodations. When they decided to stay on in Otranto, they found a small apartment in the post-war section of town. Before they negotiated their rent, they asked me what I paid for my place. Now they often brag about paying 100 euros less for their shorter stay, inferring that I'm paying too much for my month's stay.

I'm fairly sure their math skills are lacking. I don't remind them I'm staying longer, my apartment is larger, it's in the old city, and it has views of the sea. Somehow, they see it differently and will continue to tell me why they still got a better deal.

I tag along, thinking I can take a quick look at their apartment and then get on with my aloneness and my trash duties. It's quite a lengthy walk. When we arrive, Bobby rushes down the steps and assists Priscilla to the top. With pride they show me the tiny studio with kitchenette, small bedroom, tiny bathroom, and a small terrace with a view of trees. They can't move without running into each other.

The couple of small chairs in the bedroom provide no real sitting area and no privacy. Their numerous squabbles, when we're together, indicate lack of personal space. After seeing their apartment, I understand why they got such a good deal. Instead of pointing this out, I'm quick to compliment them on their good fortune.

"Come on, let's go to lunch," Priscilla says as I try without success to flee.

Eating in Southern Italy is a much later affair than in much of Europe. We've discussed this before, but these conversations have fallen on deaf ears. Nothing I say enhances their knowledge of local customs. They whine a bit when I tell them the restaurants aren't yet open for lunch.

Since it's too early to eat, Priscilla says, "Let's go to the Blu Bar for a drink."

"Thanks, no," I respond. "You need to rest. I have photos to take, but I'll stop by the Blu Bar later. If you're still there, we can make plans for lunch. Why don't you choose the restaurant?"

To my dismay, Priscilla says, "Oh, taking photos sounds like fun. We'll come with you until it's time for lunch."

My first thought is to dash down the steps, knowing they can't keep up with me. But that would be rude. My inner voice tells me I'm still that Southern girl infused with good manners.

As we walk-hobble back to the village, I ask about their interests.

"Occasionally, I paint. I was a schoolteacher for years. I had no time for hobbies. Now that I'm retired, I just want to travel," Priscilla shrills in time with her flip-flops slapping up and down on the pavement. Bobby grunts, not adding to the conversation.

I show them an obscure part of town they've not been in before and find a shop full of glitzy souvenirs. Priscilla smiles. *Hmm,* I think, *I've hit a soft spot. Perhaps I can slip away.*

As she becomes engrossed in the large array of knickknacks, I say, "If you don't mind, I'm going to a few other places. It's important for my research to take a lot of photos. But I'll meet you for lunch around one. Where do you suggest we meet?"

"Meet us at *Profumaria del Mare.* Have you eaten there? It's our favorite."

"No, I haven't. Great! I'll meet you at one o'clock," I respond, quickly moving toward the door.

Leaving them content to shop, I spend a couple of hours happily visiting local craft stores. At each shop I introduce myself to the owner and go through my routine: *"Sono una scrittrice americana. Sto strivendo un libro sulla storia, la culture e il cibo della Puglia—* I'm an American writer. I'm writing a book about the history, the culture, and the food of Puglia."

My canned introduction is readily available and easier than attempting a conversation about Idrusa, Pantaleone, or my trash-filled life. Those conversations would be too complicated. My halting Italian isn't capable of complexity. On the other hand, everyone loves to talk about their history, culture, food and wine.

I practiced these phrases over and over with my friend and Italian instructor Manuela. She was born in Sicily and taught at the University of Catania. It was my good fortune to meet her. Whatever Italian I know, she taught me with great patience and a marvelous sense of humor.

After I finish my recitation, I ask each shopkeeper if I can snap a photograph of them and their shop. They are shy, but giggle and relent with only small protests.

After taking many photos, I buy a few small gifts to take home. Continuing my walk, I rediscover a small jewelry shop I originally found on my first trip to Otranto. On that previous trip I bought a stunning red starfish necklace made from Venetian glass. The designer and owner of the shop was a talented young woman, and I was impressed with the unusual pieces she created. I'm thrilled to have rediscovered the shop because during our earlier travels, I had dropped and broken my beautiful necklace. Perhaps there's a possibility to have it repaired or replaced.

The *For Sale* in the window stops me in my tracks for a few seconds. Pushing through the door, I greet the shopkeeper, reminding her of my purchase two years ago. She embraces me as a long-absent friend although I'm reasonably sure she doesn't remember me. I ask about the sign. She tells me with many sighs and downward smiles that she has two shops and must sell one as the economy has been bad for business.

"Oh, I'm so sorry," I murmur.

Her frown quickly changes to a smile as she says, "È la vita. Sometimes things work out, and sometimes they don't. Today you are here, and that makes me smile. Is there anything I help you with?"

"Yes, would it be possible to replace or repair the beautiful red starfish necklace I bought here two years ago. I dropped it, and one of the arms broke off. Do you think it can be fixed?"

"Of course, I'll ask my husband to look at it. He's very good at repair work. Can you leave it now?"

"No," I respond, "I don't have it with me today, but I'll bring it by tomorrow morning. I'm so grateful your husband may be able to repair it. It's such an unusual piece. It's been disappointing not to be able to wear it. *Ci vediamo domani.*"

I don't linger, as it's one o'clock. Priscilla and Bobby will start looking for me if I don't meet them on time. When I arrive at the restaurant, they're already seated. They wave me over. Bobby jumps up to pull out my chair. Priscilla tells me they've already ordered for the three of us. One of their redeeming qualities is they enjoy good food. I'm reasonably sure their selections will be tasty.

A liter of white wine stands sweating in the center of the table. My glass is already full. Silent drops of moisture slide down the sides, creating a wide, wet circle design on the tablecloth. Priscilla hands me a menu, pointing out what they've ordered. But my eyes fall onto the proprietor's attempt to translate the Italian into English. There are many interesting interpretations, but my favorite is *Vino Bianco Frizzante alla Spina,* translated as White *Whine* On Draft. I point out the typo to Priscilla and Bobby. Laughing at the *faux pas,* we raise our glasses, celebrating the delicious white wine.

My musings about them ordering good food are correct. A large bowl of steaming mussels is placed before me. The broth merges white wine, parsley, slivers of garlic, and cherry tomatoes into an exquisite masterpiece. Next comes eggplant parmesan. It's crispy and stacked high with melting mozzarella, a spicy tomato sauce, and freshly torn basil leaves. We all dive in.

It's obvious Priscilla is suffering from her fall. She's quiet, and there's a wariness in her voice.

"Are you in pain, Priscilla?"

"Yes, I need to go back to the apartment and lie down," she says. "My entire body aches."

"I'll help you walk back, if Bobby wants to stay longer," I offer.

"Thanks, but Bobby's ready for a nap, too." She heaves a sigh and gingerly pushes herself up from the table. They hobble off toward their apartment, the sound of flip-flops smacking the cobbled stones.

Back at my place, I move my computer to the terrace. Sighing with contentment, I pick Eva Cassidy from my playlist, closing my eyes as the first strains of "Fields of Gold" surround me. My reverie is disrupted by a pounding on the front door. Looking over the terrace, I see Bobby, scowling and ready to pound again.

"Do you have any pain medication?" he yells up to me.

"Yes, of course," I say. "Come around to the back door and I'll let you in."

I learned, after my first trip abroad when I was in my early twenties, that it's mandatory to travel with a fully stocked medical kit. I give Bobby pain relievers.

Turning to leave, he says, "I've found someone to drive us to one of the local fairs. The only problem is we have to go tonight."

"Priscilla can't possibly go out tonight. She's in pain," I respond.

"Well," Bobby replies, "she says she's going. She's determined. I can't stop her, so we might as well go. Meet us in the square across from the *castello* at eight this evening."

"Text me if you change your mind. I hope you do," I say.

It's a dreadful idea for Priscilla to even contemplate going out tonight, but it's her choice. I admit to myself I'm excited about the possibility. Going to a festival is something I'm happy to do with other people, even Priscilla and Bobby. My only hope is that she doesn't wear flip-flops. I start to ask Bobby about details of the arrangement but change my mind. He's easygoing and unenchanted with logistics or the why or how of things. I'll show up and see what happens. I won't be disappointed if they cancel.

This evening, instead of my usual *passeggiata*, I linger on the terrace. I'm always astonished that I'm privy to both the rising and setting of the sun. It's not only the panoramic view from the terrace that grants this, but the position of the landmass jutting into the sea. I watch the sun in its busy descent, not fully comprehending that some internal eye has been awakened in me. My only sign is an ancient longing that seeps into my soul. Several years will pass before I discover a permanent place for my heart, but I'll remember it began here where the expansiveness of sky, sea, and setting sun present me with the gift of redemption.

Tonight I only know that the twilight sky unfurls cloud cloths to dust gold and red fragments from the sun's face. I imagine it's essential for the sun to freshen up before beaming through someone's morning window on the far side of the world. The red and gold-dust sparks fly on the evening breeze. They dance lightly across the rim of my wine glass. Shivering with pleasure and in anticipation of tonight's adventure, I sip nectar from the golden goblet.

Welcome to the Table

BENVENUTI AL TAVOLO

A FEW MINUTES BEFORE eight I amble through the walled village. I merge with families and shopkeepers out for *passeggiata*. Fairy lights and music splash across the cobbled streets. A secure and peaceful sensation permeates my skin as I saunter through the well-lit pedestrian area. Reaching the *castello,* I glance across the street to our prearranged meeting place. No one is there. Dark edges of night wrap around twilight.

Crossing the street, I enter the small square where a bench and the boarded-up metal shed proclaiming *informazioni turistiche* stare back at me. One dim streetlamp at the other end of the park paints grotesque images of things swaying in the breeze. I debate whether to stay in the darkness or move into the eerie glow. My indecision keeps me lingering on the curb until a shadowy movement startles me. A man emerges out of the night. Since it's just early evening, I still have a certain bravado.

I stay on the curb and call, *"Stai aspettando gli americani?* Are you waiting for Americans?"

"Sì," he responds, moving toward me with his hand outstretched in greeting. *"Luigi,"* he says.

Our conversation reminds me of the Tower of Babel. He speaks to me in Italian. I respond to him in my hesitant, present-tense Italian, interjecting a smattering of English. There's not much comprehension between us.

While I'm wondering whether to stay or leave, Priscilla and Bobby's slow, hesitant figures come into view. Priscilla's gait has a peculiar limp-hop. Pain is conveyed in each halting shuffle. Meeting them halfway, I first glance at her feet. She's still wearing the blasted flip-flops. Either she doesn't understand that flip-flops are the reason she's falling, or she doesn't own other shoes. Or perhaps, she simply doesn't care. Instead of dwelling on the flip-flops, I ask how she's feeling after her rest.

Her grimace implies pain. "I'm stiff but okay."

"It's not too late to cancel. There's an abundance of festivals at this time of the year. We can go when you feel better," I say, offering her a way out.

"But I don't want to miss this festival. We're leaving Otranto soon. I may never have another chance," Priscilla responds.

Bobby interrupts. "She'll be fine. We'll go slow. I told Luigi she's in pain."

"Do you know where we're going or what festival we're attending?" I ask.

Bobby smiles and says, "I asked Luigi to pick for us. He chose the pork festival."

I'm happy not to oversee anything tonight, so a pork festival sounds interesting.

Gazing around the square, I look for tonight's transportation. There are no cars, vans, or taxi-type vehicles parked nearby. There's only a three-wheeled contraption parked close to where Luigi stands. I don't consider this shabby vehicle a possibility. But I'm wrong.

Luigi bows grandly with an ear-to-ear smile, saying, *"benvenuti alla macchina."*

Bobby, who appears to never give a hoot about anything, pauses. His mouth opens and closes. It's a full minute before he laughs and exclaims, "Isn't this going to be grand! Come on, ladies, your chariot awaits you."

He assists Priscilla toward the miniature, falling-apart, open-sided, motorized golf cart. The contraption is something the Italians call *l'ape*—the bee. In standard Italian it's pronounced *lap pay*, but in the Southern dialect of Puglia it comes out as *omp per*. The three-wheeled vehicle has a grime-encrusted plexiglass windshield, a ripped plastic sheet for the back window, open air on the sides, plastic golf cart benches for seats, and a tattered canvas on top.

Bobby cautiously positions Priscilla onto the back seat. I follow, but Luigi indicates he wants me up front. I look pleadingly at Bobby, praying he will sit up front and let me sit with Priscilla.

"No," he says, "it's a balance thing. I would be too heavy up front. He needs someone small like you."

Luigi gallantly assists me into the cart on what should be the driver's side. I'm confused until I realize the steering wheel is on the right. I consider jumping out but Luigi has cranked up the engine, and the tiny vehicle lurches forward. I search for a seat belt or a small handle to cling to. There's nothing.

Shifting gears, the vehicle hurls down the road. There are no streetlights. The night sky closes in as we buzz through the countryside. The tiny headlights throw weak beams onto the narrow road before us. A sudden stop would launch me through the wobbling windshield. Invisible things brush against my hand as we pass swiftly through the night.

My terror escalates when the vehicle swerves, throwing me against a disappearing Luigi. His head is barely visible above the steering wheel. His left shoulder leans into the dash, and his left hand fumbles around on the floorboard. My gasp is quieted when Bobby touches my shoulder and whispers, "I think Luigi's trying to fix the CD player. Don't say anything or move suddenly. We'll be okay."

Not reassuring words, as it appears that Luigi's goal is to simultaneously drive and fix the player. Screaming would distract him, so I bite my lip and turn back to the blackness. I don't look again until music erupts. L'ape shimmies and shakes to Luigi's dance movements as we gyrate toward some unknown destination.

At some point we careen onto a main highway. Cars plunge at us, honking, braking, and aggressively passing within spitting distance. My left elbow is screwed to my side as I white- knuckle the edge of the seat. We're destined to catapult into one of the numerous stone walls we're passing at breakneck speed. Momentarily, I wonder if I can find another ride home or if I can manage to walk back to Otranto. But I decide these are premature thoughts because our arrival anywhere is not guaranteed.

Fortunately, the l'ape gods are with us tonight as we safely joggle into a little town called Muro. I quiz Luigi about when and where he'll pick us up and the cost of the ride. He says he'll meet us later—much later. I shrug and ask for directions into the festival.

He says, "Vai dritto, vai destra, c'è la fiera—go straight, go right, and there's the fair." Our ace in the hole is we didn't pay Luigi in advance, so I'm sure he'll return and find us. But I wonder if that's a good thing.

It takes a false start or two for us to figure out the dynamics of the fair. It's like a festival back in the States. We have to buy tickets for food and beverages, and finding the ticket booth is a challenge. People love pointing us in various directions. Each one is sure they are giving us the best possible information. I finally stop a man who's young enough to possibly know a little English. With a quizzical grimace, he points at the tent we are standing next to and says, "qui."

Breaking into laughter, he explains the joke to the crowd waiting in line to buy tickets. They join in the laughter, as do we. By the time we reach the head of the line, we have been welcomed in several languages and provided instructions about what tickets to purchase and which stalls have the best food.

The difference between Italy and the US collides when we discover we must buy a specific ticket for each item—red tickets for wine, blue tickets for pork chops, yellow tickets for sausages, green tickets for *panini*, white tickets for *bruschetta*. It takes a bit longer to sort through this process. We become part of the entertainment as a crowd gathers round to encourage us with our choices. Everyone dispenses advice.

"Lady, you must buy the sausages at Gaetano's stand."

"No, no," says another. "The sausage is best at Antonello's. You must go there."

All suggestions are given and received with great seriousness. We listen intently, pool our resources, and make our choices. We traipse from booth to booth, choosing chunks of roasted pork, grilled sausages, fried potatoes, and toasted bread smeared with spicy tomato sauce and topped with thin slices of crispy *pancetta*.

Laden with our full plates and large paper cups of wine, we locate community seating under a gigantic tent. The tables are filled with families and friends eating, talking, laughing, and teasing. We enter the tent, but every table is full. We stand waiting expectantly for others to leave. The crowd looks back. The noise-laden air softens. No one appears to be in a hurry. We begin to back out of the tent to look for another place when a man from one of the long community tables stands. He beckons us to join him and says something, causing all the people to shift until a pocket of space is found for each of us.

"*Grazie mille*," we say, squeezing ourselves in the vacant spots around the table. Slowly introductions are made. Each person says their name and where they're from: Antonio from Lecce; Paola from Tricase; Angelica from Maglie; Fredrika from Greece but now living in Otranto; Claudio from Gallipoli; Maurizio from Santa Cesarea Terme; Mateo and Fatos from Albania now living in Otranto.

They top off our wine glasses from a large jug and offer us large bowls of roasted chestnuts along with stalks of celery. Our fingers blacken as we peel away the chestnut husks and then cleanse our palates with the sweet stalks of celery—a new and much appreciated food experience for me.

The food and wine flow around the table as we struggle with language, sometimes failing and sometimes succeeding in understanding each other. The most poignant moment comes when one of the men stands and says to all of us, *"Noi siamo il mondo a questa travola—*We are the world at this table. We come from many different lands, but we embrace each other as friends."

Goose bumps bubble on my arms as I marvel at the simplicity of life in this moment. I glance at the faces gathered around the table: American, Greek, Albanian, Italian, and goodness knows what other nationalities. Yet, we are the same, a mini United Nations but without agenda, animosity, or angling for power.

*Siamo la gente di questa terra—*We are the people of this earth. There's a pause as I gaze around the table at each person. The man speaking raises his glass. In unison we raise ours. We all drink to friendship.

La musica drifts into the tent. We clear the table and with much laughter glide to the dance floor to watch and, perhaps, to dance. Fredrika has taken a liking to me. She hooks her arm through mine. Priscilla joins us showing no signs of her earlier tumble. Our feet move to the music as we scrutinize the whirl of dancers. The men gather 'round us in a protective semicircle. We move in sync to a predetermined choreography—a warm and pleasant gift of the night.

Wrapped in this warm, mellow place, I gaze into stars. A crescent moon rises. Music scrambles my brain, or perhaps it's the wine in combination with the night. A dark, handsome man comes from behind me, gently transporting me onto the dance floor. I'm so startled I drop my jacket. We both bend to pick it up, simultaneously, whacking our heads together. I see more stars. Slinging the jacket over my shoulder, I bump into dancers passing by. The slim, elegant man gathers me into his arms, sweeping me into the crowd of dancers. The music quickens. I stumble, stepping on his feet. His handsome face grimaces in pain.

Fortunately, the music pauses and my new friends rescue me. I laugh, understanding they are rescuing the gentleman from me. He's gracious. He bows, kisses my hand, and disappears. Priscilla and Fredrika sigh. Fredrika twines her arm through mine. We fold once again into our semicircle, swaying with the music.

The evening continues with shared glasses of *grappa, amaro, sambuca, ouzo* and probably something else. Our new friends refuse to let us pay for anything. Too soon it's time to part. We hesitate, not wanting to leave this agreeable evening. For those who live near or in Otranto, we agree to rendezvous tomorrow at the Blu Bar. This eases the sadness of ending such a memorable evening.

Luigi turns up as promised, ushering us back to our Cinderella *l'ape*. The ride home, while no less frightening, is softened by the glow of warm memories of food, wine, music, and friendship across language barriers.

It's three in the morning when I climb the stairs to the upper terrace. The night's adventure still smolders: a night of simplicity and uncomplicated moments, a night of harmoniously bringing people of different nations together. It's the age-old story of community at the table. Most of the important lessons regarding life I've learned at the table with family and friends—lessons of peaceful coexistence, difference of opinion, and respect for each other—regardless of our diversity.

Tonight, I, the intruder in this land, was welcomed to the table. It's a homecoming kind of feeling—one that leaves me gratified. My work, sorting through the fragments and trash of my life, is showing signs of progress.

Slipping between Salento sun-kissed sheets, I understand how many problems could be solved if the peoples of the world came together at the table and shared a meal.

Fredrika

WHAT WERE WE THINKING last night when we agreed to meet at the Blu Bar this morning? Clearly, we'd had too much wine. While I'm certain no one in their right mind will show up after a night that lasted until the wee hours, I drag myself out of bed. My upbringing dominates, dictating that I show up, even if I'm the only one.

Besides, a cappuccino is much needed to soothe my throbbing head. I will greet the day wholeheartedly and see which of these newfound friends show up—not that I need more people to disrupt my solitude.

I wonder briefly what happened to the "I came here to be alone" person. My days are filled with obligations and developing friendships that won't last. I'm not writing. "It's okay," I murmur. "I may not be writing, but I'm living this very simple, uncomplicated life. It's exactly what I need to be doing."

Ten o'clock. Only Giovanni is at the Blu Bar to greet me. After ordering a cappuccino, I settle at a table in the shade. Eventually Fredrika, Mateo, and Fatos materialize, showing wear around the edges. It's ten thirty before Priscilla and Bobby straggle in.

Maurizo never makes it. Everyone is a different shade of pale with green tinges.

Priscilla and Bobby have a quick coffee and leave. The pain from Priscilla's fall has intensified, and the late-night festivities have compounded her problems. She needs to rest, she says, as she hobbles away still wearing flip-flops.

Mateo and Fatos work on Sunday and only have time for an espresso before leaving.

Fredrika and I are left on our own. We stroll through the village. Either we didn't imbibe as much as the others, or we're both putting on a brave front. My head indicates it's the latter. We chat in a mixture of languages about our lives. Fredrika is a violinist. She was born in Greece but has lived in Otranto for twenty-two years and calls it home. Her aging mother lives in Albania, and she visits her often. She tells me she's been married to Mateo for a long time.

"We have no children," she says. "My career doesn't allow me time to raise children."

We meander arm in arm within the walled city. I tell her I've been looking for a book on Otranto's history.

"Which book?" she asks.

"*L'ora di Tutti.* Do you know it? It's about the massacre that occurred in 1480. I've tried several bookstores, but no one stocks it."

She nods. We continue through the narrow streets until she grabs my hand, steering me outside the village. Abruptly she stops, pivoting to check out the surroundings. Her eyes crinkle as she guides me through a small door wedged next to a souvenir shop. It's a mishmash of clothing, household items, knickknacks and books.

Fredrika tracks down the shop's owner and demands a copy of *L'ora di Tutti.* Her indignant voice announces to anyone listening, "This is absurd. My friend cannot find a copy of the most famous book about Otranto."

She proclaims to the owner that I have looked all over town. A copy is immediately found and placed in my hands like a precious jewel. I thank the owner and fling my arms around Fredrika. The book will take time to translate, but it will reveal more about Idrusa.

With *Lora di Tutti* under my arm, we march out of the shop into the brilliant sunlight.

Fredrika squints. Her shoulders slump, fatigue crosses her face. She grabs my arm, planting cheek kisses. "Now I will nap. But tonight at six-thirty you must wait on the corner by the food stalls outside the city walls."

"*Perché?*"

Instead of answering why she wants me to do this, she takes my hand and walks me to the corner. She points to a spot, "I will meet you here. We will take our evening walk together."

"*Va bene,*" I say.

With *Lora di Tutti* in my hands, my only thought is to rush back to the apartment and begin the tortuous process of translation. But I need nourishment before I start.

My blue and white veggie bowl overflows with fresh-from-the market purchases. For lunch, I select plump tomatoes, tiny green beans, potatoes, slender sweet red peppers, onions, garlic, spicy green peppers, and olives. They fragrantly sizzle in the skillet as I pour a very small glass of wine, hoping it will revive me. Balancing my plate and the wine, I almost skip to the terrace with *Lora di Tutti* tucked under my arm. Idrusa, who has become my personal guide in the village, may have other secrets she will reveal to me. The longer I'm here, the more insistent her presence. She leads me down pathways, through grassy fields to isolated parts of the sea where fishermen cast their nets, where the flickering rays of sun part the water revealing silver-gilded fish, captured but still fighting for freedom. Idrusa's story is becoming my own.

Later, I awake face down on the Arabian cushions. The cool evening air blows down my spine. It's almost time to meet Fredrika.

After washing my face and combing my hair, I add a pullover to my tank top, wrap a scarf around my neck and snatch a light jacket off the chair in preparation for the damp, chilly night air creeping in from the sea.

Strolling contentedly through the Sunday crowds, I join the *passeggiata*. I'm becoming a regular. Several people nod and smile as I wander past the carousel to my designated waiting spot.

A walk with Fredrika will be entertaining. She'll show me so much more than I've seen on my own. Perhaps we'll have a gelato, and I'll be home in time for the Italian game shows. I don't wear a watch, so I don't know exactly what time it is. But it's an easy wait, fun for people-watching. The area fills with families strolling before dinner.

Darkness deepens quickly. I wait, feeling a little conspicuous standing directly under a streetlight, something I didn't notice when Fredrika indicated the spot earlier. A young man from Pakistan wanders by with his trinkets.

"*Buona sera*," I nod, as we are on speaking terms.

Each morning he sets up his souvenirs on a blanket in the main piazza. We always nod and say good morning to each other. Now he glances up, smiling in his easy, warm manner and says good evening. He pauses as if to say something more. But a murmur of voices changes his mind. He looks around, quickly bows his head, and walks away.

I don't understand his actions until I watch him walking away. I've created some sort of diversion by speaking to him. We're being scrutinized by the locals. Perhaps in this town it's inappropriate for him to speak to me. I hope that isn't so, but here, like in every part of the world, immigration issues are rampant these days. People struggle for freedom. People everywhere want the same rights as those bestowed upon me by birth, something I never had to fight to gain or to keep.

Sad thoughts of the immigrant plight creep in until I see Fredrika approaching. She launches into a chaotic hand-gesturing explanation of why she's late. She indicates Mateo can't find a parking space, so we must walk to the car.

"Where are we going?" I ask. "I thought we'd walk together and have a gelato. Why do we need a car?"

Her rapid speech and equally rapid pace leave me clueless. I rush after her, trying to keep in step with her sprint, but several blocks at racing speed leave me trailing her. I call out for her to wait just as she stops by a dark four-door car. Mateo and Fatos are in the front seat. Fredrika nudges me into the back and follows.

Why am I getting into a car with a group of strangers? I ask myself in my mother's voice.

Because they've been kind and friendly to me, I answer her in my head. *They aren't going to hurt me. I'm not a child. It's an adventure.*

Each day I grow stronger, making choices without considering anyone else's thoughts or feelings. What blissful freedom this is for me. With a contented sigh, I lean back in the seat, ready for whatever escapades await.

The car speeds away from the curb as we bolt into darkness on country roads without streetlights. My shoulders tense as my mother's voice pipes up again. *Is this a smart thing to do?*

The two men are silent. So is Fredrika, a dense silence. I can't see their expressions in the dark. My mother speaks to me again. *Who are these people? Do you know the family? Where were they born? Who are their friends? Where are they taking you? How late will you be?*

My bravado takes a nosedive. *What if I'm being kidnapped by an Albanian, an Italian, and a Greek?*

I squirm nervously formulating a plan to save myself as the voiceless drive on a one-lane back road morphs from minutes into an hour.

Mateo and Fatos are solidly built men and could easily overwhelm me. Perhaps, as a kidnapping victim I won't be harmed if money is the only motive. But that wouldn't be the case since I can identify them—although I don't know anyone's last name.

I wonder if a finger or one of my ears will be cut off and sent to my husband, along with a note demanding money for my safe return.

Maybe I'll be robbed and thrown out on the road without means to find my way back to Otranto. Or, the worst possible scenario is I'm being kidnapped and will be forced into marrying Fatos. Last night he was quick to let me know he was available.

Questions rise and fall in my mind as I scan for road signs, just in case I'm robbed and thrown out of the car. There are none. My numerous attempts to start a conversation fall into silent spaces. Little knots in my stomach curl into big lumps. I try once more, asking Fredrika where we're going.

"*Aspettata,*" she snaps. There's no other choice. I wait.

We slow a little, after passing a sign proclaiming San Foca. We bump off the road into a parking area. I sigh gustily with relief. There are bright lights and small knots of people. Fredrika smiles, opens the car door, and reaches for my hand.

"*Siamo qui.*" We are here.

The well-lit area ahead of us is filled with people strolling through the market. Fredrika links her arm through mine. We saunter through the stalls, browsing booths of kitchenware, clothes, shoes, linens, pottery, spices, olives, and toys. Fatos and Mateo trail behind, looking at gadgets and materials for their business. It's late. The vendors prepare to close for the night.

They pack up the stalls, moving some of their goods into trucks and vans in preparation for tomorrow morning's market in another town.

Fredrika guides me across the road to the promenade by the sea. It stretches from brightness into blackness. New pavers shimmer with silver flicks bouncing off the light-lined walkway. Flowers fling off sparks of red, yellow, and orange as their wind-tossed heads bounce in unison.

We step into the finely ground, sugary sand. The long stretch to the water indicates the tide is out. We glide like Olympic champion skaters across the wide, clean beach to water's edge.

"It's the best beach in all of Puglia," Fredrika explains. "I want you to rent or buy a place in this town. That's why we came here tonight. This is my surprise for you. I'm sorry we were late. Now it's too dark for you to see how beautiful it is. We will come again. You must think about living here. You must become a permanent resident. I will help. We will be best friends."

"*Grazie mille,*" I respond.

How delightful to have just met someone, and they want to be my best friend. Is there something about not understanding another person's language that endears you to them? I can't imagine suggesting this to a just-met person back home. But I'm not home. I'm here, and the gesture is comforting, especially during this time of worldwide political upheavals and acts of terrorism.

We walk on the beach while she tells me about this perfect seaside town. The wind bites, swooping and pushing us toward the water. Our words float out to sea so that even without a language barrier we wouldn't be able to understand each other. We struggle for a few more minutes before turning back to the warmth of the car.

The drive back on the same dark road is joyful. Now the night casts a warm, friendly luminosity across the car's path. Sultry Greek music flows from the radio. We hum, then sing together in different languages while bouncing down the uneven road. At the outskirts of Otranto, Mateo stops the car and explains he can't maneuver any closer to the walled village. The streets are blocked for pedestrians on Sunday. As we exchange *ciao* and *a presto,* Fatos grabs my hand, pressing my fingers around a piece of paper.

I ramble home slowly, slipping through the soaring arch of the gate into the ancient, walled village. Murmurs of conversation and sounds of dinner ricochet from open windows—a symphony, soft and harmonious. Music presents itself in so many ways. I hum and sidestep down the cobbled path, the Greek rhythm still weaving its way into my memory.

Fredrika and I have arranged to meet tomorrow for coffee at the Blu Bar. Perhaps my self-imposed alone time in Otranto is over. If I keep socializing, my solitude and my work will be interrupted. But what is my work? *Myself? The book? Both?* Both, I think. I no longer feel the need to be in exile. There's time and room for both solitude and community.

As I turn into *via Castello*, I stop under a streetlamp and open the piece of paper from Fatos. It contains his full name and phone number. I toss the slip of paper into the trash container and think that perhaps there is a conspiracy to fix me up with him. He only speaks Latino, the language spoken in Albania, so I'm having a difficult time explaining to him I'm not available. Perhaps, because I'm traveling alone, they think I'm single. In this rural part of Southern Italy, it's not common practice for a married woman to travel solo. I've shown Fredrika a photo of Ray proclaiming, *"Lui è mio marito."* Perhaps I used the wrong words.

Tomorrow I'll explain to Fredrika once more—*domani, domani*—tomorrow, tomorrow, I hum, closing the door on another joyful adventure.

Did They Ever Return?

SONO MAI TORNATI?

HOW MANY SONGS ARE there about train rides? *Thousands,* I think, as song titles breeze through my mind while the train that was supposed to take us to Otranto didn't.

Songs like "Last Train to Clarksville," "Midnight Train to Georgia," "This Train Don't Stop There Anymore," and the one that most closely matches our dilemma, "Charlie on the MTA." Charlie's song rhythmically winds and rewinds in my head on the return journey from Lecce to Otranto—a song about a guy getting stuck on the train and never returning home.

The misadventure was hatched a few days ago when I agreed to go to Lecce with Priscilla and Bobby. It's my own fault. I'm the one who rattled on about the beauty of this Baroque city.

Of course, they want to see it, and I must come along as their guide. While I've turned them down on numerous occasions, Lecce is one of my favorite cities in Puglia. It would be less of a challenge for me to travel on the train with companions. *It really can't be too difficult to spend a few hours with them, could it?* I'd enjoy showing them the small pedestrian streets, quaint shops, and fabulous Baroque cathedrals. Plus, I'm feeling a wee bit guilty because I've been avoiding Priscilla and Bobby since the night of the festival.

It's a spectacular fall morning when I leave the apartment—cool enough for a sweater although remnants of summer are promised for later in the day. Our plan is to meet at the train station.

I can't remember where the train station is located. Paolo showed it to me the first day in town. He said something about its position being the highest point. So far my entire route has been flat. There are no hills or high points. I trot swiftly past the wine shop, the vegetable stand, the bakery, and the fish monger. The ancient caves and tombs, spilling over onto modern sidewalks, are scattered with last night's trash. But the train station has vanished. I briefly wonder if I'm late will they go ahead without me. *That might be a good thing.*

As I'm daydreaming, a roundabout appears. I trot halfway across. It looks exactly like all the other roundabouts surrounding the town. An elderly couple totter in my direction, arms ladened with grocery sacks.

"Buongiorno, mi scusi, dov'è la stazione ferroviaria?"

They smile, nodding in unison. The man says, *"va sinistra,* and you'll see the station." Or that's what my ears hear. I've discovered that asking for directions in a foreign country when you're not fluent in the language is like working a jigsaw puzzle. Most of the time you're guessing at what you're being told. It requires many attempts to accurately fit the pieces into a pattern. I nod, smile, and give a thousand thanks. I go left, eventually finding myself back at the same roundabout.

My next source of information is a man repairing a column. *"Sì,"* he says, *"va a sinistra, poi a destra e poi dritto."*

His instructions sound more hopeful. I go left, then right, and then straight. He didn't mention another roundabout, but I recognize this one from my first day with Paolo. I'm sprinting as it's only a few minutes before the train departs. As I crest the hill, the station appears.

Priscilla and Bobby are waiting. Unfortunately, they had no intention of leaving without me. They direct me to the ticket window while Priscilla fusses. When she purchased the tickets, she learned that a one-way ticket cost three euros, but a round-trip ticket is six euro and forty cents. As I slide my coins through the slot in the window, she wiggles into my space, sputtering in Spanish. She raps her knuckles on the ledge to attract the ticket agent. He doesn't wish to engage and pretends he doesn't understand a word she's saying. I purchase my round-trip ticket and walk outside. I don't want to be part of the discussion—any conversation with Priscilla can be confusing as well as long and loud.

On the platform several people struggle with large pieces of luggage as they maneuver toward the train tracks. I wonder how they managed the four flights of stairs with luggage because there isn't an elevator in the train station.

One issue still outstanding on this trip is how I get back home to South Carolina. My flight is booked from Brindisi to Rome, but I'm still in limbo about transportation from Otranto to Brindisi. The train might be a possibility, but only if there's a way to circumvent the stairs with my luggage.

Bobby wanders onto the platform. He also doesn't wish to be sucked into Priscilla's continuing tirade about forty-cents difference between two one-way tickets and a round-trip ticket. Pointing to the people with luggage, I ask if he knows how they've managed the steps.

"If you look just past those trees, you'll see a road that taxis use to deposit passengers on the upper platform," he says, pointing out the road and parking area beyond the tracks.

"The train might be a good possibility for me to take to Brindisi when it's time to leave. What do you think?"

"That might be so," he answers, "but it depends on the day you're leaving. I just checked the schedule. If you're leaving on any day other than Sunday, then it might work for you. The train from Otranto to Maglie doesn't run on Sunday."

"Crap, wouldn't you know, I'm leaving on a Sunday."

"Why don't you change your plane ticket?" he asks.

"Oh, gosh, no. I'm not willing to pay a large sum to change my nonrefundable ticket. I purposely booked the flight back to Rome on a Sunday because the price was considerably cheaper." Sighing, I continue. "I'll come up with a solution. I still have plenty of time. Today we're going to Lecce. I'm not going to think about it."

Priscilla joins us, still grumbling about forty cents. Fortunately, the train huffs and puffs into the station on time, so we don't have to listen to her. Surprisingly, there are only two cars.

Otranto, I discover from Bobby, is the end of the line for this two-car train. These tracks only go to and from Maglie. Connections can be made from Maglie to the rest of Italy. Bobby has gleaned a lot of information about the Otranto train.

He regurgitates everything he's learned. "The two railcars are privately owned and are not part of the national rail system. The private train parks itself in Otranto every night. There are six trips back and forth each day between Otranto and Maglie, except on Sundays. Sundays the train doesn't go anywhere."

The most important thing he tells us is that the last train to Otranto leaves from Maglie at five fifty-eight. It will leave on time, with or without us. If we miss it, we will have to spend the night in Maglie. The trains, unlike the people, run on time.

Priscilla memorizes all this information and repeats Bobby's conversation as if I'm hard of hearing. Clearly, she has all the mechanics of the trip worked out. I nod, emitting a vague, "hmmm." That seems to satisfy her, leaving me to focus on relaxing while they make all the decisions.

The engineer, who is also the conductor, bellows, *"Tutti a bordo."*

We are part of a group of ten or twelve people, most on their way to work, who dutifully step inside. We perch on ancient wooden benches. Each bump and jolt reminds me I'm not well padded. The windows are down, indicating there's no air-conditioning. Diesel fumes siphon off the fresh sea air, clogging my sinuses and conjuring burning tears. Luckily, the trip is short.

Once in Maglie, we ask a variety of people which track goes to Lecce. The consensus is track three. We stand on the platform and peer across several rail lines as trains rumble in and out. There isn't a crossing over or under the rails to transport us to track three. We shift our positions and observe others jumping off the platform and walking across the tracks between inbound and outbound trains. My trembling knees teeter on the edge. I only hope that when we jump on the track a train doesn't flatten us.

We wait until a large group decides to cross. We go with them. By the time we reach the other side, the train to Lecce is announced and pulls into the station. It's obvious when we board this train that it's part of the national system. The seats are cushiony and clean with plenty of legroom. Our expressions relax into the pending adventure. To pass the time, we discuss our return trip and agree that we'll check the posted schedule in Lecce for return times. None of us want to spend the night in Maglie.

It takes less than forty-five minutes to reach the station in Lecce. We sort ourselves out and amble over to the posted schedules. None of us understands it. An agent's window opens. I queue myself in line, understanding I'm not to approach the window until invited. Priscilla attaches herself to my side while Bobby brings up the rear.

In my train travels across Europe, I have determined most passengers are either midgets or giants. This observation is based on the ticket windows, which are either too low or too high. This one is so low that even I, with very short legs, have to crouch down into a semi-squat to speak to the ticket person.

While I'm asking the agent about the return trip to Maglie,

Priscilla eases into my space. She's much taller but somehow manages to poke her head down beside mine. With her height, she could more easily manage one of the giant windows. However, we are at a midget window, and there's not room for both of us.

Prior to her crouching down beside me, I'd been listening carefully to the instructions from the agent. As she squats, she leans into my space, forcing me off balance. If that isn't enough to test my patience, she takes over the conversation, happily interjecting her thoughts about the situation. She feels obligated to share with the ticket agent what we're doing in Italy, where we're staying, and why we need help with the train schedule. During her travels, Priscilla has determined if she shouts loud enough in English she'll be understood.

The agent points to the different times on the schedule. Whenever he points to a time, Priscilla repeats it in her best loud voice. I call it her "big bold print" voice. She repeats herself several times and makes this sort of clicking sound that I hadn't noticed before.

I suggest, without being rude, it might be helpful if we are quiet and listen to the agent. Priscilla pauses, allowing the agent time to rush through three different schedules in the afternoon that are sufficient to get us back to Maglie in time to board the last train to Otranto. I thank the agent, who smiles in amusement. The three of us turn and walk away from the station toward the old city.

It's been a couple of years since I've been in Lecce, so I pause to look for landmarks. Bobby walks rapidly away to the nearest bar for his morning pick-me-up. I later learn his beverage of choice is *caffè corretto*, coffee with a shot. Priscilla, still talking in her big bold print voice, stands in the middle of the sidewalk trying to determine north, south, east, and west.

A couple approaches the station. I ask them for directions. They're very attentive to my halting request. He says to walk straight and turn left.

She says, *"no, no, si deve andare a destra,"* indicating I must turn right.

They forget about me and begin to argue about the correct way to get to the old city. I say *"grazie mille,"* backing away as their bickering continues.

Priscilla continues to stand on the sidewalk, pointing and muttering. Bobby sheepishly wanders back from his morning pick-me-up. We can see the ancient wall surrounding the city and the church steeples inside, so it's just a matter of finding *un porto* to slip inside.

Lecce is called the "Florence of the South." It's much smaller than Florence but has the same eye-popping Baroque architecture. My intention is to wow Priscilla and Bobby with the beautifully decorated churches in the center of town—the ones noted for their stunning façades. Priscilla has a different agenda. The *duomo,* the main cathedral, is first on her list. No amount of rhetoric on my part changes her mind.

"If you must see one church in Lecce," I say. "Santa Croce is far superior to the *duomo.*"

But Priscilla's mission is the *duomo.* She's adamant. I bite my tongue. Since we don't have a map, I suggest we stop at the tourist office for directions. Priscilla disagrees, saying it will slow us down. At every corner she yells out the name of the street and says we must remember it. If we don't, we'll never find our way back to the train station. We both ignore her. Bobby lags. I move ahead.

Priscilla is a lovely, tall woman with cropped white hair and brilliant blue eyes. Her ensembles feature long, flowing skirts, carefully draped scarves, and gauzy blouses. The only thing lacking in her wardrobe are decent shoes. She must have flip-flops for all occasions.

I wonder why I thought she might possibly wear something sensible today. There's no point in saying anything, but I fear her choice of footwear will trip her up again.

Maybe my flip-flop thoughts create the perfect storm. Who knows? But as we approach the steps leading up to the *duomo,* she stumbles and goes down. The count now rises to three flip-flop accidents.

"I think I've twisted my ankle," she moans.

It's hard to have sympathy, but I muster a small dose.

"Bobby," she says, "find me ice or a bottle of cold water for my ankle. Go now." Bobby nods and walks off, probably to have another *caffè corretto.*

"Donna, I'm going to sit right here. You go on inside. You'll be able to describe the cathedral to me."

"Oh, Priscilla, why don't we wait until Bobby returns? Maybe once your ankle is iced you'll feel better. Or, I could help you inside. You could sit in a pew and at least see some of the artwork."

"Who knows how long Bobby will be? I'd rather stay here and keep an eye out for him. Go ahead. I insist."

I assist her to a shady spot, elevating her foot on her sack purse to make sure she's as comfortable as possible before I leave. Then entering though the towering cathedral doors, I pick up a brochure in English. The cathedral was built in 1144. Its stark, utilitarian demeanor pales in comparison to the wedding-cake appeal of Santa Croce. There's plenty to see, but I don't linger. I'm uncomfortable leaving Priscilla alone.

As I push against the oversized, ornately carved wooden doors, angry voices pelt me. Priscilla is engaged in a heated conversation with a street peddler. He towers into her sitting-down space. He's tall and gaunt, spewing angry words as his outstretched hands flail in her face.

"What going on?" I demand, approaching Priscilla from behind the man. "What's the problem?"

He swings around, hurling words in a mixture of French and some bizarre form of Italian.

"*Venti euro,*" he snarls with his hand out.

Money, of course. That's what he wants. Priscilla looks at me in pitiful tones.

"What's going on?" I ask again.

"He gave me this cross," she replies. "He said it was a gift. I tipped him a euro, but he says it isn't enough. Now he's demanding twenty euros."

"Do you want the cross?"

"No, but when I tried to give it back, he wouldn't take it. He keeps demanding money. He won't go away. Should I scream for help?"

"Please, no," I say, holding out my hand.

She relinquishes the cheaply constructed made-in-China cross. I hold it directly in front of the man's face. *"No, signor, la signora non vuole comprare questa croce,"* indicating no deal as I thrust the cross into his basket.

"Vi maledico," he snarls.

The words are harsh and guttural. I'm sure they mean something unpleasant. I respond, "Leave now or we'll call the police."

He understands and disappears.

I'm surprised Priscilla fell for this age-old sales pitch. According to her, she and Bobby have traveled the world. It's weird that she'd involve herself with someone peddling inferior trinkets. I start to ask why, but let it go when I look at her face, an exhibition of misery.

Bobby strolls across the large piazza as if he had all the time in the world. The once-cold bottle of water drips condensation. It's better than nothing, so we place it on her ankle. We sit in the shade, sharing the other bottle of water Bobby thoughtfully brought back with him.

After a short rest I suggest, "Let's find a taxi and head back to the train station."

"No, I'm really feeling so much better. You and Bobby help me up. If I can put some weight on my ankle, I may be able to continue."

With our help, she struggles to a standing position and smiles. "Look, I can walk. It only hurts a little. I'm fine so let's go."

I give her very little credit for wearing flip-flops. I give her lots of credit for being a good sport.

"Okay, with the time we have left, let's find *La Chiesa di Santa Croce.* I read an article on the internet this morning describing the church as a 'confectionary slathered with butter-cream frosting and laced with spun filigree.' Doesn't that sound delightful?"

"Is it far?" asks Priscilla.

"I don't think so. But anytime you need to rest, let me know and we'll stop," I say as we slowly hobble-walk toward the center of town. Church bells chime out the noon hour.

I ask, "Priscilla, are you hungry? Would you like something to eat and a short rest before we continue?"

She moans. "Yes, terrific idea. I can't go much further without a rest."

The nearest cafe has outside seating. We prop Priscilla's foot on a chair, and Bobby heads to the bar to order wine, or perhaps another *caffè corretto.*

"Are you comfortable?"

"Yes, of course," Priscilla responds. "Sit down. Let's order something to eat."

"If you don't mind, I'm going to make a quick visit to my favorite *cartapesta* shop. It's close by, and the owner makes the loveliest pieces. When I was here a couple of years ago, I bought a splendid Madonna in royal blue robes. Today, I'd like to find a Salento sun, a perfect memory for me to take home."

"Sure," says Priscilla. "We'll order some food. It'll be ready by the time you get back. Take your time."

Charging down the street, I put distance and flip-flops behind me.

The Salento Sun

IL SOLE DEL SALENTO

CARTAPESTA, OR *PAPIER MACHÉ,* translates as chewed paper. It originated in China in the second century and made its way to Italy by the tenth. Today this amazing art form flourishes in Puglia and especially Lecce. I drift through the narrow streets, wondering if I can locate the small shop.

I turn the corner and it's there, still tucked away in a side street. The man who makes the most beautiful artistic pieces out of shredded paper stands in the doorway. From my last visit, I remember his greatest joy was startling his clients by throwing his work across the shop. It's his way of informing the buyer about the sturdiness of his craft.

"Buongiorno, signora." His words greet me as I slow my pace. He hesitates, key in hand, ready to lock the door. It's lunchtime. Italian shopkeepers rarely accommodate shoppers after the noon hour strikes.

"Buongiorno," I respond and ask if the shop is open. *"Sieti aperti per me, per favore?"*

"Si, signora, per voi, certamente!"

"Grazie mille, signore. Sono stato qui due anni fa."

I tell him I visited his shop two years ago. He reaches for my hand and guides me inside. Upon entering, he embraces me, kissing my cheeks as he dances me further into the shop. His excitement overflows as he shows me the guest book, pointing to the signature of an American ambassador. He tells me how much he loves Americans. I don't mention he showed me the same book two years ago. Instead, I murmur with astonishment and tell him how impressed I am that an American ambassador signed his guest book.

"You and your shop must be very famous, for the ambassador to come here," I say to his delight as we examine the signature together.

Next, I show him a photo of the gracious Madonna I previously purchased from him. It's perched on top of our china cabinet. It's necessary to discuss all these things in earnest before I can ask him if he has a Salento sun for me.

"Questo tempo vorrei un sole Salento."

He asks, *"Perché un sole del Salento?"*

"In Otranto, where I'm staying, I created a mosaic of Puglia's splendid Salento sun. It reminded me of your shop and the beautiful pieces you make. Perhaps you have a Salento sun for me?"

He takes my hand, pointing out all the suns he has made. Each one is special, gracing a precise position on the walls of his tiny shop. He lovingly removes one piece of art from the wall. He stands next to me, holding the sun next to my face. Along with the art of *papier maché*, he has developed the art of deciphering which of his pieces belongs to which visitor entering his shop. He will intuitively know the right sun for me.

Suns come and go as I stand in the shadowy light filtering in from the shuttered window. He clucks and hums, twisting and turning my face. After several suns have failed, he pushes aside the beaded curtain separating the showroom from his workshop. I wait.

He returns with a holy relic—a subdued sun touched with gold, copper, and bronze framed by spiraling rays. The burst of sunbeams reaches into my heart. He lovingly places the sun in my hands. It's larger than I anticipated.

A mental list all the items traveling home with me appears: the mosaic, laptop, camera, pottery, gifts, and numerous pieces of luggage. Pausing, I consider the size of this sun, knowing it will add to the gentle distress of my travel.

Our eyes lock. We both know it's the right sun for me. He removes the radiance from my hands. It sails across the shop, landing with a thud on the wooden floor. It passes the indestructible test.

"*Quanto costa?*" I ask.

His response shocks me. It's not in my budget. I lean forward and say, "*No, no, troppo, troppo!*"

From experience, I know a credit card has no value in this small artisan shop, and I'm not sure how much cash I have with me. I gently place the sun back in his hands and say, "*Troppo, grazie mille, arriverderci.*"

He grabs my hands before I slip out, telling me he'll give me a better price. But he doesn't say how much. He wraps up the sun and places it reverently in my hands, whispering the new price. It's still too much.

We gaze at each other across the incredible burst of sun. It's not just any sun. It's the *Salento* sun. It will grace my home and lighten my heart with healing memories on rain-filled days when the glue loosens in my fragmented heart and trash piles at my door. I empty my pockets of cash.

My reward is more kisses to ensure I don't change my mind. I leave the shop with the warmth of a Salento sun radiating in my shopping bag.

Coming out of the shop, I turn left. Unexpectedly, Santa Croce rises in front of me. I had forgotten that the magnificent cathedral is around the corner from the shop. I rush back to the cafe where I left Priscilla and Bobby. They have ordered appetizers and spritzers, saving plenty for me, along with a glass of wine. Priscilla's ankle has improved.

"Do you feel up to walking to Santa Croce? It's only a few streets over," I report.

"Yes, of course," they respond in unison.

We move in time with Priscilla's hobble. I don't convey how close we are to the church because I want to see their first reaction when we turn the corner.

For once, they are speechless. The splendid Baroque cathedral in all its glory towers before them. It's worth the trip to watch them in a moment of rapture. Sunlight bounces off the lace-inspired façade, creating delicate patterns across their upturned faces. Murmurs of adoration drift on the breeze as songbirds regale us with joyful tunes.

Santa Croce is an extraordinary church. It's not the oldest and most famous of Lecce's Baroque buildings. But in my opinion, it's the most spectacular. The work began in 1353 and continued for over 300 years. The façade has the mandatory rose window and the usual decorative fruits, vegetables, wreaths, grotesque figures and cherubs, but that's where the similarity to other cathedrals ends.

The outer surface is made from local Lecce stone, which is soft and pliable like putty. It can be worked with the blade of a knife and a lathe. Once this soft, porous stone is positioned and exposed to the air, it hardens like marble. The masons from long ago spread the soft stone as if icing a cake. Its splendid façade radiates in the early afternoon sun. The delicately woven lace-like appearance sways in the breeze.

"Oohs" and "aahs," emit from Priscilla and Bobby. Immobilized, they stand and stare. Not wishing to interrupt the moment, I silently advance toward the massive doors, beckoning them to follow.

Inside, the sculptures and famous paintings shimmer in the filtered light. The central nave has intricately carved timber beams while the side naves have cross-shaped vaulted ceilings lavishly decorated with artwork. The ornate rows of massive columns capture Priscilla and Bobby's attention as they wander in silent awe.

They are disappointed when I remind them we can't linger. We have a train to catch. Our time has slipped away.

The Last Train to Otranto

L'ultimo Treno per Otranto

Earlier today we made a group decision to take the two-thirty-six train back to Maglie. It's the next-to-last train, allowing a backup option if it's needed. We discuss the possibility of staying longer in Lecce, but agree it's too risky. It's better to be early and have to wait in Maglie than to chance missing the last train to Otranto.

It's close to two o'clock. Priscilla's limp slows our progress to the station. We're thankful we purchased our return tickets ahead of time, even if we did pay an extra forty cents. By the time we arrive at the station, the train is already boarding. We're tired, dirty, and oh so happy to relax into cushiony seats. Priscilla winces but says nothing. Thankfully, she's not a whiny person.

The return trip is not the same. There are several stops between Lecce and Maglie. It's taking much longer than the express train we traveled on this morning. At each stop I listen intently, making sure this isn't our stop. Priscilla and Bobby chat about the day, sometimes dozing. As the train slows for another stop, the speaker crackles with a garbled announcement.

"Well," I say, jumping up from my seat, "we need to get off at this station for a transfer to Maglie."

"No, you're wrong," blurts Priscilla. "That's not what the announcement said. This is not Maglie."

"I'm sure the conductor announced the Maglie connection. I think we need to get off."

"No, you misunderstood," says Priscilla. "We're not getting off the train here. I don't know the name of this station, but it's clearly not Maglie. The trip back should be the same as the trip over. When we stop in Maglie, we'll get off. I'm sure I'm right," she smugly replies.

I don't feel up to disputing her as my Italian isn't good enough to say for certain what was announced. We stay on the train, but my stomach lurches as the train roars down the tracks. Just before the next stop, the conductor calls out Nardò. My heart sinks. We look at each other, silent in our own thoughts about what to do next. Priscilla and Bobby have no suggestions. The ticket agent comes through the car punching tickets. Flashing my best smile, I explain our dilemma in halting Italian. He looks at my ticket and then at Priscilla and Bobby's. His face darkens and creases into surliness.

Spittle collects in the corner of his mouth as he snarls, *"No, no, no, questo treno va a Gallipoli."* Turning away abruptly, shaking his head and muttering, he storms into the next car— possibly to report us to the train police.

"Gallipoli," we say in unison, realizing the worst possible scenario. Gallipoli is on the west coast. Otranto is on the east. Not only are we headed in the wrong direction, but the agent is going to report us. We'll be fined, and the fines in Italy are steep.

During our speechless phase, I scan the other passengers, wondering if any of them can help us. Heads are buried in newspapers, cell phones, e-books, or emitting light snores. No one returns my gaze until my glance passes over one woman. She's only a couple of seats down from me. I nod. She smiles. Gingerly clinging to the back of the seats, I edge toward her.

Her eyes are kind, so I take a chance. *"Parla inglese?"*

"Yes," she says in perfect Queen's English. "I'm from England."

She's very empathetic when I explain about the mix-up and our need to be in Maglie for the last connection to Otranto.

"Do you speak Italian as well?" I ask.

"Sì," she responds.

"Would you be willing to speak to the ticket agent and ask him how we can get back to Maglie?" I plead.

"I've lived in Gallipoli for twenty-six years, so I'm fluent in Italian. I'm so sorry for your mix-up as the trip to Gallipoli is long, and there are numerous stops. When the ticket agent returns, I'll speak to him. One advantage to this system is that if no passengers are waiting at the substations, the train won't stop."

"I'm not sure what you mean. I was hoping we could get off at one of the substations and make a connection to Maglie."

"No, that's not how it works. All the small stations along this line connect back and forth between Gallipoli and Lecce. The fewer times the train stops, the quicker you'll get to Gallipoli. You'll need every minute to make your way back to Maglie. That's your only chance to connect to the last train to Otranto."

So there's nothing more to do except wait.

"Thank you so much," I say to her. "My name is Donna. My travel companions are Priscilla and Bobby." I nod in their direction, turning to watch as they doze, oblivious to our plight.

"What's your name? Do you mind telling me your story? I'd love to hear how you came to live in Italy. It's something I've always wanted to do."

"My name is Katherine," she answers. "Many years ago while traveling in Italy, I fell in love with a handsome Italian boy. Being young and foolish, I believed I couldn't live without him. I didn't realize that leaving my family, friends, and my good life in England would turn out to be a poor decision. My fairy tale ended when I was cut off from my family, and his family didn't welcome me into their home. They made my life very difficult. He was supposed to marry an Italian girl from the family his parents chose for him. I was an intruder."

Pain then sorrow etches across her porcelain face.

"I wish to return to my family in England, but I cannot leave my three beautiful daughters. When I agreed to marriage, I also agreed to become Catholic, to raise my children in the faith. The laws in Italy say I'm free to go, but the same laws prevent me from taking my children. They must remain with their father. He wouldn't allow them to visit me in England. I would never see them again. I cannot leave."

Softly she whispers, "We're still married, but my life is no longer happy."

Asking any more questions would be an intrusion. I squeeze her hand and quietly return to my seat, closing my eyes as the power of her sadness penetrates my thoughts. My trash pile seems insignificant by comparison

As we get closer to Gallipoli, the agent returns. Katherine touches his arm, emits a beautiful smile and drops her gaze in a flirtatious manner before asking for help. She has learned, unlike me, that Italian men require assistance in chivalry. He returns her smile, agreeing to help. He indicates he'll call ahead to Gallipoli, requesting the train be held for us. When we pull into the station, we must be prepared to run to board the waiting train. It will only be held for a few minutes.

Katherine explains all of this to me and adds, "This is just the first train. You will have to take several before you reach Maglie. At each stop you must hurry as they won't hold the train for more than a few minutes."

When I share the information with Priscilla and Bobby, I tell Priscilla she'll have to do her best to keep up. Bobby will run ahead, and I'll help her.

It happens fast. The train stops. There's no time for a proper goodbye and thank you to Katherine, only a quick hug and a *grazie mille*. We're hustled out the door and run to the waiting train.

Sliding into my seat as the train pulls out of the station, I search the crowd for a glimpse of Katherine. She's vanished. Pulling inside my head, I focus positive energy toward her, trusting she'll find her way. I channel my small amount of energy remaining to the engineer, praying he'll get us to the next station in time.

I lose count of how many train changes we make, perhaps four. Each train steals a part of my spirit, giving me weariness in exchange. Over the course of our multiple train transfers, I realize Katherine's blessings extend across the miles. Each train is held for us as the story is passed down the line—the story about the confused Americans.

As the train chugs toward another station, Italy's reputation for hospitality is reinforced. It's one of the many reasons Ray and I return again and again. But this experience goes beyond hospitality. Each time the train stops, someone is waiting. They guide us to the next train, handing us off to another person who assists us aboard. It's never mentioned that each time a train is held, a minor delay is created in this precision-based transportation system. Instead, at each stop we are welcomed with kindness and assisted with patience.

Our zigzagging brings us back to Nardò. We're told when we board that the next stop is Zollino. It's the only station left with a connecting train to Maglie. When Zollino is announced, the train pauses. We step out onto the platform. No one else gets off. No one is waiting to greet us. The train rattles and huffs out of the station on its way to some other destination. We stand in dusty, diesel-laden silence.

My imagination takes flight. The late afternoon sun casts deep shadows. I shake my head, trying to erase the uneasiness draped across my shoulders. Maybe if I shake hard enough, I'll wake up in my grand Moorish apartment with the sun beckoning me to engage in a new day. But when I open my eyes, I'm still standing on the dusty platform. I'm an imaginary person on a fantasy journey without a guide. Nothing stirs until Priscilla moves.

She breaks the eerie silence with her loud voice. "Well, why isn't anyone here to meet us? What do we do now?"

In my dreamlike trance, I'd forgotten they're with me. As we huddle on the platform, a tall, dark, thin man glides out of the station. With a curt nod in our direction, he disappears into empty space. We're too stunned to call after him. Tired, brain-dead people who are dirty, hungry, and in desperate need of a bathroom are not good at regrouping. We split up to case the building, checking for facilities. There's nothing but a gritty haze covering the station. The only creature stirring is a small, speckled, tail-wagging dog. His sweet, furry puppy face offers comfort. In my exhausted state, I sink down onto the concrete platform and wrap my arms around his neck. He nestles in and licks the grime from my face. I look around, but there's only the pup, the dust, and a silent train track.

Our only choice is to wait, to listen, and to watch for the next train. We're like zombies, peering down the track for that tiny black spot to materialize into the train to Maglie. Not knowing if this will happen puts a damper on an already challenging day.

The urge to potty sends Priscilla and Bobby drifting off to look for possible places to relieve ourselves. I stay behind on the platform in case a train or a person appears. The station stands alone in the middle of a scraggly field with a few barren trees offering scant shade. It's a desolate place, reeking of abandonment. The wind swirls up a fistful of dust and flings it into my face, adding to the grit and grime of today's journey.

Bobby returns with a lopsided grin of relief.

"Hey, guess what? See those little trees over there? They worked for me. Gave me just enough cover to take a leak. Boy, do I feel better. Why don't you and Priscilla give it a try?"

"You've got to be kidding," I respond. "Those trees aren't wide enough to hide a squirrel's tail. Priscilla and I can't stand up like you can."

Priscilla wanders back, agreeing with my assessment of the tree coverage. She asks me to join her in the hunt for a less conspicuous place. I leave my beastie friend, who sniffs his way off. Bobby stays on the platform and stands guard, reassuring us he'll yell if any signs of life occur.

Priscilla veers right on the rutted path while I advance to the left. We're careful to keep the station within view just in case a train arrives. I've only walked a few paces when Priscilla squeals with delight. She's found a spot. I rush to join her. She gleefully points at a clump of cedars enclosed inside a stone wall.

"I'll stand guard first," she volunteers.

Finding a slight opening in the wall, I squat, contemplating life and its adventures. I pray there are no bugs or snakes waiting to attack me. As I pull up my jeans, I see there's some sort of stone protrusion backing up to our throne room.

When it's my turn to stand guard for Priscilla, I move to the front of the stone wall and see a simple grotto arching over, protecting a statue of Mary. She stands in all her glory, smiling benignly as we water her garden. She's watching over us because she knows how difficult these situations are for women. I nod and say, "Hail Mary, full of grace." That's all I know, but it's enough. She radiates light back into the darkness of this day.

With empty bladders, our good spirits return. We focus on the train that we hope will take us to Maglie. Timing is critical. There's only a breath and a prayer separating us from making it. We wait. Priscilla and I secure a spot on the platform for quiet contemplation. We try not to think that the man who locked the station door may have gone home, never to return. We try not to think we'll be stranded in this discarded, lifeless town.

Bobby has walked the perimeter and says there's nothing but a few abandoned houses. We try not to think about hot showers, soft beds, and gallons of water followed by food and wine.

On this occasion, Bobby is a good companion. His jovial personality is the best kind to have on a less-than-fun journey. He jokes and tells us stories. His lanky body, silly hat, and horn-rimmed glasses dance with him as he nimbly waltzes around the platform performing his storytelling antics. He whistles and hums silly tunes. Every few minutes he looks at his watch and says, "It's now five o'clock."

We peer down the track. No train.

After another series of songs and jokes, Bobby calls in his best conductor's voice, "It's five fifteen."

No train. We wait. I wander over and study the poster tacked to the wall displaying the train lines. It shows how we've zigzagged across the country. Each obscure village where we stopped is a tiny dot. As I'm committing the station names to memory, the tall, dark, thin man reemerges as if created out of air. He nods in the direction of the track. Our eyes strain until a tiny black dot pulsates into view. It's five thirty-two. There's a small possibility we'll arrive in Maglie in time.

Our spirits soar as the train pulls into the station. Not waiting for assistance, we jump on board before it comes to a complete stop. The conductor signals the engineer. The train gathers speed, chugging and coughing its way down the track. Noxious fumes spew through open windows that can't be closed. Our bodies lean forward, urging the train to go faster. It's still shimmying to a stop when we jump off. We run without thought as the conductor waves from the next track.

The last train to Otranto has been held for us. We board our long-awaited carriage, the one that will take us home. I vow to tell anyone who will listen that the train system in Puglia is a network of caring people who went out of their way to help three confused Americans.

We stand as the train pulls into the Otranto station. I'm surprised we don't applaud. The city folds into the sea as our train chugs into its evening stable. There's no one to thank at the end of the line, but we are ever so thankful.

Priscilla and Bobby, in full glory again, suggest we find a place to eat. Clearly, they are crazy. My only thought is to lock myself in my apartment, take a shower, get in my PJs, sip wine and stare into space. We say goodbye and part, they to the sprawling suburb and me to the old walled village.

Entering through the outer wall, I sigh with relief. By habit, I turn toward the sea. The breeze catches me full face, cleansing the dirt and exhaustion from my body. Pausing at the seawall, I give thanks for surviving the day with Priscilla and Bobby and our harrowing train adventure.

Tonight the sea is quiet, pulling me into reflection. This day was stuffed with trash, but I managed. Smiling wearily, I pick through the day's events, pulling out the sweet moments: when the shopkeeper places the Salento sun in my hands; when the rapturous look crosses Priscilla and Bobby's faces as they glimpsed Santa Croce; and when the last train to Otranto pulled into the station.

All the other trash accumulated during the day falls away. I study the sky, observing the last bit of the sun's red glow. It hovers on the edge of the horizon before dipping into its nightly bath. Stars twirl across the sea, knitting lace shawls to capture the last glittering rays of sunlight. They skim on the surface, lifting off again trailing sparkle dust. Darkness clutches the tiny flickers of light, depositing them into a falling star account.

Turning away from the sea, I allow the warmth from the familiar cobbled street to escort me home. A new song forms on my lips, "The Last Train to Otranto," lyrics and music by me.

Give Me the Simple Life

DAMMI LA VITA SEMPLICE

THIS MORNING I WRITE until it's time to meet Fredrika at
the Blu Bar. Idrusa has been my constant companion the past couple
of days. She whispers to me about her unhappiness in a marriage
arranged by her sister and brother-in-law when she was only sixteen.
She was told to marry or be thrown out of the house. They chose a
fisherman, thirty years older, rough, uneducated. She speaks to me of
domestic issues, how she tried to find comfort in cooking, cleaning,
and joining the other wives at the market. But she hated it. She hated
her lowly state. She hated the other women who snickered when she
joined them. She hated the drudgery of her daily chores, leaving her
tired and listless at the end of the day. All that waited for her was
another night of his groping, his calloused hands bruising her body,
destroying what little remained of her spirit. Her glorious barefoot
days of running wild were halted because it was blasphemous and
unseemly for a married woman. But when he went to sea, she ran
free, not caring. He'd beat her anyway, she tells me. The few days of
freedom she has when he's gone are all she lives for.

Fredrika and I arrive simultaneously. A surprise, since usually no one I'm meeting arrives on the same day, much less the correct time. After ordering coffee, we secure a table on the square. She, like Giovanni, insists I speak Italian. Stumbling my way through the language, I try to string enough words together for her to understand me. Through our disjointed conversation we uncover more details of each other's life. Fredrika tells me she's still confused about why I'm traveling alone. The crease in her forehead indicates that my limited explanation falls flat.

After coffee, we walk. Fredrika steers me to points of historical significance. Her musical voice lulls me into her world. Today she tells me that Saint Peter came here from Antioch.

I discuss *L'ora di Tutti* and Idrusa with her. She thinks Idrusa's name might derive from *Hydruntum* or the *Hydrus* of the Greeks. We chat and continue our walk into the center of town, moving outside the walled village. She grasps my elbow, bringing me to a stop.

Flinging her hands and arms in a wide gesture, she says, "Look, Donna. I brought you here to see this performance. It happens every year after the tourists leave."

Following the movement of her hands, I see the entire town at work. Banks, storefronts, government buildings, and parks are being revitalized. She says it happens every year to ensure the village will prosper and continue to be one of the most sought-after seaside resorts during the summer months.

She continues. "They're preparing for next year's horde of tourists."

Or at least I think she says *orde*, which means hordes. I'm never quite sure as Italian flows from her tongue like spring water down a mountain.

We survey holes in the streets being patched, and fresh whitewash slathered on the entire town. There's singing and laughter as the men work, joke, and call out to each other. It's a sound unusual in an American work environment—good-natured exchanges making work fun.

Fredrika's speech swells with enthusiasm. She explains with words and more gestures about the local businesses and who operates them. When I lose track of her flowing conversation, I say, "Please, slow down. The noise makes it difficult for me to understand you. Let's go back to the apartment. If we continue speaking in Italian, I need assistance from my language dictionary."

Fredrika squeals. "Oh, yes. I will come with you. I want to see your apartment."

She stands to the side as I unlock the door. I've traveled in Italy enough to know I must give her a proper invitation to enter.

"Please, come inside. It's a pleasure to welcome you to my apartment."

She nods and enters. She walks from room to room in silence. Finally, she says, "How much did you pay?"

"One thousand euros for a month."

"Oh, my dear, that's entirely too much. I have an apartment I'll rent to you for 300 euros a month."

"Tell me about the apartment," I say. "Is there a washing machine, a kitchen, and a view of the sea?"

She pats my cheek and says, "Those things aren't important. I'll see that your clothes are washed, and you'll eat with us every night. The apartment is small, but you are a little person. You will fit."

"You're too kind, but I must have space to write and a view of the sea," I say as I imagine the tiny bedroom-bathroom combination in her family's house. There would be no opportunity for solitude and dreaming in such a place.

Fredrika grunts, indicating I spend too much money without much thought. In her attempt to help me she says, "Today we are going to the grocery store called Euro Spin. The prices are the best in Otranto. But first we must go to the eye doctor. You'll come with me."

I agree. Somehow and somewhere during our brief relationship, she has decided I need to be looked after. I nod because I'm okay with accompanying her. It will be useful to know the location of the eye doctor. Before we leave, I pick up my dictionary and stick a small notepad and pen in my back pocket.

We stroll arm in arm, leaving the walled village. We arrive at a tiny shop lacking any indications of what it might be. Since I've been in Otranto, I've observed an interesting aspect of the culture. There's a lovely indifference to arriving on time for an appointment, which drives me up the wall. The same behavior is reenacted when we arrive at the eye doctor's office.

Fredrika smiles at the person behind the counter and says, "I'm late because I have to take care of my new American friend. She doesn't know her way around. I'm helping her."

The counterperson is sympathetic, nodding in understanding as she assesses my inability to function without Fredrika.

She indicates a chair, telling me to sit. A curtain behind the counter is pulled aside, revealing a tiny examination room. It's then I realize the counterperson is the eye doctor. The curtain remains open. Anyone coming in can observe the doctor and patient.

I'm content to scribble in my notepad while Fredrika's eyes are examined. Several other people arrive for appointments, but the doctor doesn't acknowledge them. She's totally focused on Fredrika.

Those waiting have lively conversations about work, children, shopping, or whatever else will pass the time. There's no secretary or receptionist. No one gripes about the wait. They realize they will receive the same care and individual treatment when it's their turn to be the most important person.

People here take pride in the one thing they are doing. I wonder if I could learn to do one thing at a time.

From an early age, my sisters and I were given responsibilities, most of which involved multitasking—making beds, dusting, vacuuming, setting and clearing the table, washing and drying dishes—under the watchful eye of my mother, who understood early on I was a child who spilled and broke things. She was never sure if I was clumsy or purposeful in my shattering of objects. But it was neither. I simply lived in a dream world, moving to a different time and place when faced with unpleasant tasks. That dream world captured my attention, leaving me distant and prone to disasters.

When was the last time I gave my undivided attention to one person, to one thing? When was the last time I stopped my busy work and watched a bird take flight, or a sunbeam twirl across the deck on the way to kiss the roses?

Life in Southern Italy isn't glamorous. It's lacking in so many things I consider necessary to survive back home. But waiting for Fredrika in the tiny doctor's office, I realize I haven't missed or needed any of these "necessities." I've been here long enough to have forgotten what they might be. My life back home is full of trash—obligations, commitments, schedules, appointments, and social engagements. In Otranto, the few daily responsibilities of laundry, trash, and meals are joyful events. The rest of my time is spent roaming, thinking, dreaming, existing. The days ebb and flow. It's more than enough for me.

Once the eye exam is complete, Fredrika grumbles about the cost of her new glasses. This part is the same all over the world. *"Adesso,"* she says, "let's go to the grocery store."

When I left the apartment this morning, it was chilly. The ever-changing weather prompted me to wear a tank top, shirt, and sweater with my jeans. It's a long walk to the grocery store. The sun's intensity moves into overdrive. Removing my sweater, I drape it over my shopping bag as we continue up the long, steep hill.

The Euro Spin is a huge disappointment. It's a miniature Sam's or Costco. Everything is sold in large quantities. There's not enough time left for me to use sixteen rolls of toilet tissue or ten rolls of paper towels. On my shopping list are five potatoes and two onions—not ten kilos of anything.

But since Fredrika has been so kind to show me around, my good manners kick in, compelling me to buy a few things. This show of gratitude is important to our friendship. Two large bottles of water, matches for the gas stove, and small items for the kitchen fill my basket.

We're not in the store long, but I emerge with two large, heavy sacks of groceries, one cradled in each arm. Fredrika offers to carry one. Handing her a bag, I rearrange my shirt and purse, shifting the sack to my other arm.

"Oh, shit," I say.

A startled Fredrika asks, "What's wrong, Donna?"

"I've dropped my sweater somewhere, either on our way here or in the store."

She pushes the bag back into my free hand. "Wait here. I'll go back inside and look."

She returns before I finish rebalancing the grocery bags.

"No one has seen your sweater. I retraced our steps through the store. But, no, I could not find it. Let's take the same way back down the hill, perhaps you dropped it. Okay, give me a sack so I can help you."

Once again, I hand her a grocery bag. This time her phone rings. In her haste to find the phone, she releases her hold on the bag. I grab it inches before it hits the pavement.

She speaks rapidly and hangs up, saying, "My sister needs me now."

Off she trots to give someone else the great attention she has given me all day. She calls back over her shoulder that I'm to meet her at the Blu Bar this evening at five-thirty, or did she say six-thirty tomorrow?

I shift the grocery bags until they're balanced, and begin the long walk back to the apartment. An intense sun keeps me company. My sweater is lost, not that I need a sweater. It's 110 degrees, or maybe 80, but 110 is my mental truth.

Sadness envelops me, not because it was an expensive sweater or a one-of-a-kind label, but because this sweater has a certain importance in my life. It had belonged to my sister Sue. She gave it to me more than seven years ago. She often gives me nice clothes because I tend to look ratty from time to time.

I'm used to hand-me-downs as I was the youngest of four girls. But the clothes my sister passes on to me are beautiful pieces she buys for herself but decides after one wearing the items aren't right for her. She also knows I hate to shop. She knows Ray and I owned a business that operated 24/7, and there was no time during those working years to think about anything as frivolous as clothing. When she visited, she always arrived with a bundle of lovely garments for me.

The sweater was black with two gray stripes across the top. It went with everything in my closet. It was exactly the right weight and fabric for travel—no wrinkles, no sagging, no pulled threads based on the seven-year travel history it had with me.

On our last couple of trips, I mentioned to Ray that the sweater was past its prime, and I should leave it and buy a new one. But each year, when repacking my bags for the trip home, the sweater was always tucked back into my luggage. It's my traveling sweater, much like a favorite blanket or toy I had as a kid. I've lost my pacifier. I want it back.

Grumbling, I descend the steep incline and start up another hill. The heat intensifies. The sacks gain weight with my every footstep. Focusing, I try to think positively, but nothing surfaces except the sweat trickling down my face. The sun swings higher in the sky. The grocery sacks bulge in my arms.

Finally, a good thought: I've walked so many miles up and down all these hills I'm sure I've received a butt tuck. It didn't cost me a penny.

I didn't have to go under the knife. Smiling, I sweat my way home.

After gulping an entire bottle of water, I change into shorts before putting the groceries away. With my laptop under my arm, I wander onto the terrace. There are busy noises at my neighbor's house. Glancing over the wall, I discover she's part of the community's refurbishment program. A workman whitewashes the house in Tom Sawyer style.

Andrea Bocelli rolls off my playlist in his best operatic voice as I cushion myself on the bench, sighing into the sea air. The workman next door sings with Andrea—the dueling Bocellis. A joyful noise fills my ears and eases into my heart.

Back home when I hire workmen, they never sing on the job. In Otranto, everyone sings.

This morning, while Fredrika and I walked arm in arm, she sang to me. All the workmen whitewashing the buildings in town sang. Franco sang all during the tour of historical sites. What's the mystery that makes singing a natural, everyday occurrence in this tiny village on the Adriatic Sea?

Is life here better than anywhere else? Or do these people understand that music is the food of love, binding people together? Do they know that people who sing live longer because singing stimulates the blood flow? Why have I found this continuing burst of song only in this land? Will I continue to sing when I return home?

No answers come. My mouth opens, but it's my heart that sings with the workman. He doesn't care if the words or the melody are incorrect. He sings without concern for how his voice sounds to anyone else. He doesn't fear what others think. His trash has been sorted. His freedom hasn't been compromised.

My playlist changes to Steve Tyrell's "Give Me the Simple Life"— too perfect to be contrived. The workman doesn't know Steve Tyrell, the lyrics, or English. But he finds Italian words to fit the song. His work goes quickly. He doesn't stop to grumble, to ask for more pay or more benefits. He's happy. It's a beautiful day to be working outside. He makes each moment a good moment for himself.

He continues to sing with raw, robust beauty. I slip inside, leaving the door open as I prepare lunch. Slicing the smallest eggplant, I sauté the pieces in golden olive oil until each side is crisp. I make little stacks, placing a crispy eggplant slice on the plate, topping it with a juicy, sliced tomato and then a thick slab of fresh mozzarella before adding another eggplant slice.

Each stack has three layers. Sliding the stacks back into the skillet, I add marinara sauce.

Simple things in life create happiness—Fredrika's care of me, the workman's song, the eggplant stacks, a sister's sweater, and this golden sunshine day.

It's Greek to Me

Per Me È Greco

AFTER A HOT SHOWER and a glass of Salento wine, I stand on the terrace. The healing balm of the night's softness restores me. Before walking across the street to order pizza, I revisit today's devastating Greek tour, the endless hours of stop and go, the crawling in and out of the crammed van, the melting asphalt heat, and the no-English-allowed, implying the language police were watching.

I've still much to learn about when to say *yes* and when to say *no*. It's difficult and awkward to work on oneself while not offending anyone else. Taking care of my own emotional, spiritual, intellectual, and physical needs is hard enough without everyone else's stuff trickling in. Every day there's a lesson, a choice, a way to reclaim my strength and truth.

The unforgettable train ride from Lecce to Otranto is still raw in my memory. It was a day in which I collected too much trash simply because I didn't say no to Priscilla and Bobby's invitation. It would be foolish to compare the trip to Lecce with the Greek tour because the situations were totally different. Yet, for both events, I'm forced into miserable, cramped quarters with people I have little in common with and will never see again.

The second invitation I wish I hadn't accepted occurred when I bumped into Barbara, the director of the language school, at the market. She excitedly informed me of the tour of Greek cities and insisted I go.

"It'll be so helpful for your research and writing to understand the extent of the Greek culture in Puglia," her smiling eyes and voice said. "Please, go as my guest. There's no charge for you."

I was hesitant about giving up my time for an excursion with a group of unknown people. "Will English be spoken?"

"*Sì, un poco*"—a little." She went on, "But the Italian will be simple. You'll be able to follow it. You'll enjoy the tour."

Barbara has invited me several times to join her Italian language class on excursions. I turn down each invitation, citing work on the mosaic as my excuse. My goal is to find solitude, not be part of some group outing. But the mosaic is finished, and I have more time. A deviation from my solitude to visit Greek cities sounds like fun or at least informative.

Barbara has gone out of her way to be kind, assisting me often during my stay. Whether or not the couple of hours will be beneficial is questionable. But I decide not to let one crazy day with Priscilla and Bobby prevent me from participating in the Greek tour.

But instead of a day filled with culture, history, and significant research, I suffered through a day of endless small towns without benefit of understanding what was being said. One of the participants finally whispered to me that the guide wouldn't answer my questions because instructions had been given that only Italian would be spoken on the tour.

Last night I Googled the eleven Greek cities. As it turns out, the only knowledge I gained was what I learned from that online research. From the first settlement by the Illyric and Italic people in the first millennium BC, to the unification of Italy in 1861, invaders conquered this land over and over, bringing their culture, history, food, and DNA.

Otranto is a huge melting pot, like America. This reinforces my belief that the world is a wonderful mixed bag of humanity. It emphasizes how important it is to understand the backdrop of a person's history. Traveling helps me examine my prejudices. It pries loose my stereotypical ideas of people and cultures. I'm part and parcel of the human race. My own DNA can be traced back to the beginning of time. It commingles with all people and all places. There is no purity of blood or race. We are all mixed, and the better for it.

I embarked on the tour eagerly. But from the beginning, the day was fraught with mishaps. I arrived early, waiting patiently while the others randomly straggled to the meeting place carrying bags of takeout food. There's nothing worse than being in a plane, a van, a car, or a train with strangers and a variety of food odors.

The guide forgot to put on his personality. He was surly and irritated that everyone but me, the non-Italian speaking person, was late. He paced and fussed at the people who arrived late. I kept quiet. His sparse brown hair was shaved close to his scalp. He wore rumpled blue jeans with a navy-and-white-striped polo shirt embroidered on the left side with an Italian insignia. His rimless glasses caught fragments of light in the already piercing sun.

A group of seven eventually meandered to the van, which was too small to accommodate this number without us squashing into each other. Food exacerbated the excursion. I stepped on banana peels carelessly thrown on the floor, along with half-empty bags of chips and brown bags oozing with olive oil and tomato sauce.

After a while, I gave up counting the towns and the bits and pieces of antiquity we raced past. Several cathedrals, one olive grove, one olive mill, and one crumbling *trullo* created fatigue and an endless coughing fit by one ill member of the group.

The *trullo* could have been a highlight of the trip, but this was a crumbling *trullo*. On my previous trip to Puglia, I spent an afternoon in the exquisite city of Alberobello, a UNESCO village that's famous for its *trulli* houses. Each *trullo* had been restored, and ancient symbols adorned the roofs. The falling pile of rubble we saw on the tour was a poor example.

The word *trullo/trulli* is derived from the Greek word for dome. It refers to the ancient stone houses with conical roofs built without any mortar. The first *trulli* settlements date back to the Bronze Age. In ancient times, the property of citizens was taxed beyond reason. Cleverly, the people devised housing that could be dismantled. They sent village spies to discreetly follow the tax collectors. The spies would alert the villagers when tax collectors were coming to their region. Then the houses were quickly dismantled, leaving a field of scattered stones. Once the tax collector left, the houses were reassembled, and life went on as usual.

Although the crumbling *trullo* was disappointing, there were two lovely highlights on the tour. In one of the cities, we met a ninety-four-year-old Greek man at an elaborate wedding arch, and a small black puppy eager to be petted. These were the only happy faces I saw all day.

Night had fully descended when the van stopped in front of the school. Instead of a couple of hours, the tour had morphed into six. I stumbled out of the van, mumbled thank you, goodbye, and ran down *via Antonio Primaldo*, not stopping until the door to my apartment was closed and locked behind me.

After a shower and a glass of wine and a clearing of my thoughts on the terrace, I'm refreshed and ready to say *no* to the next person who invites me to do anything—well, maybe.

Breezing across the cobbled street, I order *una pizza da mangiare a casa mia.* How beautiful the words are to order takeout. The owner wants conversation. I listen while he happily chats about his day and the end of the season. The pizza arrives, wafting fragrances of tomato, mozzarella, and sausage.

Buona notte floats on the air from the owner as I scurry to my apartment. Locked safely inside, my teeth sink into gooey goodness. I eat the whole pizza and fall asleep on the sofa.

At three I awake and grope my way to the bedroom. Pulling back the sheets, I crawl into cool freshness and blissful darkness.

Parts Down

PANTALONI GIÙ

IT'S CLOSE TO NOON when I get up, too late for my daily cappuccino and chat with Giovanni.

Since I'm here to sort through so many parts of my life, I ponder how yesterday's excursion turned out so badly. I puzzle over how I could have prevented the outcome other than by declining to go. It exasperates me that my old patterns of behavior are still entrenched, the ones ingrained during my upbringing that still shout, *"Be polite, it's not nice to refuse someone's offer. You need to mix with other people. It's not healthy for you to be alone so much."*

All my mother's words.

The doorbell ends my ruminating. My "accidental Americans," whom I haven't seen for a few days, are on the doorstep. I thought they'd left town without saying goodbye. But no, they're still here. Priscilla has been in bed because of her many flip-flop falls. They ask if they can come in for a glass of wine.

Here we go again? Do I refuse? Just say no? I can't. My Southern upbringing won't allow me to turn them away. I sort through alternatives, settling on the truth.

"I'm writing, but I can take a short break. There's time for one glass of wine, but then I have to get back to my work."

It works. A short, pleasant visit ensues because they abide by my wishes without fussing or insisting I do something with them.

Later in the evening, I check in at the Blu Bar. Fredrika doesn't show. I'm sure I misunderstood what she said when she rushed off the other day. Half the time when I think we have agreed to meet, she doesn't. I don't worry and drift into *passeggiata* with the locals. On the way back, I check again. No Fredrika. I happily return to the apartment, watch the crazy Italian game shows, fix a light dinner, and dream sweet dreams.

After a good night's sleep, I devote my day to laundry, housecleaning, and compiling a list of groceries. Priscilla and Bobby are finally leaving Otranto and moving on to Sicily. Oh happy day. It will be this weekend, so I'm having a goodbye lunch for them. Yes, I could ignore them, let them go off with a simple goodbye, but Southern manners are a lifetime commitment.

Of course, there's a small glitch. When I invite them for a farewell lunch, they respond with an eager *yes*. After a moment's hesitation, Priscilla asks if they can also stay for dinner. Bobby wants to watch the Grand Prix. Their TV doesn't have cable. My mouth drops open. A big *no* hesitates on my lips. Priscilla's eyes plead. She offers to cook dinner. I say *of course*.

With my chores finished, I turn on my laptop to edit photos. I'm fully immersed in my project when the door buzzer interrupts. I peek out the front window, hoping it isn't Priscilla asking if they can spend the night as well. No one's at the front door so I move to the back wall and furtively peek. It's Fredrika.

She speaks rapidly. Her words gather speed. Fierce gestures accompany her story. I fear she's going to fall off the narrow ledge.

Racing down the stairs, I open the door, careful not to knock her off the top step. She enters, grabs me, and embraces me as if I've been raised from the dead. The stream of words jump from her mouth, slamming into each other until my brain stalls. *Niente* is what I understand.

"*Lentamente*," I say, placing my hands on her shoulders, requesting her to slow down.

She pauses for breath. When she does, I pull her in, assisting her up the steps. She drops onto the sofa with a soft moan. From the fridge I retrieve a cold bitter. Gulping it down in one long swallow, she pushes out a sobbing sigh as bits and pieces of her story emerge.

When we parted on Tuesday, her intention had been to meet me at the Blu Bar. She wails that she couldn't because something bad happened. Words gush again, explaining what the bad thing is. The only part I can decipher is she's been ill. Her words continue to jump and jumble.

I scoot one of the kitchen chairs right next to her. Leaning forward, I think if I focus really hard I'll understand her Italian.

"Please, start again. Speak slowly."

She pushes me away, jumps up, and pulls her slacks all the way down to the floor. It happens so quickly I'm paralyzed in place. Unclear about what do next, I stay frozen in place until she taps my arm. Then the reason for pants down materializes as she exhibits the problem. A huge varicose vein had ruptured in her leg. My gasping in horror reassures her that I understand. Her speech slows enough for me to follow the rest of the story.

When the vein ruptured, Mateo rushed her to the medical clinic in Lecce where doctors capped off the vein. She's supposed to stay off her feet with her legs elevated for several days. She rested for two days, but today she became distraught because she hadn't been able to meet me at the Blu Bar and couldn't get a message to me. This morning she waited until Mateo left for work. Then she walked here.

Over and over she repeats, "*Mi dispiace, mi dispiace molto*. I'm sorry. I'm so sorry."

Assisting her slacks back up, I ease her onto the sofa. The kitchen chair becomes a place to elevate her feet, and a cool cloth on her forehead brings color back to her pale cheeks. Many times she repeats how upset she is about letting me down. It's not necessary for me to explain to her I really wasn't upset when she didn't show up. Actually, I was worried she would bring Fatos to the Blu Bar. The idea of a kidnapping and a forced marriage still lingers.

I smile, saying, *"Nessun problema,"* until she's reassured it's okay. I suggest calling Mateo to pick her up, but she's resolute: he can't know she left the house. She says that after she rests she'll be able to walk home.

"Then you must stay and rest," I say, smoothing back her strawberry blonde hair streaked with gray. Her bright blue eyes transmit discomfort. As they close, I slip away to make her a cup of tea. She rests for a while and then says, *"Ora sto bene,"* letting me know she feels better. Then she asks me to tell her what I've been doing since we last saw each other.

I explain Bobby and Priscilla are leaving for Sicily on Monday. "Tomorrow I'm preparing a going-away lunch for them. It would be grand if you could join us. Would it be possible for Mateo to drive you close to the *castello*? We could meet you and help you walk the short distance to the apartment."

"Va bene," she says, a large smile gracing her lovely face. "A lunch for Bobby and Priscilla. *Sì*, I'll make a Greek pizza. I can make the dough at my house and roll it out once I'm here. I'll bake it in your oven so it will be fresh."

Before I realize what's happening, she lunges from the sofa, crossing swiftly to the kitchen and opens the oven door.

"Please, Fredrika, come back," I protest. "Tell me what you need. I'll find it for you. Please, you must rest and keep your legs elevated."

"Oh, I must see for myself how your oven works," she exclaims. "Come and show me how to operate it."

I turn the oven on. She selects the temperature and waits until she's satisfied it works correctly. She looks at the oven pan, making faint *tsk-tsk* sounds before addressing me. "Donna, this pan isn't clean."

There's no point in telling her it's a pan I haven't used. Instead, I show her all my cleaning equipment. She smiles as I explain I'll clean the pan before she arrives.

"Now," she says, "where is your *mattarello*?" While there is a wealth of kitchen items, I don't recall seeing a rolling pin. We look through the cabinets and closets but can't find one. Once more the *tsk-tsk* emerges. She sighs, asking, "Do you have a broom?"

It's an alarming question because I suspect she's thinking about the broom in a different manner than I am. Leading her to the terrace, I point out the three brooms in the cabinet. She inspects each one carefully, selecting the one with the shortest handle. I watch in slow-motion horror as she walks over to the concrete counter and raises the broom above her head. The instant I realize she's going to break the handle to create a rolling pin, I yell, "No, no," and grab her arm. "Please don't. I'll have to replace it. I can buy you a rolling pin."

She places the broom back in the cabinet and says, "I will bring my own rolling pin tomorrow."

I nod in relief as that's a far better solution. What an amazing warrior woman. She should be in bed. Instead, she's flexing her muscles to break brooms. She's strong and creative.

Smiling, she says, "The pizza will have spinach and feta. You will like it."

"It sounds delicious. I'm happy you can come. Pricilla and Bobby will be surprised and delighted," I tell her.

Gently I suggest it's time to leave if she's to be back in bed before Mateo returns from work. "If you can tell me how to find a taxi, I'll call one for you.

"No, the tourist season is over. There are no taxis. I must walk."

How I wish I had a car or could secure a taxi for her. It would hurt her feelings if I tell her she needs to rest and shouldn't join us tomorrow. It would be a useless, losing conversation. Once an Italian decides you're a friend, there are no limits to their loyalty.

Food, the Bread of Life

CIBO, IL PANE DELLA VITA

RETURNING FROM THIS MORNING'S walk, I find Fredrika sitting on the stoop surrounded by shopping bags. I help her to her feet and unlock the door while scooping up the two largest bags. She protests with a smile as she relinquishes them. We clamber up the steps. Wheezing follows every breath she takes. Once inside she tells me she must rest before preparing the pizza. I offer her a bitter and assist with elevating her legs.

"How are you feeling today? Are you well enough to make the Greek pizza? If you instruct me, I'll try to make it the way you would."

"Today is good. There's no pain or swelling. I'll be ready once I rest for a few minutes."

In detail she describes her walk over as I finalize the antipasti. On a large, brightly hand-painted platter, I assemble vibrant tomatoes roasted with rosemary and garlic. Green and black olives, miniature balls of mozzarella, *cipollini*, prosciutto, and *piccante* salami follow. I add green beans that have been marinated with onions, tomatoes, and capers. On the outer edges of the platter, I arrange slices of hardboiled egg, roasted red peppers, piles of baby shrimp, and artichoke hearts.

I sauté long, sweet green peppers and spicy red ones and place them on a large platter next to slender leeks, creating colors of the Italian flag. Mushrooms swaddled in olive oil, garlic and parsley are cradled in a pale green crock. It's a small feast we can nibble on while waiting for Fredrika's Greek pizza.

Once Fredrika revives, she asks me to help her empty the shopping bags. She shows me each item as we unpack.

"I prepared the pizza dough before I left home. It was better to roll it out there. My rolling pin was too heavy to bring along with all the other items." For now my broom handle is safe.

"See," she continues, "the dough is stretched inside this large rectangular container."

"Oh, it's so thin. Is it phyllo"

"No, of course not. It's pizza dough. Touch it. You see it's not as thin as phyllo," she patiently explains. It looks like phyllo to me, but I keep quiet.

"Here is the spinach, *feta* cheese, *parmigiana*, onion, and garlic mixture, which I prepared this morning. Now watch. I'll spread a layer of the mixture on top and add more pizza dough," she says, her eyebrows arch into positions of intense concentration.

She spreads the mixture thickly on the bottom layer of dough and then covers the filling with a second layer. It's much like a savory Greek spinach pie I make with phyllo dough.

While Fredrika is making the pizza, Priscilla and Bobby arrive. They bring more food, wine, and a gorgeous branch of magenta bougainvillea they've borrowed from a bush hanging over someone's garden wall. We spend a delightful afternoon reminiscing about our time together in this beautiful place—with Priscilla stillspeaking Spanglish.

Sitting on the shaded terrace, we Google our home addresses to show Fredrika how far South Carolina is from California. We hope this will clear up her belief that Priscilla and I will visit each other once we return home. In Fredrika's mind we are neighbors. We show her the East and West coasts, pointing out the huge distance between our two houses. She's mesmerized by how big the United States is and how it would take days to drive across its vastness.

Fredrika Googles the apartment in Albania where her mother lives. I don't know why her mother lives in Albania. Our language differences don't allow for complicated conversations about our lives. Fredrika has never Googled an address before. Her excitement is contagious. She shows us the drab military-style apartments and tells us these used to be important government offices. Now they house the most modern apartments in Albania.

Divine aromas of garlic, onions, and cheese waft onto the terrace, drawing us back inside. While the pizza cools, we devour the antipasti. Fredrika slices thick layers of the pizza and brings it to the terrace. We clink our wineglasses, our bursts of laughter bouncing into the brightness of this celebratory day.

At one o'clock, Priscilla and Bobby go inside to watch the Formula One car race.

Fredrika and I remain on the terrace. As the sun shifts and sea breezes tousle our hair, we listen to Andrea Bocelli, Jimmy Buffett, Etta James, the Buena Vista Social Club, Steve Tyrell, Jackie Evancho, Eva Cassidy, and many others from my play list.

Fredrika can't get enough of American music. She asks about each artist and wants to know why I've selected them. She expects me to know each one personally and is surprised when I say I don't. She has such an appreciation for *la musica*. We sing along, she in Italian and me in English.

It's November, but the tropical sun still lingers. The day settles into a warm wine glow, drawing us into its web of security.

When the races are over, Priscilla and Bobby join us, adding their voices and dance moves to the music. Soon it's time for everyone to leave as a late afternoon nap is mandatory for Fredrika.

It's also become a necessity for those of us who have adapted to this delightfully slow lifestyle.

A nervous exhaustion invades my body after Fredrika, Priscilla, and Bobby leave. Instead of napping, I write. Idrusa wanders in and out of my thoughts. I ponder her place and purpose in this backdrop. I wonder why she haunts me, begging for her story to be told with no indication of how I'm to tell it. Words flow, then stall.

I nap before Priscilla and Bobby return later this evening. As I drift into that suspended space, my inner voice asks me why they're coming. *Why did I, in a weak moment, say yes when Priscilla volunteered to cook tonight's meal? Where is my "no" voice?* I'm stuffed from today's feast. My body wants a long nap, a slow walk, and then a thumb-sucking night watching game shows while snuggled into the safe harbor of the sofa.

My new strong voice rises and tells me tomorrow Priscilla and Bobby will leave on the evening bus to Sicily. It'll be the last time I see them. While I'm thankful they're moving on, they did add an interesting dimension to my time here, including some good stories to write about. There have been moments when they've endeared themselves to me. Though we won't stay in touch, and I won't miss them, these two wacky people have wiggled their way into my heart.

Before Priscilla and Bobby arrive for dinner, I return to the little shop that's fixing my starfish necklace. It's closed. Instead of returning to the apartment, I follow the sea. *Il mare* always seduces me to stop, to consider its lessons.

My gaze skips on the waves which gift me with forever sight. God was so generous when water was created. Every emotion lives in the waves, the colors, and the seasons. Water provides us with endless hours of recreation. It creates jobs, and provides life-sustaining food. It's one of our most precious resources. And it offers me solace, allowing my soul to soar with the waves.

The sun begins its descent, gently nudging me back to real time. I stroll home the long way, passing by my favorite little shop, the one that's never open but has a window display with beautiful sea glass jewelry. I window shop as I meander through the narrow streets. My feet, before my ears, experience gospel music. I halt, allowing the melodious notes to direct my steps. It's the first time in my many travels to Italy that I've heard gospel music. The familiar strands of a Whitney Houston song quiver on the air. Circling around the narrow alleyways, my feet harmonize to the source.

The musical joy beams out of the Catholic school, the one I've passed often on my morning walks. The only activity I've ever seen is the coming and going of schoolchildren. Today all the windows are open. The music palpitates. Locals walking by shake their heads as if this music is surely sacrilegious. But I dance right up to the window and peek in. There's a lovely group of young people singing with gusto. When they see me at the window, they beckon me inside. I say no, *grazie,* as I have the perfect front row seat watching them through the large, open window.

"*I go to the Rock, I go to the Rock, I go to the Rock for my salvation.*" Their voices are loud, pure, brimming over with joy.

The director comes to the window, insisting I join the singing group. But I'm a singer only in my heart. My voice would detract from their magical performance. *Perhaps,* I think, *my voice might soar if blended with theirs.* But it's wishful thinking on my part. I decline, indicating my seat on the window ledge is perfect. Looking in and listening to the voices of heaven singing just for me is where I want to be. "*I go to the Rock.*"

My dinner commitment calls me away. As often happens in life, I long to stay at the Rock, gathering strength and joy, but I must turn away. There are choices to be made, even in this small world I've created for myself.

Priscilla and Bobby turn in to the alley as I unlock the back door. Clearly, they've emptied out their refrigerator. They stagger in with bags of groceries, some for tonight's dinner and some to leave with me.

"If y'all don't mind, I need to check at the jewelry shop one more time to see if my necklace is ready. I won't be a minute," I tell them. "The shop owner promised I could pick it up today. If I don't, I'm concerned the shop will be closed for the season. Go on in, wine and glasses are on the table."

"No problem, take your time," they respond.

I jog back, taking the long way past the Catholic school. The door and shutters are closed. There are no singing voices. All is still and quiet as the shadows deepen and night comes calling.

The song granted me another sacred fragment—one I'll remember when my days run together—days when returning to the Rock is a necessity.

Rushing to the jewelry shop, I focus on not twisting my ankles on the cobbled stones. It's still closed. I turn to go home but change my mind and jog toward the other shop. Maybe it's still open. It is, and the shopkeeper's inside. She welcomes me with a hug. I ask if it's possible to pick up the necklace. She smiles, removes a bunch of keys from the counter and signals me to follow. She closes and locks the door. We walk arm in arm to the other shop where her husband, she tells me, left the necklace. She shares her day. Telling me stories about bike rides with her children. We laugh over the universal problem of *le formiche* (ants) spoiling their picnic.

Once in the shop, she searches for the necklace. She discovers a small package and shows me it says *americana*. As she opens it, the smile in her eyes slumps in disappointment. Moving everything off the counter, she places the starfish in front of me, pointing to a slight bump in the arm—the place where her husband tried to mend the break.

She shakes her head and says, "No, I cannot give this to you. My husband was not able to fix it. It's not acceptable. Please, choose any piece of jewelry in the shop. It will be yours."

But I want the red starfish with the bump. It's another reminder of the imperfection of my life. It's like the humility stone in my mosaic. I love it. I try to explain this to her. She looks at me strangely, nods, and reluctantly hands me the starfish. She refuses to let me pay for the repair.

She sees the starfish as trash, something to be discarded. I see it as something worthy of being restored, saved from the trash pile. I secure the necklace around my neck. Its red glow hangs warmly against my skin. Smiling, I touch the bump, give the shopkeeper a hug, and rush back to the apartment.

When I return, Priscilla is in full swing in the kitchen. She's preparing a meal of pasta with tomatoes, garlic, onions, and broccoli. She's comfortable in the kitchen, permitting me to relax. The pasta is excellent, the wine heady and intense. When we finish, Bobby shoos us out to the terrace and cleans up all the dishes. They redeem themselves in these final hours we're together.

It easier to relax knowing I won't have to listen to any more possibilities about the trip to Sicily. It's a reality. They're leaving. They have their tickets. Priscilla is no longer obsessing about what to do. The evening is soft, mushy—filled with humidity, warm breezes, and friendliness.

It happens over time. You get to know people a little better. They trust you with some of their secrets. You have a better understanding of why they are the people they are. A lot of Priscilla's know-it-all attitude is a way she protects herself. The same with Bobby's constant "silly man" antics. They're people who want you to like them but are ˜ vou won't. They prepare themselves ahead of time for the brushoff.

Slowly I've come to care about them.

They have given me many gifts—wonderful characters to write about, the ability to speak English with them, their love of good food and wine, and the enjoyment of deep discussions on politics and religion without either of them being defensive. The good of them far outweighs the not so good. I hope they've discovered the same about me.

My life in Otranto is winding down and wrapping up. Though my going-home shoes are being polished, there's still time left to grow stronger. Letting go of such a joyous time in my life will be difficult. It's important I pack all the good things about this golden time in the Salento sun.

Sicilians, Beware

I Siciliani Guardano

YESTERDAY AT OUR GOODBYE celebration we all agreed to meet one last time at the Blu Bar at 11. After all this time, I'm still optimistic someone from the group will show up. *Ma no*, no one does. I go back at eleven-fifteen and again at eleven-thirty and still no one. Back at the apartment, I prepare lunch and decide that last night was our goodbye. I've just put the first forkful of food into my mouth when I hear Bobby and Priscilla.

The refrains of "Oh, Donna. Oh, Donna" waft through the courtyard. I consider not responding, but the singing continues, interspersed with yells of, "Come out, come out, and play with us."

Poking my head out the window, I say, "Wait by the *castello*. I'll be down in a few minutes."

I cram the rest of my lunch into a couple of bites before joining them where they wait perched on the surround.

Priscilla gleefully chuckles, "Well, we're at your mercy until our bus for Sicily leaves tonight. We didn't realize we'd have to check out of our apartment at noon."

"Where's your luggage? Do you need to leave it in my apartment?" I offer.

"Oh, no, the lady at the travel agency said we could leave it there until it's time to go. We just need a place to hang out. We know you won't mind."

Oh shit, I think, as all the warm, fuzzy feelings I had about them disappear. My mind whines about another day without solitude, but I say, "Sure, it's not a problem."

The *no* that's so ready on my tongue stalls as I consider how I would want to be treated if it were me that needed a place to stay. Compassion can't be turned on and off. It's either there or it isn't.

"Stay until it's time for your bus to leave. There's a bottle of prosecco chilling in the fridge. We'll continue to celebrate all the adventures we've had together, and we'll toast your new adventures in Sicily."

Priscilla launches into her hymn of praise about how smart she is to have found such an inexpensive, comfortable bus to take them to Sicily. Ahh, so much for compassion. I think, *Why did I offer to let them stay here?*

"I'm so excited. Do you realize we'll ride all the way across Southern Italy to Villa San Giovanni on the west coast?" She doesn't stop for comment. "Then the bus will drive right onto the ferry, which will take us to Messina. Did you know we'll be in Catania by early tomorrow morning?"

I nod and make *hmmm* noises as I put out snacks and open the prosecco. Her monologue continues. I listen with my eyes but not my ears. Around four-thirty, Fredrika rescues me by banging on the door. She huffs and puffs her way into the apartment asking why we weren't at the Blu Bar at ten this morning. "I waited and no one came," she says, her eyes and sighs interspersed with sorrow.

We laugh until our sides ache. Not once have any of us managed to understand what time we're supposed to meet at the Blu Bar. The best part about staying in a small village is that eventually you can find each other without any assistance from technology.

I fill a glass with chilled prosecco for Fredrika. We have another toast to our good times. We push away sadness and embrace as Fredrika leaves for her doctor's appointment.

Priscilla and Bobby want to eat before they board the bus. They've convinced themselves there'll be no food stops. It doesn't matter that I've told them numerous times there will be stops along the way and there will be bars and restaurants on the ferry. Not once has any of this information taken root. Unless Priscilla says it's so, it isn't.

Priscilla nods through me and says, "We really want to eat one last time at the pizzeria across the street."

"You know, they don't usually open until late."

"Oh, I'm sure they'll open for us as often as we've eaten there. Don't you agree?"

"All we can do is ask," I respond, ushering them out the door. It's certainly a better alternative than staying here.

Darkness descends early as fall takes a step closer to winter. Misty evening fog shrouds us as we shuffle across the cobbled street. Bobby knocks on the side door, one we've never used before because the weather has always been conducive to sitting out front on the wooden deck.

The owner pokes his head out and says, *"Si, si entrare prego,"* delighted to open early for us.

Into my memory file I tuck yet another act of kindness. Bobby and Priscilla have an 11-hour bus ride ahead of them. A full stomach and a glass of wine will ease their way. The restaurants in Otranto are tiny, but most have large outside areas that are utilized most of the year. During my stay, I've learned many restaurants have a tiny seating area inside. It's usually sequestered in the back by the kitchen. The locals know this and claim these in-house spots for long, leisurely meals when the weather is bad, like today.

It's one of those cool, damp, fog-covered evenings, enough to whitewash our clothes and hair with moisture, granting us a shiver of weather to come. The owner opens the door wide and gestures for us to enter. He seats us close to the pizza ovens. In a few minutes, we are cocooned in the luxury of warm, delicious odors accompanied by the sizzle of pizzas in the old brick oven. For antipasti we share a seafood salad that still, in late fall, tastes of summer sunshine. Next, a *caprese* salad arrives with fresh mozzarella, big chunks of fresh tomatoes, and fresh basil. There's a plate of sheer, raw tuna surrounded with lemons and sprinkled with chunky sea salt.

We order two different kinds of pizza—cheese, tomato, sausage, and freshly picked herbs for one; green olives, onions, parmesan, and mozzarella on the other. A large carafe of wine and water complete our meal. This yumminess costs less than forty-five euros for the three of us.

When we finish, Priscilla and Bobby gather their belongings. We group hug, not sharing our private thoughts.

Priscilla looks at me and says, "You've given me such a beautiful gift of friendship. People don't always like me."

I hug her again. She says her time in Otranto has been the highlight of their travels. They are uncomfortable with lingering goodbyes, so they quickly close the door on Otranto to begin their Sicilian adventure. Perhaps Priscilla will meet her match in Sicily.

I stay behind in the pizzeria to finish my wine, chatting with the owners. The husband, who at first seemed like such a grump, now beams every time he sees me. In the morning when I leave the apartment for my walk, his wife opens the window and greets me with, *"Buona giornata, signora."*

I will miss these small daily rituals. I've been given more gifts to take home—the gift of strangers offering me many kindnesses during my stay, and the gift of recognizing and accepting people wherever they are on their journey, including myself.

There are only twenty giant steps from the restaurant to my apartment. I take the smallest steps possible, lingering to savor these gifts, packing them in my heart for a safe journey home.

Refocus

RIFOCALIZZARE

I RECLAIM MY LIFE of solitude. My walks lengthen as the days grow shorter and twilight comes earlier. Daily photography sessions take me to every point of the old city. There are so many places and people I want to photograph, but my camera balks. The problem started during the Greek tour and has escalated. These past few days I've only been able to squeeze out one or two photos before the camera locks up.

Lacking a good grasp of the language becomes more of a challenge. I don't have the language skills to explain what ails my camera. I packed an extra memory card and recently swapped them. The camera works for several shots. Then it stops again. Today I'm asking for help.

I write down several phrases in Italian. *Sometimes my camera works, and sometimes it doesn't.* That isn't clear enough, so I stretch it out. For my next option I write, "*My camera is broken (la mia foto camera è rotta).*" Too vague. For simplicity I choose, "*I need a memory card (Ho bisogno di uno schema di memoria),"* thinking perhaps the cards I brought with me are defective.

Before beginning an endless search for another memory card and before visiting Wednesday's market, I stop for *un cappuccino.* Giovanni might know where I can purchase a memory card. He advises me to first check the souvenir shop by the sea. If they can't help, then try the *farmacia* as it's possible the pharmacy could sell them. However, his hesitation indicates he's not sure. It doesn't bode well when a local isn't sure.

Thoughts of wandering through the market distract me from dealing with the camera. The tourist office is on the way to the market, so I stop, inquiring if Franco is in. No, I'm told, but he's at the market, which is small enough so I can easily find him. He wants to know about the hurricane hitting the East Coast of the US. He's worried I'll have problems flying home.

At that moment, it registers I've been living without interference from the outside world. I was unaware a major storm was creating havoc in the States. To put his mind at ease, I tell him by the time I fly home the weather will be fine. He tells me Carlo is vacationing in Spain but may be back on Saturday.

"È possibile per noi tre per il pranzo?" I ask, hoping I can repay their kindness by taking them to lunch.

Franco says, *"Certo!* But Carlo is young, and it's not definite he'll return on Saturday."

"I'll check in a couple of days," I respond. "If Carlo is back, we'll make a date for lunch."

A major highlight of my time in Otranto was the day I spent with Franco and Carlo. Taking them to lunch would be a small way to show my appreciation for our day spent with antiquities, legends, and songs. I would have missed the tawdry beauty of the cross, the fragile shell of the old lighthouse, the green pond, Pantaleone's monastery viewed on the run, and the joy that these two men bestowed on me.

At the market I buy olives and veggies. On the way back, I stop at the grocery store, purchasing water, yogurt, bitters, my favorite juice and a couple of sausages. Hurrying home, I put away the groceries. It's a dismal, overcast day, creating a need for me to slip into a jacket before pursuing my memory card search.

All my ramblings take time. It's after eleven when I leave the apartment. I set off at a brisk pace. It would be terrific if I could solve the problem before lunch, or at least before the storm descends.

The souvenir shop is first on my list. Of course, they send me to the *farmacia*. Patiently, I wait behind the green line. When it's my turn, I ask for a memory card. The pharmacist comes out from behind the counter. Taking my hand, he walks me out the door and points to a big KODAK sign that everyone in the world must be able to see except me.

After many thanks, I walk into the camera shop, only to discover it's not a camera shop. It's the eye doctor's office where Fredrika brought me for her appointment. One thing about shopping in Italy that will forever remain a mystery is how to know where to shop for routine items when they are so often sold in unexpected places.

A few years ago I searched high and low for a hair dryer. I finally enlisted the help of one of my Italian friends who took me to a large appliance store, one that sells washers, dryers, ovens, and refrigerators—and hair dryers.

To find a memory card so quickly in this unusual place is an unexpected pleasure. As I pay for the card, I smile, knowing Fredrika would tell me that I had paid entirely too much. True, but I don't care about the cost if the camera works.

Sitting on the stone wall right outside the optometrist shop, I open the memory card package. The card pops out and falls to the ground. There's no little plastic protective package to hold it in place like the ones I buy in the States. In my haste to pick up the card, the camera slides out of my hand. I snatch it midair.

My hand hits the battery door, scattering batteries across the sidewalk. I scurry after them as they tumble in all directions. After all have been rescued and wiped off, I put them back in the camera and insert the memory card. Clutching my other packages, I run across the street to take my first picture. It works.

Jumping up and down with joy, I run to the sea to capture the scowling, smoky blue-gray texture. Positioning myself in my favorite dreaming spot, I steady the camera on my knee and push the button. Nothing happens. I push again. There's no click—only silence. My camera says it's taken 9,999 pictures. It refuses to take any more.

Ever since my camera became erratic on the Greek tour, I've tried without success to fix it. I've deleted every picture, I've reformatted the memory card, and I've changed the batteries three times. Nothing works. The camera is broken or locked up in some way I can't figure out. I have tried downloading the manual, but it tells me nothing about how to fix this problem. Google provides no solutions.

With great sorrow and a big sigh, I put my camera away. Sinking back into my dreaming place, I shelter in the small spot between the wall and the sea. I refocus. My eyes sweep across the sullen sea that captures every color, every wave, every shade of dark and light.

Storms march above the sea from Africa. The seasons change just as I have during my stay.

I close my eyes. My brain shutter clicks and stores away the moment in the memory card inside my head.

PART IV
JOY

Weeping may endure for a night, But joy comes in the morning.

~ PSALM 30:5

Madonna of the High Sea

MADONNA DELL'ALTOMARE

BEING ALONE IN OTRANTO has expanded my life in all directions. There's a freedom in my heart, a largeness and depth of spirit that awakens me with excitement and anticipation for each new day. *Joy* is the only word coming close to expressing that internal longing that brought me here. Each day I'm surprised when joy grabs me like a hummingbird darting in and out for nectar. I'm up early, greeting the sun's warmth and fierceness after the intensity of last night's storm.

My first stop is the Blu Bar for morning cappuccino. As usual, with Giovanni's encouragement, I have memorized my activities in Italian. He's kind enough to fill the blanks in my halting sentences. He does this in such a gentle manner I barely know I'm learning.

After cappuccino, I walk through the main street of the old city, stopping as always to admire the local crafts. Sometimes Idrusa walks with me. The shops are tiny but packed to the rafters with treasures. Today, with Idrusa's help, I select a small pitcher in the fierce red of tropical sunsets. It's adorned with a bunch of lush purple grapes. There are two matching cups—the perfect size for *limoncello* or *amaro*—and small enough to tuck in a corner of my luggage.

With the package under my arm, I continue my walk, debating which path to take. In my first weeks in this village I've found sacredness in many corners, an abundance of solace and inspiration. Each shrine I visit is magnificent. But my favorite is the tiny chapel I discovered the first day on my own. I find Idrusa there more than anywhere else. At first it surprised me until I remembered her husband was a fisherman. She would have come here with the other wives to pray for his safe return home, or perhaps her prayer was for something different.

Chiesa della Madonna dell'Altomare—the Church of the Madonna of the High Sea. The stairs I climb to reach the chapel extend out of the sea. The church totters on the edge, reminding all who come here of the perils of a life spent on the water.

Stopping at the top, I reread the sign posted out front. It describes the massacre of 1480 and the Otrantini women who were captured and enslaved by the Ottoman caliph and his warriors. During the mutilation of the people and the city, the Ottomans stole the statue of the Madonna from Otranto. One of the captured women, who'd found favor with the caliph, begged not for her own freedom but for the freedom of the sacred Madonna.

The caliph Acmet eventually relented, putting the statue in a boat without a crew and pushing it into the sea. The woman was inconsolable, fearing the Madonna would be lost in the vast stretch of water that separated her from Otranto. But after days, weeks, or perhaps months, the Madonna found her way safely back to the beach below this church. It's a miracle that is celebrated every year.

The festival lasts fifteen days, the number of days Otranto was under siege by the Ottomans.

Every August during *La Festa dei Martiri Hydruntini*, the Madonna leads the procession from the church through the town and along the seawall. She's placed into a small boat, but this time she has a crew to ensure she finds her way across the sea. After sailing from the church to the old village, she's lifted onto the shoulders of the young men of Otranto and carried with great reverence through the town and into the church. There's music, food, dancing, singing, and fireworks—a joyous celebration of a small victory in the face of the massacre's devastation.

Today, as with most days, the church is empty, embellishing its tranquility, solitude, and sacredness. The mosaic floor cannot be compared to Pantaleone's masterpiece in the *duomo*. It's far simpler in size and decorative impact. Yet, the stars and shipping knots were crafted with the same level of intensity and creativity. Slipping into the last pew, I'm surrounded by the wives of the fishermen who have been coming here for hundreds of years, kneeling on these same mosaic stones to pray for the safe return of their men.

There's much to absorb in a chapel so small. Today the sun slowly dances across the mosaic floor and up the wall, tipping my gaze toward the ceiling. A ship's wheel suspended from three long chains bolted into the ceiling sways in time with the waltzing sun. Another ship's wheel holds steady, wedged under the altar between hexagon-shaped marble supports. Its wooden spokes are burnished and buffed to a rosy glow. Crisp, white altar linens shimmer as the morning light pours holiness into this place.

My eyes sweep across the whitewashed walls, bringing the *Madonna del Mare* into view. Robed in a red gown embroidered around the hemline with gold threads, she stands in regality. Her long, slender neck rises from the draped softness of a gold scarf. Her gown, partially covered by a royal blue cloak, glints with the same gold threads.

Baby Jesus nestles in the crook of Mary's arm. He's about two years old with curly brown locks clustered on his head. He holds a book in his left hand. Mary looks down on him with a mother's love. Her lovely bare toes peek out from under her royal robes. Potted orchids and freshly cut roses positioned at her feet nod in adoration. Behind her hangs a red banner held aloft by two giant sea creatures. To her left an anchor hangs against the wall. I imagine it's a safety net in case she loses her balance and requires a place to steady herself. A seahorse hovers nearby to guide her safely on her journey. He holds a swinging lantern from his mouth to light her path. She will never lose her way again.

The tiny chapel wraps me in silence. The holiness of this place soothes away my cares. The fragments of my life find their way into lovely mosaic patterns as I soundlessly leave.

Joy accompanies me.

Gifts

I REGALI

SEVERAL DAYS AGO, FREDRIKA and I agreed to meet for *un cappucino alle dieci.* She doesn't show up at ten. It's customary for her to miss our rendezvous so I'm not concerned. I head back to my apartment with this gift of additional time to write and sort through emails. As evening approaches, the weather snarls, promising rain. I hate missing the evening *passeggiata,* but it's a night to stay inside.

Swapping out jeans and a long-sleeved pullover, I slip on pajama bottoms, faded red with black roosters. It's the first time the weather's been cool enough for shabby flannel. To the old, faded PJ bottoms I add my rattiest black tee, covering it with an extra-large, soon-to-be-discarded denim shirt. To complete my ensemble, I pull on thick black socks. My hair is in its natural state of frizzy from the humid sea air. The TV's on the game show channel as I pour a glass of wine and poke through the fridge for tonight's meal. Suddenly, a pounding noise outside startles me, and I whack my head on the door.

I peek over the back wall and find Fredrika on the back step, spewing forth a mixture of Italian, Greek, and Latino.

"I couldn't meet you this morning at the Blu Bar. I forgot I had a physical therapy appointment *per le mie vene*," she yells.

"What? What about your veins?"

"*Ero esausto* and stopped to rest at home before meeting you. I'm so sorry because I fell asleep. I woke up, rushing to the Blu Bar. *Ma, no, era troppo tardi*, you were not there. Next, I come to your apartment. You were not home."

I'm still stuck on what it means to "reinvent her veins" as her gush of words gallops into language confusion for me. The intensity of listening exhausts me. I'm never sure if I have the correct story. I have added the language of gushing veins, "*vene zampillanti*" to my repertoire of Italian, but today's story is told with such drama and rapidity there's no time to interpret all the new words.

"Come inside," I say, "the air is damp. I don't wish for you to catch cold or increase the pain in your leg."

She enters the apartment. Before she sits, she lovingly places a little silk bag in my hands. Inside I find an enchanting bracelet with silver and pink glass beads. A silver elephant, just like the one in Pantaleone's mosaic, dangles from the middle loop.

"It will bring you countless years of good luck, plus you will think of me," she says with a grand smile.

I have no words. I hug her long and hard. She wants to sit at the kitchen table, so I push the clutter to the far side. She accepts a glass of wine and begins to examine my paraphernalia.

"*Quanto costa?*" she asks. Back home it would be rude to ask anyone the price of something they own. But I'm not offended as she does this with such innocent charm. Over the course of our relationship, I've discovered she asks me the cost of everything so she can tell me I've paid too much. After I tell her the price, she always says if she had been with me I would never have made such a mistake. This covers everything from a pedicure to a gelato.

Initially, I asked what I should have paid. There is never an answer. She passes over the question, implying I should have better sense. It took me a while to realize that I'm missing the point of these beautiful comedic conversations. In these exchanges, she reveals my lack of experience while exposing her abundance of it. In these few remaining days I learn to *tsk-tsk* and let her know how much I appreciate her good shopping sense. It's a charming ritual, and our mutual connection and appreciation of each other has risen through its practice.

Today she focuses on the calcium chews along with some vitamin D tablets. She wants to know what they are for, how much they cost, and if she can eat one of the chews. She giggles, telling me something so good shouldn't be healthy. Next, she examines all the vegetables residing in the big blue-and-white bowl. This test I pass easily—she smiles a lot as she pats each one.

She moves from the vegetables to the piles of paper. There are maps, books, journals, and photos. She touches them reverently and asks me questions about the ones that interest her. Once all the items on top of the table have been addressed, she asks about the tablecloth. She is captivated with the story of my mother-in-law and how I bring her to Europe with me by way of one of her tablecloths. She takes my hand and presses it to her cheek.

"I must leave now," she says as she wraps me in one of her generous hugs, kisses both cheeks, and gives one an extra pinch. "It will be dark if I do not hurry. At the end of the week, we will meet at the Blu Bar. I will wait for you."

My chest tightens as I watch her walk briskly away. I won't hold my breath about seeing her again as I have adjusted to her in-the-moment attitude. If she doesn't show up, my memories of her will retain their beauty. It will bring a smile to my face to recall the sincere plans she makes to meet me and the stories that emerge when the plans don't work out. When it's time to leave, she'll be the one person I'll miss. Joy pulsates from the elephant dangling from my wrist as I lock the back door and return to my safe place on the sofa.

The wind sighs heavily as a loose shutter keeps time like a one-note band. The comfort of the warm, food-scented kitchen surrounds me. The sofa snuggles me into the soft spot I've come to call my game-show seat.

A sharp pain, not associated with my health, enters my heart. I'm astonished my adventure is ending. I'm not ready to leave. I could stay here forever. But the lesson is knowing when to leave, when to rejoin the life I left behind, when to go forward.

This time has been a joyful stopping-off point for me. Having the time to identify my fragments and sort through my trash has provided me with strength to return home, to seek forgiveness as needed, to remove myself from toxic situations, and to continue to work on becoming myself. It's time for Ray and me to find our heart place together. We need a place that offers us solitude and community in equal parts.

I curl into coziness as sounds of rain reflect the teardrops in my heart. Sighing heavily, I turn on the TV and prepare for game-show overload, a warped form of joy.

The Hill of the Martyrs

La Collina Dei Martiri

SHORTLY AFTER MY ARRIVAL in Otranto, Paolo showed me the location of the Hill of the Martyrs. It's away from the walled village, and we didn't have time to stop. But Paolo urged me to come back and explore. It's been off my radar until today. As I continue to unravel myself, I've discovered more time to do research and think about my book. Today I'm going to tackle this gruesome hill where 800 boys and men were massacred.

It's a sultry day without breeze. Rain hovers in the air without falling. I stroll through the city, away from my area of comfort. I check out the surroundings as I walk, noting landmarks so I can find my way back. It's close to siesta time. A drowsy, sinister haze covers the village, shrouding all activity and keeping the villagers inside.

The walled enclave where I live cradles me in security. I go about each day without any thought to my safety. Now, outside those secure walls, I sense a foreboding that clings to the back of my neck.

Wear and tear permeate this part of town, speaking of difficult times. Graffiti colors the bland buildings, litter slumps in the streets. An unidentifiable, precautionary stillness circles my footsteps. Intently I scan the area in all directions, not sure what I'm sensing. I'm so caught up in the dismal surroundings I almost miss the turn that takes me to the hill.

The first sign appears identifying *Santuario S. Maria dei Martiri*, The Sanctuary of Saint Maria of the Martyrs. At one time the sign was bright yellow with bold, black lettering. Now its scarred, torn face scrutinizes me in silence. Rocks have pitted the surface, attempting to scratch out the name. It's another reminder that these amazing historical sites do not have caretakers.

Numerous stone steps confront me. They are pocked, filled with rubble and weeds. Two plaques engraved into stone pillars on either side of the steps reveal ancient script, possibly Latin. The words have faded from years of wind, rain, and rock throwing. The first carving says something about 1480, when hordes of Muslims invaded the area, killing the citizens. The second indicates there's a holy olive tree planted on the grounds, honoring the 800 who were viciously massacred. I surprise myself when I'm able to interpret bits of the ancient language based on my few years of high school Latin.

The steps span upward in a graduated incline. I wonder if it was purposely built this way for pilgrims. There are ten steps. Then there's a wide stone landing for a pilgrim to pause and reflect before undertaking the next set of ten steps. I lose count of the many sets of steps and landings as I move toward the top. It's easy to imagine pilgrims on their knees slowly and tortuously making their way, fingering their prayer beads.

Later, a Catholic friend explains the rosary to me—five groups of ten beads for Hail Mary and then a large bead where the Lord's Prayer is said. She thinks the five series of ten steps and then a landing was created to repeat the five cycles of saying the rosary.

In retrospect, it makes perfect sense. But on this day I simply move with the rhythm of the place, not fully understanding. I traverse each step, pausing in reverence on each landing. About halfway up, a stone spike spirals into the sky. It represents the location where an Ottoman soldier, after witnessing the bravery of the men of Otranto, asked how he could convert to Christianity. He was suddenly considered an infidel by his fellow soldiers. They beat him, and then impaled him on a spike, leaving him to die.

Shuddering in the oppressive air, I continue my steady climb upward. Silence thunders in my ears. Nothing moves. At the top, weeds and vines tangle in their effort to overtake the grounds. Neglect hangs heavy in the humid air.

The hill sits on the edge of Otranto surrounded by roads and traffic. Yet, no sounds reach this high place. The oppressive air clutches at my shoulders. No breeze breaks its grasp. I'm enclosed by death, trapped in some afterlife of sorrow. The 800 who were beheaded here must have felt the same as they waited in line for death.

After the massacre, the bodies were scattered across the hill or buried in shallow graves. Several years passed before the remains were gathered and moved to the cathedral. The original beheading stone, or a facsimile, was found and placed in the cathedral in the Chapel of the Skulls. It's still there, over 500 years later.

I continue to climb as the legend plays out in my mind. After the Ottomans breached the fortress and gained control of the village, they rounded up all the citizens. The women and children hid in the cathedral until they were discovered. Their sanctuary became their prison. The invaders locked them in, later killing infants and small children and enslaving the women and older children.

Men and boys who weren't fortunate enough to escape were led away for beheading. The Ottomans determined the men were too dangerous to be spared unless they converted to Islam. They were given the choice—conversion or beheading.

Legend identifies Antonio Primaldo, a tailor and devout Christian, as the man chosen to speak for the men of Otranto. He told the Ottoman captors that the men of Otranto had fought bravely to defend their homes and families. But now the fight was far greater as they were being called upon to defend their souls and their faith.

According to the story, Primaldo stood tall and said to the Ottomans, "Christ died on the cross for the salvation of the citizens of Otranto. So it's appropriate we should now die for Christ. We will remain firm and constant in our faith, even unto death."

Antonio Primaldo was first to place his head on the beheading stone. As the sword separated Antonio's body from his head, he crumpled to his death. But instantly his headless corpse stood up. It remained standing until every man of Otranto has been decapitated.

I imagine 800 young boys and men trudging to their death. The decapitated body of one man standing washes over me. Trembling, I place my hands on the ground, blood and severed heads saturating my every thought. This isn't a sacred place for me. Its haunted hush isn't peaceful. It's full of agony, suffering, pain, and endless restlessness.

I jump to my feet when a crash and rustling in the underbrush explodes right next to my prone position. My heart gallops until a glimpse of gold fur, green eyes, flattened ears, and a swishing tail emerge. Leaning against the closest tree, I gasp with relief as a large cat silently slinks back into the black matted maze of bushes and vines.

I'm thankful for my strong knees as I fling myself down the steps back into civilization.

Slowing at the bottom, I teeter on the last landing, composing myself. A fragrant bed of rosemary grows near the last step. It emits a cleansing and comforting aroma. I remember Paolo's words about anything growing in public spaces is to be shared, even fruit and flowers hanging over a wall.

I grab a bunch of rosemary, stuffing the fragrant sprigs into my pocket. My body relaxes as the pungent scent drifts on the dense air. It transports me from the gore of beheadings, guiding me back into the reality of the twenty-first century.

I dash toward town and safety. Just before I turn the corner back into the city, I pause, looking back. Death drapes over the hill, hovering in thick, hopeless despair. There is no joy in this place.

The Chef

Il Cuoco

SCURRYING OVER THE COBBLED stones, I rush to early morning mass. I'm not Catholic or religious, but the churches in Europe feed more than my soul. The ancient buildings, themselves worthy of examination, overflow with spectacular museum-quality art. Even the smallest chapel has exceptional paintings, sculptures, mosaics, and ornate pieces in silver or gold. When my soul is needy, I seek solace in antiquity and the beauty of masterpieces which are rarely found in churches back home.

I'm anonymous in these cathedrals and chapels. After our appalling church experience back home when our friends were shunned, we've had no interest in religion or its institutions. Yet, when I travel it's the first thing I seek out—not so much for healing as for restoration and immersion into artistic beauty—bringing balance in a chaotic world.

The cathedral is almost full. The locals who attend are lucky because they belong to this cathedral and to this town. They walk on the mosaic floor and sit in the roped-off area, places I cannot go.

Today the priest is using a microphone. This is unusual since the acoustics are excellent in these skyscraper cathedrals. They had to be all those years ago before microphones were invented. This is the first time I've seen a microphone used in a service in the cathedral. The priest must be new. Instead of enhancing his voice, the microphone creates hard echoes. His words bounce in and out of my ears in a loud, painful cadence. As his voice booms, he gestures wildly into the air. Mesmerized, I watch his hand crash against the microphone, knocking it off its perch. Staccato notes boomerang up to the ceiling, spiral down to the floor, echoing until I think the dead might awaken. Altar boys rush to grab the microphone, which creates more confusion and disharmony.

I don't wait for mass to end. Instead, I slip out the side door with a kaleidoscope of sound rotating in my ears. It's time to leave anyway because I'm meeting Fredrika for cappuccino. On the way to the Blu Bar, I stop by *Il Cantico dei Cantici* and ask Francesco if today is the day I may watch the chef prepare food. Francesco and I have been discussing this possibility for several days. He assures me the chef will be honored to demonstrate his cooking for me.

"*Quando?*" I ask.

"*Presto,*" he responds.

I love this possibility. I ask when and he says soon. It may not be today or tomorrow, but it will happen. It's a joyful thought as I continue to the Blu Bar.

Fredrika is waiting. We chat in Italian. She corrects me often, insisting I learn the correct pronunciation. We share our plans for the day and discuss when we'll meet again. She has a doctor's appointment in Lecce and must leave soon. We agree to meet on Saturday for coffee. We're both unhappy as the time of my departure comes closer.

"You must come to Tirana to see me," she says. "I go there frequently to visit my mother. You will love the city. You will find Albania an interesting place."

"Oh, Fredrika, I'd love to come for a visit, but not this year. Maybe one day my research will take me to Turkey. If it does, I could fly to Albania."

"Why would you go to Turkey?" she asks.

"Remember when you found me the book *L'ora di Tutti*? It was the Ottomans who massacred all of these people in 1480, so it's important I travel to Turkey. I want to understand why they sailed to this area with intent to kill. Each story has two sides. I must listen to both."

"Well, I wouldn't want to know their story," she says, wrinkling up her nose. "But I suppose a writer must do these things. If it will bring you to Albania, then okay."

"If I go to Istanbul, it would be possible for me to fly to Tirana. We'll stay in touch. Maybe there's a possibility for us to meet again. I'll wish for this."

"*Va bene.* The flight from Istanbul to Tirana is only two hours. I would come to the airport to pick you up. This is a good plan," she acknowledges with a smile and a nod.

Once she's satisfied, we embrace and go our separate ways. On the way back to my apartment, I stop by the restaurant again. But, no, the time is not right yet.

I turn toward *via Castello* and home. The shopkeeper who makes the beautiful jewelry catches up with me and loops her arm through mine. I've seen the sign in her shop window advertising a fifty-percent-off sale, so I ask her when the shop will be open, thinking I can find gifts to take home.

She says, "*Adesso,*" pulling out the key and opening the shop just for me.

I spend a grand hour picking out lovely one-of-a-kind handmade jewelry. Since the Venetian glass pieces are not on sale, I select from the porcelain, silver, ceramic, and stone. As I sort through the unusual pieces, she asks me to describe each person I'm shopping for. She then helps with my selections. She apologizes when I hand her my credit card. She can't accept credit cards on sale items. Hesitating, I begin to search my pockets for cash, not sure I'll have enough.

"Please don't to worry. You can bring the money anytime."

She wraps each piece of jewelry individually, totals the bill, and hands it to me. While she was wrapping the gifts, I pulled money from all my pockets and found just enough for my purchases. There's 2.40 euro change left—more than enough for a *cappuccino*.

On the way to the apartment to drop off my purchases, I pass by *Il Cantico*. Rounding the corner, Francesco calls out to me, *"Vieni qua lady. Il tempo e' adesso."*

Now is the time for me to watch the chef. I can't miss this opportunity, so I tuck my packages under my arm and follow. He guides me through the courtyard and the small dining room. We enter a kitchen the size of a postage stamp.The cleanliness and organization of the small space is impressive. It appears to be about eight by twelve feet, but I'm not so good at mental measuring.

The kitchen is occupied by the chef, two sous-chefs, and now me. All of us squeeze into a room filled with sinks, workstations, a large gas stove with six burners, a grill, a refrigerator, numerous storage shelves, and food for today's menu. It seems impossible, but everything fits.

Every time I've eaten here, the chef has made an appearance. He stops by each table to ask if the meal was pleasing. His concern and dedication to the art of cooking inspired me to ask if I may watch him prepare some of his specialities.

Today is my lucky day. He gives me a choice between two dishes. One dish is the seafood antipasti, which I have eaten before. I choose the one I don't know, *spaghetto festoso*. Making myself small and inconspicuous, I observe over the chef's shoulder. He sorts through a container of zucchini, placing some on the grill and some in boiling water.

One sous-chef chops and dices tomatoes, onions, garlic, celery, parsley, and arugula, creating a lineup of colorful veggies. The other soaks and rinses a variety of shellfish: mussels, clams, shrimp, and squid. They scrutinize me with sideways glances under half-closed eyelids.

The chef drains the boiled pieces of zucchini, setting them aside. In a skillet he pours a generous splash of different flavored oils— garlic, *peperoncini*, and basil. After adding the boiled zucchini, he smashes it with a wooden spoon, creating a thickening agent. Next, he tosses in quartered cherry tomatoes along with beautiful red shrimp and a handful of chopped parsley. The skillet sizzles. Sea aromas encircle the small space.

While the shrimp are cooking, he deposits freshly made spaghetti into boiling water. He tells me how important it is to always have a pot of salted, boiling water on the stove. He takes a ladle of pasta water, drizzles it over the shrimp, and then covers the skillet. The shrimp is cooked briefly, then the skillet is removed from the burner.

Into the still-sizzling skillet he adds the pasta. Once it's swirled to perfection, he arranges the contents on a large white plate. The spaghetti mingles with flecks of red tomatoes and green parsley. On top of the pasta he tenderly positions each red shrimp into a spiral pattern interwoven with the grilled zucchini. All is generously sprinkled with more parsley and a scattering of sea salt. My mouth waters when he passes the plate under my nose. It's a work of art.

Francesco sticks his head in the door. When the chef nods, Francesco enters, gently scooping up the plate with one hand and guiding me out of the kitchen with the other. He seats me outside. The owner joins us, admiring the plate. Locals begin to fill the tables. She tells them about my observation in the kitchen, pointing out the meal that has been prepared for me.

With *spaghetto festoso*, Francesco adds a glass of sparkling white wine, a frosty bottle of water, and a basket of my favorite bread stuffed with olives. Food heaven embraces me as I reverently relish every morsel.

Francesco beams and hovers nearby, ready to respond to my command. We discuss the beauty of food. He tells me of his desire to go to New York. He says first he must go to London to perfect his English, which he does not consider good enough to obtain a job in the States. I don't question his choices, but his English is easy for me to understand. His lovely smile and charming manner would make him a welcome addition anywhere he traveled.

The sublime food fills me. There's no room for anything else. But I ask Francesco if the chef will let me watch him prepare a squid dish. It's something I eat often when in Italy but don't have experience preparing.

Before Priscilla and Bobby left, the three of us had dinner here. The chef prepared a scrumptious dish with squid. The exquisite presentation featured slivers of grilled peaches and squid married in a balsamic reduction arranged on a bed of arugula. It was both elegant and delicious.

Back in the kitchen I ask the chef if he will prepare a squid dish for me. He suggests the dish with the peaches. I pause. I don't wish to offend him, but I want him to create a new dish for me.

Smiling I say, "The squid with peaches was unique and delicious. But for today, is it possible to prepare a dish not on the menu?"

He thinks about it. Then he asks what ingredients I would like to be paired with the squid. I suggest something simple with olive oil, red pepper flakes, tomatoes, parsley, white wine, and a scattering of olives and capers.

I watch while he tests the sharpness of his knife before carving the squid into the thinnest bands. He slips them into a bath of warm olive oil. After a minute, he splashes in white wine, a pinch of parsley, a combination of sweet and spicy peppers, cherry tomatoes, and a ladle of pasta water. He reminds me the water is salted, indicating this is why he doesn't add salt to the dishes after preparation.

He covers the skillet, turns the heat to high, rapidly reducing the liquid. He stacks arugula on the plate, then a whirl of pasta. For the last step, he slides the squid, peppers, and tomatoes on top of the pasta and generously scatters parsley, capers, and olives over the top. Francesco whisks the plate and me back to my waiting table. Another glass of wine appears. Again, I settle into food paradise. My stomach emits a tiny whimper, searching for food space, but I ignore it.

"Francesco," I exclaim, "please ask the chef if he has a name for this magical creation." Francesco leaves. When he returns, he says *"seppia con i pomodori."*

I think about this and then say, "Would he consider changing the name? Squid with tomatoes doesn't convey the creativity of the dish. It must be playful and full of joy."

Francesco goes back to the kitchen and returns with the name *seppia del mediterraneano.*

"No," I say again. "Mediterranean squid is too ordinary. It must have a special name like *spaghetto festoso.* It must speak of the creative process. Please ask the chef if he will allow me to name the dish."

Francesco returns and says, *"Sì,* the chef is pleased for you to name the dish."

Another scrumptious bite slides into my mouth. Flavors erupt while I consider the possibilities. Each taste includes a bit of pasta, a sliver of squid, tomato, peppers, olives, capers, and arugula. The combination harmonizes into a dance in my mouth. Smiling, I signal Francesco. I tell him I have a name for the chef to consider.

"Le danze di calamari—the squid dances," I pronounce.

Francesco nods in agreement. He enters the restaurant and returns saying the owner and the chef are delighted with the name. Maybe they are being kind, but a lightness lifts me higher in my chair. The restaurant continues to fill. The once pouting sun spills into the piazza, washing the ancient walls in hues of gold, peach, and taupe.

Francesco continues to watch over my every wish, observing with interest as I scribble in my notebook. Calling him over to the table, I ask him, "Why was *Il Cantico dei Cantici* chosen for the name of the restaurant?"

"The name," he explains, "comes from the Song of Solomon."

"Yes, but tell me more. Why was The Song of Songs chosen?"

Francesco thinks until understanding spreads like a dove's wings across his face.

"Oh, *signora*," he says, "this name means there is perfect union between food, wine, and love. In the book of Solomon it says this: 'The love for the fruit of the earth is special. It is necessary in life to have good food and wine to experience the fullness of love.'"

"*Sì*," I say, "*capisco*." And I do understand. I'm in love with this place, these people, this food and wine, this land of sun and sea.

After such a meal a nap is essential. I ask Francesco for the check.

"No," he explains, "there is no check."

"This can't be. Please let me speak to the owner."

She walks to my table and asks if I will send her a copy of the book I will write. That will be enough payment. I try again to pay, but she refuses. The hospitality I've found in Otranto fills my heart with gratitude.

Misguided Rain Tour

TOUR DELLA PIOGGIA FUORVIATO

YIKES, I'VE SCHEDULED ONE last tour with Barbara. Yes, of course, I should have said no, but I didn't. This evening's tour includes further explanation of Pantaleone's mosaic floor and more information on the massacre. Barbara is well informed about local history. Speaking with her always enhances my knowledge of the area, and I still have a few lingering questions about the massacre. The information could be useful for my book.

Well, there's that other reason for not wanting to refuse. Barbara goes out of her way to include me and doesn't charge me. I'm still enough of my mother's girl to think saying no to such gracious hospitality isn't acceptable.

Since the tour is within the walled village, it won't be difficult to slip away from the group anytime the tour turns sour for me. We're scheduled to meet at the cathedral later this evening, but Barbara texts saying bad weather is moving in. She wants to start the tour earlier, so I agree to meet her at four.

When I step out the door a few minutes before our scheduled meeting time, wind slams around the corner, dumping buckets of water in my face. My first thought is to turn around and go back inside. Game shows, wine, and a warm blanket around my shoulders as I snug into my TV seat is a much better alternative than facing the elements. But on I go.

Our designated meeting place is the *castello*. I don't know who else is on the tour until I arrive and see the sick lady from Canada, the one on the dreadful Greek tour. She says she's feeling much better. The Swiss guy, who was also on the Greek tour, shows up as well. We chat in English until we see Barbara crossing the street. Conversation quickly changes into Italian.

Barbara greets us with *"Andiamo."*

Italians are not noted for rushing or for greeting each other without kisses, but Barbara foregoes the civilities and vaults toward the cathedral. So we pick up our pace, splashing through flowing streams of water.

There's a group of nine Spanish tourists waiting for us. A large group is not what I had anticipated, but I puddle into the church thinking it will be easy for me to disappear without notice.

The tour is gratifyingly different from the miserable Greek tour. Barbara speaks beautifully. Her quiet, lyrical voice draws me into the mystery of Pantaleone's mosaic floor. She speaks slowly and distinctively in Spanish, Italian, and English, stopping often to see if everyone understands.

I stare at the floor until it blurs. My eyes examine it differently than they did a month ago.

Pantaleone created this work so that every person considering the design could find themselves in its glorious pattern. It's the complete story of my life told in precious, broken fragments that have been unified. The mosaic floor represents the great mystery of my birth, and the work I must do each day to continue my journey. I won't know what I have become until the end of my life. I now know that on that last day, when all is summed up, I'll have done the work.

The complexity of the symbols in the mosaics manifests my own complexity while it defines the path of all sojourners. We're all on the same journey. We just use different symbols to interpret our individual patterns.

I come out of my reverie when shuffling feet indicate the group is moving toward the chapel with the skulls. On the way, Barbara explains the pipe organ, the intricate railing that protects the altar of the skulls, the cherubs holding up the heavy columns, and the famous painting of the Ottomans murdering the men of Otranto.

The painting reveals the beheaded corpse of Antonio Primaldo standing upright, just as legend describes. His decapitated body is rigid. His head lies on the ground. Agony outlines the faces of the waiting martyrs. Triumphant sneers are plastered on the faces of the victors.

Barbara invites us to examine the bones behind the altar. She points out the small skulls, those of the young boys who were part of the massacre. She wants us to remember what evil, left unchecked, can do. When I look closely, I discover the uniqueness of each skull. Each has a story waiting in silence—a story never told. Maybe one day I will tell their stories.

She invites us behind the altar, demonstrating how it's possible to touch the stone where so many were decapitated. A cold shiver courses through my veins when my fingers brush across the place where heads would have been separated from bodies. It's a chilling moment, underlining the fragility and swiftness of life.

By the time we leave the church, the piazza has turned into a rolling stream. Water swirls over and under our feet. Those with umbrellas are swept into the wind, struggling as gusts flip umbrellas inside out.

From experience, I've learned umbrellas are useless during *scirocco* or *tramontana*. My light, waterproof jacket with a hood works well under these circumstances. The Spanish people converge into a group, telling Barbara they don't wish to continue the tour.

They sprint off into streets of flowing rivers disappearing behind gray waterfalls. The four of us stand in puddles.

Barbara asks if we want to continue.

"*Sì*," we say in unison.

"*Andiamo*," says Barbara, leading the way.

We sprint to the fortress in the heavy downpour. Halting under the eaves, we examine the perimeter of the ancient wall surrounding the village. Barbara explains its inability to withstand the attack of the Ottomans. It wasn't until 1485, five years after the massacre, that Emperor Frederick II reinforced the castle and the walls.

Before we continue, I ask about the *chiesa* of San Piero. This small historical church has been under restoration during my stay. Barbara says we'll check it out. We rush to the church, but it's locked, as usual. We flatten ourselves against the structure while rain washes across our vision.

She tells us this tiny church is possibly the oldest in Otranto. Its Byzantine façade originates from the ninth or tenth century. It's shaped in a Greek cross around a square base and has three semicircular apses. She says the interior is beautiful with clean lines and many frescoes. Scaffolding surrounds the foundation. Since my arrival I have tried several times unsuccessfully to see the church. It's always locked as it is tonight.

Barbara takes off at a fast trot. We fall in line behind her, slushing through slick, cobbled streets, our shoes spraying water from our rapid movements. I momentarily think about slipping away. But I'm already soaked through to my underwear, and Barbara can make the rain merely an inconvenience. Fortunately, the rain is pleasantly warm.

Scirocco and *tramontana* have been battling it out this past week. Now as the moisture licks my face, I know *scirocco* has won.

Barbara stops in front of another church, giving a historical perspective of its role in the massacre. The steady drizzle turns into unrelenting waves of water. She smiles at our upturned, rain-washed faces and says, "*un momento*." Checking her mobile phone, she indicates the rain will continue to be heavy. She says it's time to stop the tour and go home. We laugh, applauding her decision.

As we scatter, she calls after us. "Remember, tomorrow we'll go for pizza and a *pizzica* festival. *Domani sarà una bella giornata,*" she advises us, as we puddle through small ponds, that tomorrow will be a beautiful day. She obviously has an inside scoop and must know the weather police.

I wade home to dry clothes, a glass of wine, and Italian game shows—sheer bliss. The simplest things bring the greatest joy.

All Souls and All Saints

TUTTE LE ANIME E TUTTI I SANTI

TONIGHT WILL BE MY last evening with Barbara. If I ever come back to Otranto, I'll take Italian language classes from her. I'll listen to her melodious voice, and I will learn Italian. My heart and head already speak this beautiful language, but my tongue waits to learn the music.

Our rendezvous is scheduled for eight this evening because no self-respecting Italian begins a night of fun and festivities any earlier. This allows me time for the evening *passeggiata*. Venturing out, I expect to find the streets empty at this early hour. Instead, the town swarms with people.

I've not kept track of the date, so it takes a while for me to realize it's October thirty-first, the night of the feast of the dead, or All Souls Day. In Italy it's called *i morti*. Tomorrow is *ognissanti* or All Saints Day.

There is an Italian rule about returning to the city of your birth during these two holidays to honor family souls and saints. I'm sure there are souls and saints police to remind everyone of their obligations. The tradition is ancient. All Saints originated around 853 AD and All Souls in the tenth century. Around this time, the church fathers observed the older country folk still engaged in ancient pagan feasts. They decided the best way to reach these people was to incorporate the feasts into the liturgy, merging paganism into Christianity.

The pagan belief that the dead could return among the living on these special feast days was pervasive throughout Italy. The southern regions, in particular, practiced these traditions with a mixture of religious and pagan superstition. Tonight, the children will knock on doors saying, *"morti, morti"* to receive cakes, nuts, and money. It's much like our Halloween.

My walk becomes a game of survival. The clogged streets include herds of young boys whose faces are covered in ghostly white masks. The boys randomly hurl firecrackers, some landing close enough for me to jump out of my skin.

To avoid the crowds, I push through to the Madonna of the High Sea. It continues to be my favorite refuge. Once I leave the walled city behind, there's only silence in the fast-approaching night.

I tug open the massive wooden door. I'm surrounded by flickering darkness that welcomes me to enter. Masses of candles lit in memory of the dead shimmer splashes of brilliance across the white walls, haloing the Madonna in holy light—an explosion of quiet beauty. Easing onto a bench, I center myself in this sacred place.

My thoughts return to Idrusa, who has arrived with me. She doesn't kneel beside me but swoops through the chapel arranging flowers, flicking dust off statues and straightening the altar cloth. Fascinated, I follow her movements until she vanishes. The thud of the door opening and closing indicates someone else has joined us. Wanting them to enjoy the same solitude I find here, I silently slip out, easing the door closed with a soft swish of air. Idrusa is lost to me. I step into a sinking sun as it splashes its last rays across Grecian-style white houses.

Bursts of burnt orange, poppy red, and camellia pink reflect against the alternating hues of violet and navy blue hovering across the sky. Night waits in the background as the sun plunges deeper into the sea. A touch of homesickness tugs at my heart—the first since my arrival. I don't linger as there's still time to attend mass at the *duomo* on this hallowed night.

Following the crowds back into the walled village, I find a vacant seat on the back row inside the *duomo*. Pretending I'm a member of the congregation, I close my eyes, imagining my younger self snuggled against my mother on this same bench. Later I see myself dressed in white, taking my first communion. As a young girl, I was chosen to trail behind the Madonna when we annually celebrated her return. Flowers would be entwined in my hair as I serenely followed the Madonna parading through the village. I would know everyone. Everyone would know me. I see my wedding gown kissing Pantaleone's mosaic floor as I approach the altar. My bridegroom waits in the shadow of martyred saints.

My meditative state is interrupted as a late tour group clambers into the sanctuary. They burst into the nave, pushing and shoving to get inside. Contemplating the swarm of tourists, I watch with an insider's eye. They don't notice they've jolted the congregation from its quiet reverie. No one has told them this is a sacred night. The group moves forward as one large mass. They talk loudly, casually walking through the cathedral. They look and touch the antiquity as if it's on sale tables in Macy's bargain basement. They pause as if to consider buying a twelfth-century candelabra or an ancient altar cloth. They walk in through the church and in front of the priest, maintaining their loud conversations.

Sadness wells up in my throat. On this night to honor those who have passed into another dimension, their lack of respect seems particularly callous. Sacredness vanishes. I steal quietly from my seat, tiptoeing out the side door.

I walk back to the apartment with ample time to meet Barbara. Settling at the kitchen table, I add notes to include in my book from last night's tour of the *duomo* with Barbara. Idrusa had been present in the cathedral as well, reminding me it's where she died by her own hand rather than submit to oppression.

She is the warrior woman, the one standing in the piazza guarding the harbor. She is all women for all time. She tells me to have courage, to keep on my journey, to write, to live, to love, to be strong. She and I merge into one.

The beauty of my meditative space is invaded when hundreds of firecrackers go off under my window, followed by young male screams of glee. The man who lives across the alley comes out of his house, yelling at the boys. Their giggles scatter from hidden places. Peeking out the window, I see a group of boys ranging in age from ten to fifteen. They huddle against my front door. All are adorned in the ghostly masks, their arms entwined. Their excited, whispering voices plot their next explosive move.

I feel edgy about my decision to go out. Meeting Barbara at eight in the evening isn't the problem. It's the idea of walking home alone in the wee hours of the morning that sends my imagination into dark places. After all, it's the night of the dead. Intellectually, I know it's safe here. But tonight I feel fidgety, not intellectual.

Boys and booms come and go. In a quiet moment, I grab my jacket and head out the door. I'm going to tell Barbara I'm opting out of the adventure because I don't feel safe walking home alone later. Making this decision provides me with instant relief. With resolve, I rush into the dark alleyway.

I Hope You Dance

SPERO TU BALLI

MY DNA, MIXED WITH American punctuality, has me
arriving on time or early for prearranged meetings. Now, a dark and
lonely fifteen minutes loom ahead as I shift from left foot to right
without sight or sound of another being. No lights from the school
brighten my waiting spot. It's locked up tight. Waiting in daylight is
tiresome, but waiting in darkness tenses every muscle. My heartbeat
booms louder than my thoughts of no one showing up.

Just as I decide to return to the comfort of my apartment, a
coughing, smoking, rusted, cracked-windshield car pulls up. Balding
tires add angst to the worn-out piece of rubble confronting me.

A young man with dark, flowing hair unfolds his long, lean body
as he leaves the driver's seat. The passenger door opens to reveal
a shimmering white-blonde beauty. They approach me, speaking a
variety of languages—French, Italian, English, and a bit of German.
His gentle voice conveys his intention isn't to kidnap me, so I lean
in to listen.

Hushing him, the blonde speaks up, thinking her English is passable. She introduces herself and laboriously attempts to persuade me to get into the car. The request isn't exactly inviting as I regard the disintegrating vehicle. My hesitation lasts long enough for the Canada lady and, of course, the Swiss man to join our little group. He seems to go wherever she goes.

They switch into speaking Italian since all of them are enrolled in the Italian language class. They tell me they aren't allowed to speak any language but Italian. I break into their all-Italian conversation.

"Sorry, but I won't be going tonight," I say slowly and concisely, hoping someone will understand.

"*Perché?*" they ask.

"*Perché*, I don't want to walk home alone when I am dropped off at some unknown hour," I respond.

With cries of outrage, they insist I go. They assure me I'll be dropped off at the *castello,* and someone will walk me home. Before I can change my mind, I'm in the car and we're speeding off into darkness. I'm wedged into the back with the Canada lady and the Swiss man.

The cramped quarters remind me of the van on the Greek tour with too many people and too small a vehicle, forcing unwanted intimacy. Torn seats spill bits and pieces of upholstery padding, adding white speckles to my black jeans. I'm thankful for my sturdy shoes that crunch against tins, newspaper, and things that crinkle as I smash myself between the door and the lady from Canada.

The group continues to speak only Italian. The conversation is slow and tedious. I follow along until I realize they're talking about calcium and the benefits of the sun. Maybe calcium was today's lesson. Later, I learn that the lesson was Dante's *Divine Comedy.* No amount of thinking will reveal to me why anyone would discuss calcium instead of Dante.

While the others chat amicably, the Canada lady whispers in English that she hasn't done well in class, and the others are far ahead of her. I murmur empathetic words, thankful she's no longer green and coughing.

We drive on into darkness, each mile revealing that the driver is very unfamiliar with where we are and where we're headed. I avoid looking through the grit-coated, cracked windshield. It only offers another obstacle in reaching our unknown destination. Adding to the cramped situation, I begin to itch as if some nasty little bugs have placed me as the main entrée on tonight's menu.

At long last, we pull off the road and into a dark alley. The driver says we're at Barbara's house. He texts her that we're waiting. A crack of light from a door slices across the darkness. Barbara glides out along with a short, balding man. I stifle a moan as he steps into the headlights, revealing the guide from the Greek tour. I'm speechless when he's introduced as Barbara's husband. His stature and stoicism accentuate the vivacious Italian goddess, Barbara.

Her luscious, imperial black hair whose long beauty has recently been sheared into sassy shortness in the back, trails into shoulder-length on the sides. When she tosses her perfectly shaped head, her hair harmonizes into place, accordion-style. Along with this thick, glossy crown follows a figure that men look at longingly with quivering sighs. Her smile radiates sunshine and flowers. Her dark, flawless skin conveys exotic images of unknown spices—gold, incense. I later learn she is half Italian and half Egyptian. Cleopatra would find her to be stiff competition.

Barbara and Angelo indicate we are to follow them. They rush away before I have time to seek solace in their car. Instead, I'm smashed back into the rumpled bug-infested vehicle. We follow at nail-biting speed, never stopping at stop signs, never slowing. We drive through dark streets into tiny towns and out again, into long stretches of night where crumbling white stone walls stand guard in half-hearted manner. I peek out the window for road signs or names of the towns but see only nothingness.

Angelo slows and pulls off the road. We pull in behind him. Snippets of understandable conversation indicate we have arrived somewhere to eat pizza. We bunch together on the dark street, shuffling off to an unknown destination. There are no signs, which is typical for the best restaurants located in the countryside. The owner expects us. We're seated, and drinks and pizza are ordered. A long discussion ensues about the correct beverage to order with pizza.

There are seven of us. Three of us, including me, have wine; the rest, beer. The wine group is clearly in the wrong, but we refuse to cave. I mentally add *beverage police* to the list of mounting policing duties.

The conversation settles into small details of our personal lives. The shimmering blonde is from Germany. She's a dog trainer, which leads to a lengthy discussion about our pets. I happily contribute stories of our three rescue boys. Barbara is also a rescuer and has four dogs.

The German woman and the young man from Austria have each left their home and country to travel the world. They decided to stop in Puglia for a year. She works at an animal clinic and rescues strays. I begin to itch again, realizing the animals she rescues are probably transported in the rusting-out car. It makes sense now—the nibbling bugs are probably fleas.

At the restaurant, I sit next to Barbara. She showers me with kindness. She stops to explain, in English, bits and pieces of conversation so I can contribute. Soon blistered-from-the-oven pizza slides onto the table. Chewing is the only language spoken.

Back into the falling-apart, bug-ridden car, we drive on into the night. The car jiggles and moans as we slow for a flashing sign indicating the town of Carpignano. We park and stumble through unlit streets, avoiding gigantic potholes and crumbling sidewalks. Concentrating on not twisting our ankles and not falling into black holes eliminates any conversation.

Ahead, numerous stalls of food, games, and souvenirs spill brilliant light onto the dark pathway. We flounder on cobbled streets toward the main piazza. The way is constricted with like-minded festivalgoers. *La musica* rolls around my feet, lifting my body into lightness. In unison we become off-course line dancers. There's no choice but to join in the rhythm. The music compels me to dance.

As I move with the others, images of my dad surface. He was a grand participant in the dance of life. He taught me, his youngest daughter, to do the same. In one of the last photos of him I have, he's dancing with one of the caretakers in the Alzheimer's unit. That long-ago photo and this trip have encouraged me to put my dancing shoes back on. I must continue in his footsteps with joyful dancing, joyful music, and a joyful life.

Arriving at the crowd-packed *piazza,* I'm transfixed by a large stage assembled in the center. Musicians and traditionally costumed dancers move with the haunting beat. Barbara explains the musical instruments, saying, *"un tamburello* (large tambourine with hairy black spider on the front); *violino* (violin); *chitarra battente* (a large four- or five-string Italian guitar); and *organetto* (small accordion) are all required for the *pizzica."*

The singing voices are deep, guttural tones infusing the soul with internal magic. The dancers move mysteriously, slowly, then with increasing speed.

Barbara insists we dance with her. She demonstrates three basic steps of the *pizzica* along with a few seconds of instruction. Grabbing our hands, she pulls us into *la musica.* My last dancing experience at the previous festival, where I cracked my dance partner's head and stepped on his feet, does not compare with this. There are hundreds of people in the piazza with *pizzica* bands from all over Puglia, many dressed in traditional costumes. Everyone dances.

Initially, I watch. Then I bob around a bit. The music is faster than anything I can imagine keeping time to. Its cadence controls body and soul. Now that I know the story of the affliction from the bite of the spider, I understand that only collapse will end the dance. It would be unwise for me to collapse, so my dance steps move in half time.

Barbara spins into the crowd. Lusty male eyes gravitate toward her. For a few seconds they look at the weird group of people dancing with her, but we're quickly dismissed. The men feast only on her. She never stops. She never collapses. She knows every step, even the complicated ones using scarves to weave heart-wrenching stories of love and loss.

She is boneless to my stiffness. Her body is the music. My body hears the music but can't follow. Soon my heart races into heart attack danger zone. I retire to the sidelines with Angelo. I'm content to watch the golden goddess and her groupies.

As the night wears on, the men get bolder—perhaps from the wine. They move in on our little group and dance just with Barbara. She doesn't notice. She has no thoughts for mortal man. One by one, members of our group drop out of the dance, holding sides and clutching chests. The Swiss man holds out the longest. His twisted, without-rhythm limbs suspend into space like some Halloween skeleton dangling from a stick. I don't laugh because his dancing flows from a heart bursting with a magical music he has not heard before.

We would still be dancing today if Angelo hadn't stepped in front of Barbara and said, "It's time to go."

She shakes him away, not wishing to return to earth. Her eyes and body linger in the dance world. He pulls at her arm. With a sigh, she returns to us. She's been dancing for hours, never perspiring. The rest of us, who stopped dancing hours earlier, are still fanning and mopping sweat from our foreheads. Painfully, the group walks back in darkness to the car, careful not to trip in potholes.

Barbara dances back.

Angelo tells the driver of our car to follow him, saying he'll indicate the road where we turn toward Otranto. We cheek-kiss, saying our goodbyes as we pile into the flea-ridden car. Angelo signals when it's time for us to turn away from them. We slow, blowing kisses out the window, shouting *arrivederci* into the wind.

We enter the roundabout and notice the sign indicating Otranto, thirteen kilometers. Laughing hysterically, we joke with the driver about how far out of the way we drove on the trip over. The driver is gracious, delivering me safely to the *castello*. We say our goodbyes again. The German girl wants my business card and wants to friend me on Facebook. I think she says she wants, when her year is over in Otranto, to come to South Carolina, possibly to live with us for a year. I nod, agreeing to something I don't understand. Everyone but the Canada lady piles back into the car. She's the designated person to walk me home. She doesn't seem like much protection from the dead. We stand silently, watching the taillights grow dim and then disappear.

"Gosh, I don't want to inconvenience you. How far away is your place?"

"It's just outside the walled village," she says, pointing down the hill.

"Oh, you have farther to walk than I do. Why don't I walk you halfway? There's plenty of light, and all the dead souls seem to have left. I'm okay to walk alone."

"I have to use *il bagno*," she whispers. "I'll never make it down the hill if I don't find one quickly."

We giggle, increasing our pace. She's eager to see my apartment because I've raved so much about it. Upon entering, she soaks up its spaciousness and rainbow colors. I'm sure she will return to Otranto on her next vacation and will move into my home. She tells me I have a remarkable deal. I nod in agreement.

I insist on walking back with her as far as the *castello*. Leaning into the early morning air, I watch her saunter down the hill, disappearing into shadows.

As I walk back to the apartment, creeping morning light curls as faint gray lines push at the night. But the star-studded blackness is stronger, sucking the gray light back into darkness. I saunter, unafraid. All the dead souls have disappeared. The saints haven't awakened yet. I close the door on another hard-to-put-into-words night. Contentment and pleasure surround me. My heart beats to the music that has been permanently downloaded into my spirit.

Another gift from this journey—the joy of dance.

Transportation

TRASPORTI

THIS MORNING AFTER CAPPUCCINO, I consider packing. But I'm not ready. I leave my luggage hidden away while I sort through books, gifts, and miscellaneous items to determine what to pack and what to leave behind.

The bottle of *reserva grappa* for Ray requires extra protection since it will be in my checked luggage. I cut up cardboard, making sturdy covers for the grappa and for a red and gold ceramic sun I purchased last week. The mosaic and ceramic suns, and my laptop will go into the blue carryon sack. My transportation is tentatively arranged, although in a much looser structure than I prefer.

Before I left South Carolina, I had asked several Italian friends for help in securing transportation from Otranto to Brindisi, where I will catch my flight to Rome. The cost of 130 euros quoted was too much. At the time, it seemed feasible to wait until I was situated in Otranto before considering transportation possibilities. But that was before I knew rental cars, taxis, or trains wouldn't be options.

Only recently, when Priscilla and Bobby were leaving, did I think about transportation. Priscilla told me I wasn't a good planner. She said it was ridiculous that I didn't know how I was getting to the airport.

For a few minutes I thought about what she had said. Then I dismissed it because my time in Otranto was for living—not planning. The spontaneity of each unplanned day has been a big change from my anal, list-making self. Fretting and checking off items on a list has had no room here. The joy that had been missing from my life has returned with the simplicity of each day here. Without schedules or lists, I've had no guilt if a task isn't accomplished.

Now less than a week from departure, transportation has spiraled to the top of my nonexistent list. In my other life, the trip home would have been mapped out before I left. In this life, the question of finding transportation is an inconvenience, a nuisance, something not worth thinking about until now.

One unsettling thought does, however, persist. *What if I stay? What if I continue my life's journey here?*

That question looms large as I make half-hearted attempts to find a ride to Brindisi. Ray's eyes and voice, when we Skype, tell me he's wondering if I might stay—not ever return. If I made that decision, I wonder if he would join me. But first we'll need a conversation about finding our heart place. We can't continue to live in a place that no longer sustains us.

These are difficult thoughts to consider. But I do consider them.

As my journey draws to a close, I understand that my commitment to Ray and the life we have together grows stronger. My mind and heart know I'm going home even if my heart will linger in Otranto for a while. Too much thinking doesn't conjure a pumpkin and four white horses to transport me to the airport.

I consider the bus as an option; but the more I think about it, the less inviting it seems. All sorts of additional steps would be required, like how to get myself and my luggage to the bus stop in Otranto. The bus would drop me in Lecce. I would have to transfer with my luggage to another bus for Brindisi. Once in Brindisi I would have to find a shuttle to the airport. This would not be a pleasant way to end my journey. The logistics of transportation is always the challenge when traveling.

A few days earlier I emailed an Italian friend, asking if there was the smallest possibility he could think of another mode of transportation since we last corresponded. He responded, *no*. He says the only company is the private transportation firm, the one costing 130 euros. He says he'll book it for me if I want him to. Although my days are running out, I still say no.

Silence follows for a couple of days. Then another email arrives. My friend has discovered a new company called Airbus Salento. They will come to Otranto and drive me to the airport in Brindisi for thirty-eight euros. I ask for details of this magic ride for such a reasonable price.

He responds with two sentences: *Do you want me to make the reservation? Airbus Salento will pick you up at 11:45 Sunday morning.*

A bit of my old anal self surfaces. I send him back a list of questions. He responds with one line. *Can I give your mobile number to Airbus Salento?*

I jettison my anxiety and say *yes*.

The next email says, "*Airbus Salento is confirmed for you. Thirty-eight euros cash and a tip if they help you with luggage. Wait in the park by the castello.*"

Blind faith will be my transportation. But I check out a local hotel, just in case my magic carpet doesn't arrive and I have to spend one more night in Otranto. I practice putting the vague transportation plan out of my mind by clicking off the anxiety tape. Nothing can ruin these last few days.

Tonight, I order pizza from the little restaurant across the cobbled street. The night's warm, garlicky breath drifts with sausages, tomatoes, and mozzarella as I zip across the cobbled stones to the restaurant to collect my dinner.

The weather, despite *scirocco* and *tramontana*, has been spectacular during my stay.

After devouring the pizza, I stand on the terrace without jacket or sweater. It's delicious November weather.

Earlier, when I'd picked up the pizza, the moon had hung low in the sky, brushing the night with a bright orange glow. Now it's climbed higher, painting burnt orange clusters on galaxies hovering nearby. *La luna* dances off the whiteness of houses, dusting me with fairy glitter.

Turning off all the lights, I am in perfect darkness surrounded by perfect shades of night. The inky sea gently laps the shore. Children, dogs, and cats are called in for the evening. Garlic, onions, and chili peppers mingle in the evening air. Outside on the terrace, I stand in community, merging into the sounds and colors of dark and light.

Broken Beauty

BELLEZZA SPEZZATA

EARLY MORNING ON THE terrace, I yawn and stretch high into the sky. Pink ribbons pull the reluctant sun into rising. No sound exists except migrating birds on their way to Africa. They raise their fussy voices at me because I'm up earlier than they are. I'll miss their sweet chirps and morning serenades. Their voices sing to me of Terry Tempest Williams's book, *When Women Were Birds*:

> *Once upon a time, when women were birds, there was the simple understanding that to sing at dawn and to sing at dusk was to heal the world through joy. The birds still remember what we have forgotten, that the world is meant to be celebrated.*

How often over the years have I forgotten to celebrate my life and the universe. This month I've flown freely into the music of this joyful place. Many transformations have stormed my soul. The simplicity of life has reinforced my determination to return home with less technology invading my life, with more community at the table, and a conversation with Ray about leaving Columbia to find a place that suits who we are—a heart place for the two of us.

It will take practice to reduce my preoccupation with pretension and busyness. It's easier and more comfortable to slip back into the old familiar ways, even if they are stressful and torture my soul.

During my stay, I often thought about Terry Tempest Williams. Reading her books gave me inspiration to come away alone, to reflect on my life. Her book *Finding Beauty in a Broken World* helped me rediscover beauty in myself, in the mosaic fragments, and in the piles of trash that accumulated over the years. Her words have guided me in sorting through the debris.

They've taught me to live in this moment where the land, the sea, and the strangers, whose journeys paralleled my own for a moment, merge into wholeness. Beauty of life has surrounded me in my solitude. This time for contemplation and meditation has eased me into letting go of old habits, into viewing my life with fresh eyes, and into renewal of my weary spirit.

Not everyone has the need to pull away from their lives. Others thrive in their daily activities. But, for me, flying free is a necessity from time to time, a way of renewing my spirit, conquering my fears, a way to be silent, to listen, and to respond to life-giving messages for my soul. My warrior woman, who had risen so bravely all those long years ago, had forgotten her inner longings, forgotten the gifts that must be nurtured, forgotten to sing and dance. My joy had been concealed under layers of daily living.

Soon I'll leave this magical place and return home. Away from daily responsibilities, it's easy to live in an uncomplicated world. There are no tugs or pulls on my time. Each day belongs only to me, to plan or not plan, to let life flow as I follow its path. When I return home, the same old conflicts will be waiting. Faith and family isolated us, leaving us adrift in a place that didn't really suit us. But after a month away I'm returning as a person in progress, a person with knowledge of myself, a person who understands that life is a continuous journey of discovering and becoming. Ray and I have each other. Together we are strong.

Leaving on the terrace the bright rays of sun and my clarity of thought, I tinker again with the idea of packing. But my heart hurts. Turning away from my luggage, I leave clothing scattered on the floor and sofa. A few days remain. I will live them without hesitation.

I wander down *via Castello* to meet Fredrika for our last cappuccino. Her friendship is an unwrapped gift waiting to be revealed. Scenes of dancing under the stars, sharing food and wine, and our linguistically challenging relationship bubble up. My fear of her family kidnapping and holding me for ransom has faded into the beauty that has evolved from our time together.

Gathering my farewell gifts for her, I leave the apartment. Since it's still early, I plan to visit the cathedral before I meet her at the Blu Bar. This will be the last time for the Chapel of the Skulls and the beheading rock. My intention is to sketch the ancient columns and sneak a quick glimpse of the Madonna, if there's time. The Madonna in the cathedral, unlike the gentle one in the small chapel, has been a puzzle to me. Her aloof eyes seem angry, searching for answers, yet fierce and defiant, ready to protect her child and herself.

Tiptoeing through the side door, I creep to the beheading stone. Barbara's gift showed me I can steal behind the altar and touch the stone. Furtively I scan the pews, the aisles, and the main altar. No one stirs when I cross the threshold into the Chapel of the Skulls. Slipping behind the altar, I position myself to touch the rock. My hands slide over the indentation where heads were hacked off. Their bravery astonishes me.

Life is so precious. I'm not sure I wouldn't have converted to Islam in order to live. I hope never to be put to the test. I offer prayers for all the people in the world who face adversity.

Sensing movement with the soft thud of a door, I leave the side chapel and continue down the aisle to the four monolithic columns by Riccardi in 1524. They're lined up against the wall. No placard indicates why they're here. The columns are characteristic of ancient Egyptian temples and seem out of place in this cathedral.

A monolithic column is made from a single piece of stone instead of a series of vertical sections. Using one long continuous stone produces considerable difficulties in quarrying and transportation. Most often, these columns were used to make a statement of grandeur, signifying the importance of the building.

There's no indication that these columns were ever part of this cathedral. Perhaps they are some recent discovery. Maybe the cathedral is the only place large enough to accommodate them. Maybe it's a mystery without answers.

Leaning in as close as the roped-off area allows, I sketch the designs on the first column. It has intricate, twisted vines and playing children. Moving to the second column, I'm frozen by the image of a young man being impaled. Shuddering, I quickly move on to the third column. It's adorned with circling and hissing snakes. I'd like to bypass this column as well, but I've learned through research that snakes symbolize rebirth, transformation, and healing. The problem is that learning and believing often don't mesh.

I've feared snakes all my life because of my mother's story regarding my birth: when she was in the last throes of her pregnancy with me, she visited her parents in a rural area of Virginia. As she turned to step off the front porch, a poisonous snake lay coiled at the bottom, ready to strike. She, with no time to think, jumped over the snake and fell on the other side. She would continue the story by telling me her labor pains started soon after. The image of that coiled, hissing reptile instigated numerous nightmares over the years.

I've long embraced that old, dark story of snakes as a foreshadowing of evil. With a child's mind and a church background of hell, damnation, and Satan disguised as a snake, I was sure my destiny was ill-fated. Now I stand before this column, recognizing the creative life force. The shedding of old skin. The cloaking of myself with new.

My feet advance to the fourth and final column. It's adorned with angels. While sketching the delicate wings and cherubic faces, images crowd my thoughts of all the guardian angels who have moved in and out of my life during my sojourn in Otranto—these are memories I'll preserve.

The cathedral doors will soon be locked for siesta, so I put away my sketch pad. Pausing on my way to the other side, I scan the wide expanse of the mosaic floor. The magnificent elephants stand motionless as the tree of life springs from their broad backs. The dangling elephant on my bracelet from Fredrika touches the mosaic floor when I kneel one more time for a closer look. These magnificent elephants are weary from their difficult task. I thank them, asking them to please continue to do this for me and for the whole world.

Pantaleone's ancient signature catches my eye as it always does. I marvel at his genius and cunning. It seems so long ago when my journey with Paolo's commanding oration revealed this mosaic floor and its ancient stories.

Increasing my stride, I hurry past the main part of the cathedral and turn up the long aisle to the left chapel where the Madonna awaits. I glance toward her space.

She's gone.

Holding my breath, I blink rapidly to clear my eyes. Even the marble base where she stood is gone. There are no marks on the floor, no shading or scuff marks to indicate where she, I'm sure, has stood for hundreds of years. There must be an explanation, but there isn't anyone to ask. There's a huge void where she was standing—as empty and vacant as the space in my heart.

Soon after my arrival in Otranto, I became a frequent visitor of this Mary as well as the other Mary in the small chapel by the sea. During one of my earlier, weepy visits here, I was sure she moved.

Later, I tried to convince myself that my tears had blurred the scene, and it had only been a figment of my imagination. Only one of the photos I took of her that day came out. It was blurry.

Now she's gone. Perhaps she's being restored, perhaps she is visiting another cathedral, perhaps she will return—perhaps.

I take her disappearance as a sign. She's telling me nothing is permanent. I can't stay in Otranto forever. Mary is telling me it's time to travel to the next chapter of my life. These thoughts are more reassuring than my thoughts that I'm hallucinating.

Mary has left the cathedral. Her job—to light the way for me during my stay—is over. She leaves me with gifts of humility, humanity, and hope. Kneeling at the altar of the Holy Sacrament, I pray for our safe journey home—hers and mine.

One day perhaps we will both return.

The Sorrow of Parting

IL DOLORE DELLA SEPARAZIONE

LEAVING THE CATHEDRAL, I rush toward the Blu Bar thinking maybe I've missed Fredrika. But she's waiting.

"Today only Italian will be spoken," she says.

I fear she's become part of the language police. It makes my head hurt, but I honor her request on this last day we have together. We walk arm in arm, giving each other many hugs, promising to remain friends *sempre*. She reminds me I must contact her when I visit Istanbul. She will meet me at the airport. We will go to her mother's home in Tirana. In Fredrika's mind it's all settled. She calls Mateo, insisting I say goodbye to him.

He says, "*Arrivederci*, nice lady."

Tears flow as we pull apart. Fredrika says, "*A presto.*"

Arrivederci is the normal parting term when you won't see someone for a while, but Fredrika's "I'll see you soon," clears the tears and returns my smile.

Walking away from her, I simmer in the sweet juices of my time in Otranto. I stop to say goodbye to the shopkeeper who makes the beautiful Venetian glass jewelry, the one whose husband gave me the gift of the imperfect starfish.

She embraces me, saying, "I will see you again next year. *Devi tornare.*"

Giving another wave to Giovanni as I pass by the Blu Bar, I stop next door to make reservations for tomorrow night at *Il Cantico dei Cantici*, my last evening in Otranto.

Francesco says, *"Una tavola per uno, signora."*

"Sì," I respond.

"We will make it a beautiful evening for you, signora."

I nod, knowing he will.

My walk continues through the ancient altars, down the rickety wooden steps, and across the sea front to the tourist office. Franco's gigantic smile embraces me. He says Carlo has not returned from his holiday in Spain.

"I'm sorry because I want to take both of you to lunch. But you and I can go. What's your favorite restaurant?"

Whatever I say is wrong because Franco's smile slips from his face. We are lost in translation. He calls to the woman I met when I first arrived, the one that Franco said could speak English but couldn't. This time I understand enough of what she's saying to determine Franco cannot go with me to lunch because Carlo isn't here. I think it's because Franco needs Carlo to translate. I tell her to tell him it's okay. He and I can manage without a translator. The lady repeats this to Franco.

He becomes increasingly agitated and says, *"no, non posso andare."* I understand what he says and ask, *"Perché?"*

They have a long conversation. The lady's eyebrows arch into surprise. She heaves a guttural laugh from the belly and says Franco does not have permission from his wife to go with the American lady unless Carlo is with us. I laugh. Franco shifts. His smile ceases. His face flushes. My laughter stops.

"Would it be possible for me to buy you a coffee or *aperitivo* at the bar next door?"

He shuffles his feet in uncomfortable silence and finally gives me a dejected nod. We stand at the bar, sipping coffee. It's awkward for both of us when I thank him for his generosity. When it's time to leave, he finds permission within himself to give me the traditional cheek kisses and an embrace.

"Please return," he says, "and please send me a copy of the book I know you will write about my Salento."

Today he doesn't sing. But it's the memory of his singing that most captures his warm, generous spirit. It's the image I post to my memory board.

I continue to spread my goodbyes to the village. My final stop is the Blu Bar. Giovanni deserves many hugs, cheek kisses, and *grazie mille* for his generosity to me.

In slow motion I climb the steps one last time to the little chapel, Madonna of the Sea.

Relief sweeps over me when I find her standing steadfast in her usual spot.

My internalized photos of sailing knots and star clusters gather as I say goodbye to her. She smiles. Images of her small sailing vessel crossing the sea surround me. This enduring thought of her will accompany me home. It's satisfying to know that although each year she leaves her home, she always finds her way back.

Entering the gates into the old village, I'm immersed in the weekend antique market. Treasures lie in wait. Spread before me are all the items I would buy to outfit my little house here—a home of my own, if I stayed in Otranto forever.

There's a large pottery bowl embellished with a faded rooster. Fresh-from-the-garden vegetables stacked high and spilling over would roost in this bowl on my kitchen table. Next is a traditional wine jug proclaiming *beviamo insieme* (together, we drink), with pottery cups to hold the wine.

Hand-painted dishes depicting village life would fill my cabinets. Wine glasses in red and espresso cups with angel wings would sparkle behind the display glass in the china cabinet.

There are crystal and brass sconces for the walls to light my way. A massive hand-burnished armoire would fit in the hallway. This antique statue of some long-ago saint would guard the doorway.

Aged and well-worn pots, pans, and kettles would fill my kitchen cabinets. An ornate screen of flowers and birds would keep the sparks inside the fireplace. An old chest from an ancient sailing vessel would store my soft, sun-kissed blankets.

A Victrola for playing opera would be placed by the front window to share music with my neighbors. Huge terra-cotta pots would fill the garden with herbs and flowers.

Running my hands over ancient books, I imagine them stacked on the floor and tables, easily available for reading. Finally, I come to a stall piled high with gently used linens, so fine I'm sure royalty slept on them. I cradle the exquisite silkiness of threads well cared-for, whispers from long-ago dreams.

But my time for dreaming has come to an end. I cannot stay. My Italian home begins its descent as Ray and my American home rise.

Back at the apartment I sauté the last of the luscious fresh produce for lunch. With a glass of wine, I stand on the upper terrace for a last check-in with Albania. But Albania has already said her goodbyes. I will not see the white shimmering country rise again. Like Mary, Albania has left, signaling it's time for me to go as well.

My eyes burn. My nose and head hurt from weeping. I wipe away my tears. My heart says it's time to leave. If I stay too long, the enchantment might disappear. It's important to leave while the beauty of this time and place remain in perfect harmony. My packing is almost finished. The reality of leaving aches its way into my heart.

The Last Supper

L'ULTIMA CENA

DESTINY LED ME TO *Il Cantico dei Cantici*—to that first bite of perfection signifying this would be my special *ristorante*. The owner, the chef, and Francesco have been generous. The food and wine surpass expectations.

But it's the magnificent name from the Song of Solomon, *Il Cantico dei Cantici*—Song of Songs—that continually nourished my soul during my stay. *Il Cantico* is a community where strangers are embraced and welcomed to the table. Food, wine, music, and a culture different from my own is a gift—a gift that bestows joy on the giver and receiver.

For my last supper in Otranto, *Il Cantico dei Cantici* is the only choice. Tonight is the last night, my last supper at Song of Songs.

Via Castello escorts me down the cobbled path. My eyes study the way with purpose and resolve, drinking in every detail. Evening's hush caresses the village, birds snuggle into their nests with last bits of tweets and twitters, caramelized onions and sweet, roasted garlic float on the tender breeze, benevolent laughter circles and the music—always the music. It moves with my breath, it lifts a single drumbeat into my heart, creating mosaic melodies—notes drifting out to sea, enticing tears to my eyes.

The November night seeps under my light sweater. Francesco waits for me. The best table on the patio is mine—the one nestled by the gas heater. It's a strange, elegant contraption featuring a long glass tube encased in an ornamental brass fixture. Flames waltz lazily up the glass, rhythmically tuned to the ancient music. Flickers of light create crossword-puzzle patterns across the white tablecloth. Coziness and warmth surround me. Francesco smiles his way to my side.

He seats me, saying, "Lady, your meal has been planned. You will trust me this one last time to select your food and wine."

"*Sì, grazie mille.*"

His dark eyes smile into crinkles as he continues. "Lady, tonight you will have best meal ever. You will remember this meal and return to us *a presto.*"

I would weep if I spoke, so I nod and imprint his face into my memory bank. The owner greets me warmly. She's seated with a man I don't recognize. This stranger maneuvers himself to my table, speaking rapidly in the local dialect, making it difficult to understand. His pointing finger darts at my neck, stopping just short. Hearing the word *collana*, I realize he must be the shopkeeper's husband, the one who repaired my starfish necklace. He mumbles out an apology, telling me he's disappointed he couldn't make a smooth repair.

"The Venetian glass is too delicate. I was afraid I would break the starfish if I continued. I am so sorry I ruined your necklace," he says, or something to that effect.

I thank him for the bump in my necklace, telling him I like it and that the necklace is more beautiful because of the imperfection. He doesn't understand my thinking. As an artist, he cannot find beauty in the imperfect. Perhaps he hasn't learned the lesson of finding beauty in broken and fragmented pieces. He shrugs in confusion at my remarks and returns to his table.

If only I had the power of his language, I would tell him my story of imperfection. Instead, I tuck the words away for another time and place.

Francesco brings me water and a wonderful local red wine. He knows even with seafood I prefer red wine to complement the dense, luscious sauces found in this southernmost part of Italy. The intense sun-blessed reds are the perfect pairing for most of my meals. Francesco positions the crimson-filled chalice before me. I no longer ask for the names of the wines he selects. His response would remind me I cannot purchase this wine in America.

The first sip swirls against my tongue, revealing dense blackberry spiciness spilling into earthy richness flamed by scirocco winds. One small taste replenishes my soul while dissolving everything I know of life—embracing yet, pushing away. It breaks me into mosaic fragments, while restoring me into a work of art.

Francesco has learned to read my withdrawals into another place. He waits until I resurface before leaving my favorite bread baked with whole black olives including the pits. He has asked the chef to prepare for me *carpaccio di tonno*.

"Lady," he says, "you will love this."

His dark eyes glow in the lazy gas flame as he struggles with the English words. He thanks me for letting him practice his English with me and tells me my slow Southern way of speaking is easy for his ears to understand. He melts away softly—part of the night.

The music flows on the outer edges of my soul, stirring some primitive spirit in me. Its haunting vibration from some exotic location lingers in my memory. It spirals with the breeze down the cobbled street, merging into the ruins, floating out to sea, supplying new songs to the sirens waiting to lure sailors onto the rocks. The ancient sounds of another time and another place, drifting on the night, tangle my heart into knots.

The first plate arrives with much fanfare. The music fades because the food strips all my sensibilities. The tuna is arranged over an upside-down, cup-shaped leaf of lettuce. Shaved to sheerness, the dark pink flesh drapes across the lettuce cup in overlapping simplicity. Large, juicy caper berries add dark green accents. Cherry tomatoes and microscopic onion shards play peekaboo among the pungent arugula leaves. A generous sprinkle of large-grained sea salt crowns the top.

A half lemon carved into a basket with a handle cleverly twisted out of lemon peel sits on the side. My hesitation to consume this masterpiece is brief, perfection waiting to be devoured. I squeeze the big chunk of lemon over the tuna. My anticipating lips sink into the first bite. My tongue sorts through the bursting sea sensations rendering echoes of a hallelujah chorus.

"Lady, tell me what you think. Is good?"

Perhaps my amateur Italian has confused most during my stay, but I have the right words for food. Even if I didn't, my eyes tell him I'm in love with the plate in front of me. I lose myself in the moment, the food, the music, the gentle night, people strolling arm in arm, whispers of *buona sera,* and the gas flame flickering brightness into the darkness.

Francesco beams. The chef peeks out from the kitchen, raising his hand in salute. I tuck this dream night into my heart, mind, and spirit.

Francesco returns to whisk away my bread-wiped plate. There's time to linger in the music as leisurely eating is mandatory. The wine glass shimmers in the gaslight. It's been refilled without me noticing. Francesco moves silently and with precision, intensifying the pleasure of the meal.

When he next appears, a plate of *orrechetti* (tiny ear-shaped pasta) enriched with mussels, clams, and tiny red shrimp glides in front of me. Francesco leans in close and whispers that the portion is double for me. Oh, I groan inwardly as I tuck my thumb into my waistband, praying for wiggle room.

This plate is a wonderland of the sea. Shellfish of every variety are piled high. My mouth explodes with the full force of tangy sea breezes. I polish off every bite of seafood, but I can only manage a forkful of pasta. This will upset Francesco, the chef, and the owner. I whimper in disappointment because there's no more room as indicated by my earlier thumb test. Francesco feigns sorrow at my still full plate.

"I'm saving room for dessert," I tell him. He nods in appreciation.

A warm, lemon-scented towel is pressed into my hand. Dessert choices are discussed. I choose, because Francesco says so, the chocolate cake with chocolate filling and chocolate glaze.

While Francesco is in the kitchen, the owner presents me with a plate of her famous almond cakes. I have already disappointed them once because I couldn't eat all the pasta. Now I must suck in my protruding tummy and devour two almond cakes along with the slab of chocolate cake.

With this over-the-top meal, a digestive is necessary for my ailing innards. Francesco leans down, whispering choices to me. Our heads meet as we discuss the options. Somehow none of the choices are right for tonight. Before I can say this, Francesco says no to his own suggestions. His concentration sends deep furrows across his frowning forehead. Slowly his face relaxes, and a smile returns across his sun-bronzed face.

"Lady, I have the right drink for you. Wait and see."

I wait. The drink arrives in a sculptured glass. Inky black liquid glistens aromatically.

"Lady, you taste. If you do not like, I find different drink."

I sip the velvety, magic liquor. There are hints of almond, the intensity of dense red grapes, and a splash of spicy sherry. The taste conveys the essence of my time here, the richness, the simplicity, and the goodness of it all. It's a perfect ending in this splendid place. I close my eyes feeling the liquor, luscious and warm, in my throat.

Night sounds mingle with the ethereal music, spinning dream webs to follow me home. Tears spill over as I open my eyes. The salty breeze gathers up each teardrop, flinging them out to meet the crest of the sea. In a moment of clarity I ask what the drink is and where can I buy a bottle.

"It's called *Elisir di Primitivo*," he tells me. "It's a mixture of *primitivo* wine, black sherry and almond liqueur. You cannot buy," he says, "it's only made in this area. The owner knows the man who makes it."

"May I buy a bottle from the owner?"

"No, lady, is last bottle for this year. It's special for you this last time you come to us. You must return to taste again."

The beauty of time and place etch into my memory on this last night in Otranto.

Francesco slips into darkness, leaving me to sip the magic potion. My spirit longs to linger suspended in this moment, sitting at this table, savoring all I have been given. If I could, I would push a pause button and remain forever. The best I can do is capture the moment in my mosaic heart and take it home with me.

Now it is time for me to dissolve into darkness. Leaving—an impossible task.

Yet, the night comes to an end. It won't add extra hours for me or for my dreams. I've hurried through my life, forgetting the need for renewal, for solitude, and for nourishing my creative spirit until the pain of living poorly surfaced. This month has given me what I so desperately longed for—a time of my own, a time for rebirth.

I murmur, *"arrivederci, grazie mille"* to the owner, the kitchen staff, the chef, and most of all to Francesco for this last supper.

The last cheek-to-cheek kisses fade into darkness as I float on the cobbled street bathed in the antiquity of moonlight. The whispery words, *buona notte, lady, per favore ritorna* linger in gut-wrenching sweetness.

"Buona notte, il mio amico," I murmur, my words trailing into soft blackness.

PART V

REENTRY

Once you have traveled, the voyage never ends,

but is played out over and over in the quietest chamber.

The mind can never break off from the journey.

~Pat Conroy, *The Prince of Tides*

Leaving

IN PARTENZA

THE BIG PIECE OF luggage sprawls across the floor. I cram in the last bits and secure the zippers with little plastic tags Ray left behind, the ones that are supposed to prevent unwelcome intrusion into my luggage. When finished, I heave the luggage upright. It immediately falls over facedown. Gazing at this unbalanced, overweight vessel, I'm reminded of a very short, wide woman with breasts weighing twenty-five pounds each. She totters, unable to stand in an upright position on her own. I call her *big lady* bag. It's my way to cope with the inconceivable fact that today I'm leaving. It will keep a smile on my face as I began the arduous journey home.

After much effort on my part, *big lady* is finally in an upright position propped against the sofa. Perspiration saturates my smell-of-the-sea-breeze shirt, turning it into a wilted mess. I sit down for a few minutes to regroup before moving *big lady* into the dreaded elevator, the only practical way I can leave with luggage. I open the front door. The drop-down step appears. I had forgotten it was there. Grabbing *big lady,* I successfully maneuver the step while maintaining her balance and mine.

Holding her with one hand, I open the elevator door and wheel her in. "Oh, shuck a duck, I don't have the elevator key with me."

Leaning her against the side of the elevator, I step out to retrieve the key. As soon as my hand releases her, *wham,* down she goes. Snatching the key from the desk, I rush back to rescue her. She's spread-eagled over the entire surface of the elevator. There's no room inside for me. I grab her feet and pull. She resists. Sweat slides down my face as I ponder my next step.

Repositioning my hands on her feet and her bottom, I give a big old jerk. She reluctantly slides halfway out of the elevator. Straddling her, I pray no one is peeking over the terrace to see me in this awkward squatting position. One big hop lands me on the far side of the elevator. I freeze in place, fearing I have upset the elevator's delicate balance.

My panting is the only sound filling the elevator as I grasp the bag's shoulders and haul her into an upright position. Hanging onto her with one hand, I close the door, slide the key into its slot and hold my finger on the button. The elevator descends in halting huffs, puffs, and moans. But it delivers me safely to the lower level.

I drag *big lady* off the elevator. We practice walking up and down the courtyard until I find the right gait and balance, one that allows me to pull her without too much effort and prevents her from toppling over. Before I go back for the rest of my luggage, I secure her firmly in an upright position.

Back in the apartment, I retrieve the black carry-on and the blue sack. The weight of these combined bags almost equals *big lady.* The thought of this overweight luggage doesn't bode well on this long travel day. Both bags go with me on the elevator. Once we reach ground level, I position the blue sack on top of the black carry-on. I take the handle in my left hand, using my right hand to grasp the handle of *big lady.* I move forward, but the bags don't follow. An intense conversation ensues where I explicitly tell them, "*When I move, you move!*"

"All together," I roar, no longer concerned the luggage police might be in the neighborhood. This time the bags reluctantly follow.

The mind is such a wonderful thing because today it ignores the fact I'll be flying two days on three different planes, and I'll be in charge of all this luggage. For now it's enough for me to focus on just getting all the bags to move at the same time in the courtyard.

Back in the apartment, I check all the rooms, ensuring I'm not leaving anything behind— other than the fragments of my heart. Placing the keys on the desk, I pause one last time, reflecting on my magical stay. My eyes caress every corner of the colorful Moorish apartment— this place I have called home, this place I wish to live in forever. There's no time for tears or regret. Shutting the front door solidly behind me, I punch the button that lowers the metal door. One thing I don't regret is this last trip in the elevator.

When I close the big doors to the courtyard behind me, I can't return. My transportation to the airport will soon arrive. This is my only thought as I turn the key and press the red button for the final ride down. Yes, I'll even miss this cantankerous elevator.

Before I leave, I address the trash for the last time. With great care I gently move the correct container outside the door, lining it up on the ledge. I peek inside where my beautifully tied bags rest in harmony. The art of sorting trash and recycling in the containers and in my life has given me strength to return in better shape than when I left.

Collecting my luggage, I shut the big green door, listening as the lock falls into place. My stomach lurches, fat tears peel into my hairline. I'm locked out of my home and my Italian life.

The longing to stay is great, but so is the longing to return home. Today is not for grieving. Instead, it's a day to face travel challenges. Assembling my luggage into a manageable caravan, I pull all to the end of the cul-de-sac.

I pause on *via Castello* to consider my travel outfit. Italians are well known for their chic put-together look, especially when they're traveling. My red skinny-leg jeans with rhinestones on the back pockets, the snug black tee, gauzy black shirt and black and white scarf create a passing grade—I hope. It's my feet that don't. No, not flip-flops, but my ugly, heavy-duty black walking shoes.

This morning I put on a great pair of Italian black leather flats. But at the very last moment reason kicked in, forcing me to change my elegant footwear to ugly walking shoes. I'm not exactly Italian chic.

As I view the steep incline up *via Castello* that I must traverse with a gaggle of luggage, I congratulate myself for making the shoe switch. There's no way those leather flats could have gained enough traction to haul me and the luggage up the incline. My happy heart never realized the entire time I lived here how steep *via Castello* is until this moment. Today my heart is sad. It notices obstacles and starts to collect trash.

I'm lost in thought when across the cobbled street, the door to the pizzeria swings open. One of the young waiters emerges. He surveys my pile of luggage, shaking his head. *"Buongiorno signora. Today you leave us?"*

"Sì."

He crosses the street, grips the handle of *big lady* and pulls her up to the top of *via Castello*. I follow with the black and blue bags.

At the top, he says, *"arrivederci.* Please come back to us next year."

I try to tell him he's my angel (*angelo*), but perhaps I say he is my angle (*angolo*). He smiles in understanding anyway. We shake hands. I linger, watching as he walks away.

There's still a short distance to cover before the bridge, but the ground is level. The ancient bridge is full of holes partially covered with plywood. It's not an easy bridge to navigate, even without luggage—although I hadn't noticed this during my stay.

Traffic stops, allowing me to cross the street into the little park. It's the same park where I met Luigi and took the wild ride to the pork festival with Priscilla and Bobby, and where the little tourist shed that never opens is located. It's now my place to wait for Airbus Salento.

The luggage and I assemble ourselves on the corner and wait.

Traveling

IN VIAGGIO

Travel isn't pretty. It isn't always comfortable. Sometimes it hurts, it even breaks your heart. But that's okay. The journey changes you; it should change you. It leaves marks on your memory, on your consciousness, on your heart, and on your body. You take something with you. Hopefully, you leave something good behind.

~ANTHONY BOURDAIN

PUNCTUALITY HASN'T DESERTED ME during this month's stay. I arrive at the park twenty minutes before Airbus Salento's scheduled arrival. It's unseasonably warm for November. My waiting spot has no shade from the intense tropical heat.

It's Sunday. Friends and families gather for weekend activities. Traffic whirls past me as four streets converge around the little park. Reviewing my transportation decision, I wonder what possessed me to go with a new, unproven company—one I've had no direct contact with. My Italian friend had very little information. Not once did he reassure me or tell me not to worry.

But I am worried.

As I consider my somewhat reckless decision to arrange transportation with an unknown entity, flies and bees swarm. Burning sweat mixed with mascara trickles into my eyes. I can't let go of my bags, fearing they'll topple. To pass the time, I pretend each vehicle whizzing by is my ride and will be stopping for me. Minutes pass. No one stops. Time lags until I'm sure I've been waiting for longer than twenty minutes. In a moment of panic I hold *big lady* with one hand and lean the handle of the black bag under my armpit so I can check the time on my phone. Only five minutes have passed. Another long fifteen minutes to go, and that's only if my ride arrives on time—or at all. This is a tricky subject in Italy, as American time and Italian time significantly differ.

The flies and bees are pleased I continue to hang out on the corner. For a moment I forget my wayward luggage and swat. All the bags topple. The heat intensifies. I'm sure I've been abandoned. I shift my position and consider other options. Magically, someone calling, *"Signora Armer"* parts the clouds. My sanity reestablishes.

The car is black, the man nondescript. He doesn't speak English. He doesn't have a business card. He doesn't wear a uniform or have any identification. There's no sign on his car telling me that he's Airbus Salento. While I'm contemplating the situation, he swings my luggage into the trunk as if they were stuffed with cotton balls. He doesn't indicate where I'm to sit, so I choose the front seat. We pull away from the curb, and he says we'll be stopping in Maglie to pick up another passenger. Memories of the fateful train ride from Lecce soar along with my imagination. Stopping in Maglie is a bad omen.

I work on exorcising all bad thoughts as we pass the walled village I have called home for a month. I take one long last look and whisper *"arrivederci, Otranto,"* wondering if it's a promise I will keep.

I encourage conversation, but the driver shrugs. Either he doesn't wish to talk to me, or he doesn't understand my Italian. I morph into silence. After about an hour, he veers off the main road into a stark, rural area. The kidnapping theme once again invades my fragile mind. He parks. As we wait for the other passenger, I glance around the area. It's desolate, without trees or houses. For comfort, I take out my notebook and write. He stares straight ahead.

From time to time I sneak peeks at my cell phone and try not to worry about missing my flight. My thoughts run through the few complete sentences I can recite in Italian, none of which include, *How much longer are we waiting?*

The driver's cell rings. He speaks rapidly, terseness in his voice. He points at his watch and holds up five fingers. Moments later a sleek black car barrels toward us, slowing long enough to deposit an elegantly dressed man onto the field. He gets in the back seat. He is silent. It's a long, empty-of-conversation ride to Brindisi.

When we arrive at the airport, the driver walks *big lady* to the entrance. I manage to get all the luggage through the door before it swooshes closed behind me. Brindisi is not a large airport, so I quickly find the right line. When it's my turn, the agent frowns and shakes her head. She points to *big lady* and says, "No, signora, your bag is too heavy. It weighs thirty kilos. The limit is twenty-three."

There's nothing I can do but agree to pay for the extra weight. She's kind enough to check *big lady*, placing her on the carousel with a thud before handing me a piece of paper. She points me toward an office, indicating I'm to give the paper to the person at the window. She says it's sixty euro, and they take credit cards. How grateful I am for that. Once paid, I'm given a bunch of forms to complete. I dutifully sign each page, agreeing to whatever is placed before me.

Breathing with relief, I find my way to the security checkpoint. Taking the mosaic out of the blue bag, I place it in the tray. I breeze through only to be stopped on the other side. The security people congregate around my mosaic. They lift it up, turn it over, and give it a little shake. They pull both my bags off the conveyor belt, signaling I'm to follow. We stop at a table off to the side. All my bags are searched. It takes a while for me to convince one of the officials to read Barbara's letter. After much discussion and numerous readings, I'm allowed to proceed.

My stomach emits an appalling howl. It's been hours since my early morning yogurt. Only snacks and drinks are displayed at the meager food stand. I grab a bag of chips and a bottle of water. I pay the cashier and find a seat close to my gate.

"Good grief," I say too loudly when I look at the bag of chips. They are Wacko's. I open the bag and peek inside to determine what Wacko's might be—aha, triple-fried potatoes in the shape of Zorro masks stare back at me.

It's a surprise I fear will be my undoing if I eat them. Giggling, I shake the bag and discover a surprise package in my Wacko's: a tiny Mr. Potato Head with all the little parts. I plug in the miniature pieces to create a pocket-size potato head. Since I don't have room in my bags for Mr. Potato Head, he lands in the trash with the Wacko's.

After a month of such beauty and peace, I'm feeling wacko as I make my way back into the world I had escaped. The rest of today and all of tomorrow I'll be traveling. It will seem like a lifetime, while my month in Otranto disappears in an instant.

The flight is called. Hordes of people stampede toward the gate. Italians are not prone to lines, so there's no indication which part of the moving mass I need to join. Squeezing into the middle, I and everyone else push forward. When I get to the front of the line, the agent glances at my ticket and nods toward the door on the left. On the other side is the tarmac and a waiting plane off in the distance. There is no covered walkway, only portable stairs attached to the plane.

Just before the steps, my shoelace comes untied. As I bend over to tie my shoe, my bracelet snags on the black bag's zipper. Passengers behind push into me. I yank. Black and white beads scatter across the tarmac. Retrieving them would be impossible. I stare at the rolling beads as the crowd surges forward, pushing me along toward the plane's stairs.

The blue bag goes in my left hand and the black bag in my right. Pretending I'm in a weightlifting competition, I suck in my breath, tuck my tummy, and focus on the door at the top of the steps. People, luggage, elbows, and shins all tangle into a mass of humanity moving forward in a strangely rhythmic, disjointed dance. We move—one step, stop, lean forward, two steps, stop, lean forward. We stumble into each other as luggage bounces off body parts. If one person falls, we will all flop like dominos. During this group dance, I notice all the Italians have on chic leather shoes.

Finally, I reach my seat, but the passengers in front of me have stuffed their bags into my overhead bin. Trudging down the aisle, I find an empty overhead and *heave ho* my black bag into the bin. Searing pain grips me, the kind that will linger.

Oncoming passengers make the trip back to my seat a battleground. There are no winners. I drop into the seat with a thud, crushing the blue bag against my chest. Pain radiates down and across my back, plunging into my legs.

My mind skips ahead to deplaning in Rome. I mentally make a to-do list: *retrieve my black bag from the overhead, find the baggage area to pick up big lady, walk to Terminal Three and find the shuttle bus to the hotel.* I hope the pain pulsating along my back can be kept at bay. It's not one of my better moments, and I find myself reverting to old habits. I close my eyes, replacing the pain with a Salento sunset.

The throbbing twist of nerve endings continues to pound new pathways, but no amount of pain makes me regret my time in Otranto. Every sunset, every *passeggiata*, every glass of wine, every bite of seafood, every gesture of friendship reinforced the necessity for this sojourn. Those precious days gave me solitude to find my fragments and glue them back in place.

Perhaps the most difficult part of this journey was forgiving myself. At no point during my life had that concept been taught to me. I'd always been ashamed of my past life, embarrassed to tell even my closest friends about the mess I made of it. This time alone has given me courage to acknowledge my past, forgive myself, and let it go.

Forgiving myself allowed me to understand that forgiveness is an act of creation, an act of freedom. My last look at the warrior woman fortified me. In her last whisper, Idrusa told me she would be my guide.

As the plane descends into Rome, sunshine rushes away to someone else's world. Ominous clouds enclose the aircraft, isolating us in thick, gray fog for the final minutes. The landing gear clunks as streams of rain strike against the window.

The usual mad scramble at landing generates additional stress. Pushing against the eager-to-deplane passengers, I retrieve my carry-on. With pain storming up and down my spine, I gather the blue bag, then put on my jacket. Standing on the slick stairs, I marvel at my good sense to wear sturdy walking shoes. Sometimes it pays not to be chic.

The cascading rain puddles on the aircraft steps. I cautiously secure each foot before stepping down to the next level. There's no need to rush with bumper-to-bumper bodies blocking my way. With all the pushing and shoving of people and luggage, it takes a while to slosh to the waiting bus. Rain swirls, darting around me as my wet-doggy look expands. The bus doesn't leave until we are packed body-stuck-to-body. Night descends in all its dreary November wetness.

At the baggage area, I wait with hopeful anticipation for *big lady*. When she arrives, I wrestle her off the conveyor belt. She lands on her face with a thud. Huffing and grunting, I force her in an upright position. Upper body pain digs in with a vengeance, but whining won't mitigate the hurt. Rearranging my luggage, I remind the bags we need to work together. Slowly I shift forward. The luggage follows without protest. My skin crawls as the sticky wetness of my clothes spreads like fast-moving lava across my body.

The baggage area empties near T-1. A large sign points toward T-3 and hotel shuttles. To avoid the pelting rain, I walk inside the terminal. The walkway is roped off, ending abruptly before T-3. Ducking under the rope, I push *big lady* in front of me. The other bags trail behind. Clearing the rope and raising my head, I thump into a major roadblock. Looking up into a stoic security uniform, I grimace. The uniform tells me I can't do what I'm trying to do. It tells me I must go back to T-1 and walk outside in order to reach T-3. I obey, adding *airport police* to my long list of unspoken Italian rules.

The way back is much longer with my wobbly bags and whimpering back. At T-1, I wearily trudge outside. The wind coats my face with warm rain. The three bags compete to ride up my legs, slowing my pace. My hair, which had been coached into straightness this morning, has snapped back to its usual humidity-induced frizzle, swirling corkscrews into the wind.

I consider a taxi but realize it would cost a small fortune. The shuttle bus, if I ever find it, only costs six euros. I move forward, fearing that if I stop I'll never start again. Finally, a sign indicating hotel shuttles appears. It can only be reached by crossing the four-lane road surrounding the airport. The traffic snarls past me. Taking a deep breath, I step off the curb and wait. When a small opening appears, I run. Rain hisses from the sky and from windshield wipers at full speed. Cars, trucks, and buses don't slow for my passage across.

On the other side, there's no walkway to where the shuttle buses are to park. Gushes of water dive into my shoes as I cross open grates. Big buses bear down, propelling waves of water in my direction. I make a final effort. Out of muggy mistiness a ramp appears. Plowing my way to the top, I pause. There are signs for shuttles, but there are no shuttles. My rain-splattered glasses hinder sight, but finding something to wipe them with would be my undoing. If I let go of the bags, chaos would ensue.

A sniveling voice speaks. I realize it's me, asking for assistance from people rushing by. Shrugs are returned as they splash around me. A kind man stops, reminding me it's Sunday. The shuttle service is slower or sometimes nonexistent. He suggests a taxi and points across the street, telling me the taxis to Fiumicino Airport line up there. He says they won't charge as much as the taxis at the main terminal.

Cost is no longer a factor. I'm desperate to be safe and dry. The only thing lifting my spirits are my ugly black walking shoes. They've splashed through puddles and survived being swamped by vehicles.

I drag my luggage across the street to the taxi stand. The wait is only a few minutes. The driver jumps out and opens the back door. He grabs *big lady*. Nothing happens. He looks at me wide-eyed while spewing a string of new-to-me Italian words.

I shrug, folding myself into the back seat. He continues to rant about the heavy luggage, saying he should charge extra. After handing him the hotel's address, I ignore him by retreating into that safe, vacant place under the table on my parents' back porch—a place that doesn't hear unkind words and doesn't allow misery inside.

Night arrives in force. Blackness without streetlights prevents me from seeing where we are going or what the neighborhood looks like. Eventually the taxi driver halts his tirade. It's not long before we stop in front of a small building. He unloads my luggage on the sidewalk and starts to walk away.

I say *grazie mille* and give him a large tip, refusing to let him add misery to the day. He pulls change out of his pocket.

"No, it's yours—all of it."

The look in his eyes changes. He walks past me and rings the bell. The door slides open. He takes my bags inside, leans *big lady* into the wall, nods and leaves.

This Isn't the Ritz

QUESTO NON È IL RITZ

"*BUONA SERA*" DRIFTS ACROSS the reception area. Twinkling eyes peer at me over a high counter, followed by a mischievous smile and a cordial greeting. The counter conceals all but the voice's head. Leaving the luggage, I stand on tiptoe to meet my greeter. I observe his dry clothes and the soft blue sweater that matches his smiling eyes.

He asks for my reservation confirmation and my passport. After inspecting them, he pushes a registration form across the counter, indicating where to sign. My glasses drip and steam, creating double forms and pens. He leans across the counter, passing me a big wad of tissues. Combined with raindrops, the tissues smear lint on my glasses. This further diminishes my sight. Somehow I manage to see the line where his finger points. I sign.

"*Parla inglese?*"

"No," he says.

Turning away, he reaches inside a wall of cubbyholes and pulls out a key card. He motions for me to follow. I grab for my luggage, but he shakes his head no. We tread down the hallway, turning right into steep marble steps. Trudging up, I ask if there's an elevator. I won't be able to haul my luggage up the stairs with my screaming back.

"*No, signora, non c'è ascensore.*"

At the top of the stairs, he turns left and moves swiftly down the hall. He stops, sliding a key card into the slot. The door swings open. A pocket-sized room stares back, one entirely too small for me and the luggage. My guide doesn't realize this and continues to demonstrate how the key card must be inserted into the slot next to the door for the lights to work. Puddles gather round my feet. I focus all my attention on not sitting in the puddle and having a good cry. He pauses when he notices I'm not listening.

I indicate the room is too small by saying, "*No, questa camera è troppo piccola.*"

We stand in the doorway. Turning in unison, we retrace our steps. He slides behind the reception counter and sits. Stretching into my tiptoe stance, I lean across the counter. My misery and exhaustion gather strength as wet droplets fall from my hair onto the counter and floor. The rip between my shoulders transfers to my eyes. He nods, understanding I haven't had a good day.

Methodically he sorts through dusty key slots, selecting an old-fashioned skeleton key. He beckons me to follow. This time we walk past the steep stairs. At the first door, he inserts the key. It's a large room, or at least big enough for the luggage and me to fit.

Grazie mille, I say, watching giant-sized drops of water collect on the floor around my feet. I don't inquire about price because I'll pay whatever I'm charged. My lighter steps follow him back to the reception area. I grasp *big lady* and demonstrate how the blue bag fits on top of the black one. We saunter down the hallway. The luggage slides easily into the room. Smiling, he softly closes the door, leaving me in silence. I gulp deep breaths until my pulse steadies.

My wet jacket drops to the floor. I unwind the soggy scarf and it puddles on top of the jacket. A hot shower will revive me, but my

parched throat cries out for water and a glass of wine. Back I traipse
to the reception area.

"Per favore, è il ristorante aperto?" Although it's eerily quiet, I'm
hopeful the hotel restaurant is open.

"No," he says. "We're closed for the season. But there's a pizzeria
close by. If you're ready to eat, I will show you."

"Dopo, per favore," I say. "Is it possible for me to buy a bottle of
water and a glass of red wine?"

"No," he says.

I walk away from the desk. Then, I stop and go back. "Please. I'm
so tired. The day has not been good to me."

His eyes consider me with gentle kindness, *"Aspettate*—wait."

He returns with a designer bottle of water. Its emerald green
glass sculptures into a swan's neck with an exotic label attached. I
imagine if I look close enough a vintage year will be displayed. He
places a large wineglass on the counter and leaves. He returns with
a bottle of white, explaining it's the only one open.

"That's okay," I respond.

He removes the cork and pours. A trickle drizzles into the glass
before the bottle empties.

"Un momento," he says.

This time he returns with a full bottle and fills my glass to the brim.
I have no intention of asking him how much the water and wine cost.

"Grazie mille." A weary smile accompanies my words.

Back in the room, the cool trickle of water eases my parched
throat. I drink until the glass is empty. Then I take a big swallow
of wine. It lies in my mouth like silk, smooth and mellow as a
Salento day. Although I'm longing for a shower, exhaustion prevails.
Positioning the water and wine on the nightstand, I crawl onto the
bed and sink into nothingness.

It's late when I wake. My first thought is a shower, but I need
food. I pick half-heartedly though my corkscrew curls and return to
the front desk. The man takes me by the hand and leads me out the

door. The blackness is relieved only by the glow from the lights in the hotel lobby. The rain has stopped. A warm, moist wind blows. He points down the street and says the restaurant isn't far. I ask for the name.

He considers this for a moment and then says, "There's no name. It's just a pizzeria."

The hotel door closes with a small thud, darkness descends. I concentrate on not falling off the broken sidewalk. It's only two blocks, but the eternal darkness makes it seem much longer. The well-lit restaurant welcomes me. There's a large glass case featuring worn-out pizza slices—perhaps left over from lunch. I already know this won't be one of my best dining experiences. I ask the young man if I can sit at a table and order a freshly made pizza and a glass of red wine.

"Yes, of course," he responds.

The wine speedily makes its way to the table. Taking the first sip, I gasp, fighting to keep it down. *Kerosene!* I push it aside. The pizza arrives bubbling with cherry tomatoes, basil, and olives scattered across the crispy, thin crust. After a few bites, my hunger subsides. Exhaustion wins again. Stumbling back out into darkness, I cautiously tackle the crumbling sidewalk. When the hotel comes into view, the front desk man is waiting with the door open.

Back in the room I empty each suitcase, setting aside books, toiletries, and clothes that will be left behind. Before I can finish, my body slumps, simply refusing to continue. I crumple onto the bed. I awake at three in the morning. My glasses are tangled in my hair, the TV hums, and the lights blind.

A long, hot shower revives me enough to tackle the repacking. Since the two smaller carry-ons won't be weighed, I move all the heavy items from *big lady* into them. I don't question the increased weight I'll be strapped with all day. Sixteen extra pounds is hard to gauge, but when I lift *big lady*, she feels slim enough to pass muster.

Around six in the morning, I move all my luggage to the lobby. The same man is still working the front desk. I ask for a taxi. He nods, makes the call, then disappears into the back. He returns with a cappuccino—my last in Italy until I return. It warms every part of my body and my spirit.

I ask for the bill. The charge for the designer water and the large glass of wine is only eleven euros. The price for the big room is the same as it was for the little one. I thank him, saying how much I appreciate his generosity.

He asks me how long I've been in Italy and why I came. My scripted *"Io sono scrittrice americana"* falls easily from my lips. He happily corrects my Italian and provides encouragement. He asks when will I return.

A presto, I say.

The taxi arrives. The man behind the counter stands, takes my hand and says, *"signora, spero che torneai*—I hope that you will return."

Arrivederci, I say, saluting him and his generosity.

Going Home

ANDARE A CASA

GREETING THE TAXI DRIVER, I warn him about the excessive weight of my luggage. He checks out *big lady*, picks her up with one hand, and pitches her into the open trunk. He's young and strong. His smile says this is going to be a good day.

He pulls away from the hotel, turning up the car radio. It's playing happy Italian music for early morning—and for going home. The taxi merges into heavy traffic. Clouds scatter to song notes. The sun penetrates the murky sky, changing the day from steely gray to palest blue.

After being dropped off at Terminal 5, I inventory myself and my luggage before turning toward check-in and home. Cautiously I lift *big lady* onto the scale. She registers two pounds overweight. The smile in the agent's eyes lets me through without charging extra.

Once onboard the flight, I find my designated prison cell for the next eleven hours. My seat mate doesn't jump up to assist when I struggle with my luggage. Instead, he turns away, facing the window—not a good sign.

It takes me forever to get situated. Finding the safest place to store the mosaic during the long flight proves difficult. First, I try to slide it under the seat in front of me. It doesn't fit. I try under my seat without success. Then I lumber up onto my seat, grabbing the edge of the overhead bin to keep my balance. I wrap the mosaic in my jacket for extra cushioning, and position the black bag next to it as a protective barrier. The blue bag stays with me. It contains all I will need during the long flight home.

My seat mate pretends not to notice the wiggle-worm person who is going to be his travel companion on the long flight. Sliding down into my seat, I catch him watching me out of the corner of his eye.

Smiling, I say, "You must think I'll never get settled."

He responds, "It's not a problem," and turns back to the window.

"I'm a quiet person, most of the time," I continue. "I promise I won't bother you or talk to you unless you start the conversation. But at some point, I hope you will. Otherwise it's going to be a long, boring flight."

The corner of his mouth twitches with a smile, but he remains silent. I resolve not to speak first. We both gaze out the window and watch preparations for departure.

We are only minutes in the air before the drink cart comes by. I'm ready for a glass of wine. My seat mate hesitates. Then he asks for a beer. Before I can take my first sip, he salutes me. Returning the salute, I smile but still say nothing.

Finally, he asks, "How's your wine?"

That's all it takes for the words to flow between us. My seat mate, John, is a Catholic priest. He's in charge of global administration for the Catholic Church. He travels the world. He's from Ireland but lives in both Rome and Pittsburgh.

He fumbles around in his pockets, producing his passport. Its dog-eared pages are full of foreign stamps, an impressive display of travel. There are countries stamped on top of countries. He points out interesting and artistic stamps from Angola, Vietnam, Croatia, China, Burma, Russia, Cambodia, and numerous other countries— each stamp telling a story of this man's life.

He now works in administration, a job requiring him to travel to every diocese in the world on a three-year rotating basis. His favorite place to visit is Africa, where he was posted as a young priest.

We exchange life stories and grumble about the lousy airline food. We talk, nap, take aisle walks, eat, read, and think our private thoughts. Time passes swiftly.

I'm startled when the last sandwich lands on our trays from a midair toss. We giggle, reading the long list of additives and an expiration date of one year. Gleefully, we decide it would be dangerous for our health to eat the sandwich. Instead, like naughty children with no supervision, we only eat the ice cream.

At touchdown in Atlanta, there's the usual mad scramble. My seat mate and I say our goodbyes and part. He travels without baggage, explaining to me he keeps three similar sets of belongings in the three apartments he maintains for his job. His passage through customs will go quickly. For me, there are long lines for passport inspection and declaration papers.

Finally, I'm through. I find the baggage area and search for *big lady*. The carousel spins round and round. No *big lady* appears, but I'm not concerned because there are three hours between flights. Eventually she surfaces out of the gaping hole, flopping down the ramp and onto the conveyor belt. As she passes, I stretch to grab her. My ripped back bellows in protest as she slides from my grasp. An airport employee across the way, watching me struggle, catches her as she moves around the carousel. The generosity of the many strangers who sustained me during this trip has followed me home.

Tucking away another act of kindness, I turn toward customs. My luggage follows easily, as if they know we'll soon be home. I breeze through customs and recheck *big lady* for the last leg of our journey.

Once through the final security check, I find my gate. The gloomy, drizzly evening wraps around me, heavy with humidity and creeping exhaustion. Stopping at a bar, I order a glass of wine, find a quiet table, and face the fading gray of evening into night.

A call to Ray lets him know I'm back on American soil. We chat for a few minutes as lovers who haven't seen each other in a while, choosing words carefully so as not to spook each other.

I murmur, "My flight is scheduled to depart on time. I'll see you soon."

He says with a voice full of tenderness, "I'll be waiting."

The red wine is mediocre. I picture the last glass of *primitivo* I drank in Otranto, tasting of sun-drenched grapes kissed by the Salento sun. I consider my time away and all the beauty in Otranto, in the people, and in myself. The world may be broken, but I'm resilient. I've been mended into a mosaic of great depth, beauty, and strength.

The statue of the warrior woman stands before me as does the mosaic floor, the moving Mary, and the cluster of stars in the shipping knots. The shadow of Idrusa crosses my vision. The soft salt-laden breeze brushes against my cheek. The sun gently caresses my shoulder as I nestle one last time on the terrace, watching the pale gray of dawn burst into flames.

The loudspeaker announcing my flight intrudes, the memories dissolve. I open my eyes watching the warm Salento sun set and the dreary Atlanta evening close in.

I board the plane. Strapping myself into my seat, I clasp the mosaic in my lap and immediately fall asleep.

Home

A Casa

THE LANDING GEAR SMACKS the runway, jolting me awake. The plane taxis into place, shuddering to a stop. Tucking the mosaic under my arm, I gather my belongings and deplane. In the waiting area, I sidestep the crowds, kneeling to slide the mosaic into my bag. The *blu* Salento sun struggles against the overstuffed bag. Rearranging the contents, I take another look, knowing it will stay tucked away until I show it to Ray.

That last look returns me to Otranto. For a moment, my heart lives again in the walled village where the sun touches the sea. Where the sea kisses the rocks. Where the rocks warm my bare feet. Where my feet walk in sacred places. Where sacred places healed my heart. Where my heart lingers on the terrace.

"Otranto," I cradle the word, the place, the food, the wine, and the people into my memory. On days when rain falls in my heart, the mosaic will remind me of those sun-kissed days full of grace. Otranto will always be a part of me.

My hand touches the rough edges and the raised humility stone. Idrusa looks over my shoulder whispering, *the book*—we'll meet again in *the book*. With one final push the mosaic is safely stored. Idrusa slides in as I zip the bag closed.

I realize this is not the end of my journey, but the beginning—a continuous beginning.

Taking a deep breath, I exhale all sadness from my mind and body. I'm exhausted but exhilarated as I turn toward the long passageway leading to the terminal.

Ray awaits. His smile encompasses me like a gigantic wave. My bags swing in unison as I rush toward him. He enfolds me in arms as warm as the Salento sun.

I am home.

Epilogue

No story is a straight line. The geometry of a human life
is too imperfect and complex, too distorted by the laughter
of time and the bewildering intricacies of fate to admit
the straight line into its system of laws

~ PAT CONROY, BEACH MUSIC

WHEN FACED WITH THE choice of going home or staying, I chose to go home.

Ray later told me he wasn't sure what my choice would be until he saw me. He understood how much I wanted to stay. He understood my need for a place where I could thrive. We talked about the importance of place as I shared my story of Otranto with him. I was sorry I had felt the need to get away from home without telling him the reason. Even after the upheavals with church and family, I believed he was content to remain there.

At first, when I admitted the lie to him, which of course I did, he was hurt. But we've talked through our feelings. He's come to understand and acknowledge my intent was not to hurt him but to protect him and to save myself. I put myself first. I was depleted, still angry from past inequities. If I hadn't gone away to rest and regroup, our marriage might have been the thing that wrapped up. That would have been a dreadful mistake. Now our bond is stronger than before. The yearly contracts continue with our thirty-seventh celebration this year.

The mosaic class gave me the gift of bringing home a memory, one I can touch every day. My mosaic is not perfect. The edges are sharp, and more stones have risen to remind me of the need for humility. My bloodstains still linger in the crevices. But the mortar continues to bond the fragmented pieces together, reminding me of my mended heart.

Real trash—refuse—and my personal trash will never be neatly wrapped and disposed of, totally. It's a global issue for all of us to consider, and a personal one.

Trash has morphed into a gigantic problem. We are the designated stewards of the earth. It's our job to sort it, recycle it, and place it in the correct bin.

In the fall of 2018, Ray and I spent five weeks in Sicily, surrounded by trash. We even had one of our five trash bins stolen. And in Rome, where we spent another two weeks, trash spilled out of large containers into the streets. There wasn't a single dear lady with silver hair and starched white apron to command the trash center. It's a sad reflection when the whole world forgets how important it is to use less, buy less, and recycle what we have.

Since my return from Otranto, my personal trash is examined often to avoid accumulation. Over the years it's become manageable. My sifting through and discarding has become an empowering experience.

Another package that wasn't wrapped up was writing *the book*, the one I lied about—the one about Idrusa or Pantaleone, the one that still swirls in my thoughts and dreams.

When I first returned home, there were strong, lingering memories of my time in Otranto. Everything that came my way fell easily into the category of joy. Thanksgiving approached, and the holiday season geared up with the Salento sun still smiling on me.

Ray and I chose to spend the Christmas holidays searching for our place. We had decided on a South Carolina coastal town. Our friends Sandy and Carl encouraged our decision and went with us. Christmas dinner on a balmy wind-swept terrace overlooking the ocean brought us hope. I told myself I would write *the book* after the holidays.

But instead, darker days appeared on the horizon—days without light, days with despair, days when my travel shoes were tucked away into the farthest recesses of my closet, and we didn't have time to search for our place. It was only those sun-filled memories of Otranto that saved me when the calendar pushed ahead into the new year, and I received one of those dreaded phone calls—your sister Jean is ill. Come now.

My sister Sue and I had been working on our strained relationship. Together we drove the long highway from South Carolina to Virginia, accompanied by intermittent conversation with long stretches of silence. There was little information about what had happened. We only knew our sister was in ICU.

"She had to have an emergency colostomy," said the doctor. "But it's much worse than we thought. That's why I asked you to come. I've called in an oncologist. She's covered in cancer."

Our oldest sister Jean, still in the prime of her life, was struck full force with late-stage ovarian cancer. For eight months we cared for her. Sue and I drove back and forth—sometimes together, sometimes alone, sometimes with husbands, sometimes with our sister Claudia. Our lives didn't matter. Neither did our differences. The small amount of time remaining for Jean was our only focus.

During those eight months, anniversaries, birthdays, friendships, children, and husbands were all relegated to the back burner of our lives. Our beloved George, one of three rescue children, the furry kind, needed to leave Ray and me—setting me back further. There was no time for Ray and me to grieve together.

And, after months of surgeries, hospital stays, and chemo, Jean said, "Enough."

We brought her home. On the first of August, hospice came. We called Claudia and said "Come. Now." On the night of August 12, we gathered on the bed of our lovely sister Jean, a frail skeleton of her full-bloomed life. We held hands along with Maurice (one of Jean's rescue cats who rarely left her side during her illness), his small black-and-white paw always touching her hand.

We reminisced about the days we playacted *Little Women*. The four sisters of that long-ago and much beloved novel—Meg, Jo, Beth and Amy—were forever sisters just like us—Jean, Claudia, Sue and Donna.

As children, we had laughed when Sue became angry because she was stuck playing the role of Beth, the sister who dies midway through the book. She felt cheated when she was left out of the remaining scenes.

But it was Jean leaving us this time—*our Jean*—our butterfly sister of a thousand talents, the sister with the glorious voice and the nimble fingers who could stroke a violin into life and sing like an angel. She could design intricate purses from thin air and stitch delicate baby clothes with ease. And when she wasn't engaged in these activities, she baked. She had been a model in her younger years and had developed into a glamorous fashionista. At birth she was given the smile, so radiant that long after baby cuteness evaporated, people noticed her and wanted to know her.

The morning of August thirteenth, just before dawn, she left us. Maurice retreated from the room, never to enter it again. We wept.

But grieving wasn't allowed. There were simply too many tasks to accomplish: obituaries to write, a cremation and memorial service to arrange, death notifications, wills and estates to work through, endless phone calls, bills to pay, thank-you notes to write, friends to take to lunch for all they'd done for her—and the most painful task of all—sorting through her life to determine which parts to dispose of and which to keep. Numbness locked in, pushing grief away for another day.

Finally, in October 2013, I returned home.

While caring for my sister, my much-needed eye surgery had been scheduled, postponed, and rescheduled. Although stressed and full of grief, I showed up—only to have the surgery go horribly wrong. My right eye hemorrhaged during the procedure. I lost my sight. The light from the *blu* Salento sun went out.

After weeks of agonizing pain and fear, I regrouped. Ray and I searched for and found our forever place in Beaufort, South Carolina. It worked its magic on both of us. Tiny rays of the Salento sun rekindled. We made an offer on a house built in the late 1800s in the Old Commons neighborhood, a few blocks from the waterfront. On Christmas Eve, 2013, we celebrated at Griffin Market, not realizing at the time we were at Pat Conroy's favorite restaurant in town—a chance reservation and a second meeting of a grand man with a grand talent. The lie I had told earlier now found a home to write the truth.

But there was still more grieving to do. Our beautiful orange tabby cat Wrecks, decided it was time to join his brother, George. So, another one of our furry children left us.

There were more eye surgeries in the new year, each one bringing extreme pain but gradually more sight. We moved into our Beaufort home in April 2014 with our last rescue child Barney, not knowing he would leave us in the fall. These beautiful creatures provided so much love for so many years. We were left in a large, vacant cavity, lingering in grief, a solid year full of mourning and changing direction.

And one day, when that year was over, while cleaning out my closet, I found my traveling shoes.

"It's time we celebrate," I said to Ray as I showed him the article—the one about Andrea Bocelli's annual concert on his family farm in Tuscany.

"Let's go," I said. "We need a change—a celebration of life, don't you think?"

He grabbed my hand, whirling me around the room as he said, "Yes!"

And once more, the Salento sun shrouded me with its soft, warm cloak, gathering me up for another journey.

I haven't stopped sifting through, rearranging, or discarding my trash. There are some days when everything is neatly tied and placed in the correct receptacle. Those are glory days—days when Ray packs a picnic lunch and tells me to stop working on *the book*. We gather chairs, towels, books, sunscreen, and a large umbrella, driving the short twenty minutes to Hunting Island and the Atlantic coastline. We spend the day moving in tempo with the ebb and flow of the tides, our toes curling in and out of the sand.

Do I long for Otranto and the Salento sun? Sometimes, but as the years pass, not too often. The memories are always in touching distance. Moving to Beaufort gave me my forever heart place, one that matches the magic of Otranto.

But even better, Beaufort is a heart place for both of us. Ray loves this quaint coastal town as much as I do. We're in awe of the Spanish moss trailing from giant angel oaks and the river's swift current, bringing ocean breezes to ruffle the yellow Lady Banks roses, the white oleander, and the brilliant red hibiscus flourishing in our courtyard.

Beaufort wrapped its arms around us. Our new family of friends keeps expanding. We're thriving in a community of art, culture, history, and Lowcountry food. If we need an adventure other than Hunting Island, we're strategically located between Savannah and Charleston for easy day trips.

Otranto was my heart place for one amazing month. It was a pivotal point in my life. If I hadn't taken that time to be alone, to regroup, I wouldn't have had the strength or courage to care for my sister Jean, to survive her loss and the loss of our boys. The month away taught me that fragmented hearts can be repaired and that trash can be discarded. It gave me tools I would need to endure all the dark spots and bumps in my journey. It gave me the power to surface once again.

I haven't been back to Otranto. I needed it in a different time and place in my life. The joy of that experience remains with me. Each time I glance at the middle shelf in my office, I recognize the woman who created the *blu* Salento sun out of fragmented stones.

If my spirit lags, I can transport myself to my special place on the seawall, the indigo waves lapping the rocks below, the salt breezes tickling through my hair, the warrior woman standing strong, Idrusa whispering in my ear. That enchantment stays with me—magic, martyrs, mosaics, and the music.

When I returned home, I brought my mended, intact heart with me. There's a peacefulness as I move toward the last hoorah of my life. There are more mysteries left to discover, more books to read and to write, more I love yous to say, more hugs to give, more food and wine around the table, and more adventures for Ray and me to share.

Otranto was my Atlantis, rising out of the sea at a time in my life when I needed to see it and believe in it. It will always shimmer for me. It will always be the place where I regained myself and the place where *the book—this book*—was conceived.

But the birth and baptism of *this book* belong to the people of Beaufort, South Carolina. Beaufort is home—our home, our place by the sea.

Grande Gioia—Great Joy!

Donna Keel Armer, January 2020

Acknowledgments

THE BIRTHING OF A book requires a community. My community expands this grand country of my birth and reaches across the ocean to Italy—my two heart places: Beaufort, South Carolina, and Otranto, Italy. These two towns and the generosity of friends and strangers gave voice to my writing spirit, which led to the creation of *Solo in Salento: A Memoir*.

Grazie mille to all the gracious people in both countries who offered assistance and support on my writing journey.

The first readers were a small group of friends who received my 2012 travelogue and encouraged me to write *Solo in Salento* from those notes, photographs, and sketches.

Jeff Baker read *Solo in Salento* when it was just forming with a few chapters and Connie Kling read the book when it had expanded into forty-four chapters.

The Sea Island Spirit Writers, led by the wondrous Katherine Tandy Brown, have been part of *Solo in Salento* since its inception. Ellen, Emily, Ginny, Jackie, and Kim and later Deb, June, and Susan all provided tough love and honest critique.

Gail Greene, my friend and double-duty beta reader, requires the deepest level of thanks. She has read every one of the numerous versions of *Solo in Salento*. It was our mutual love of Italy that brought us together. Her thoughts, suggestions and unwavering belief in my story have been countless. *Grazie mille la carissima amica.*

Deb Duer and Kris Peterson read the new and improved close-to-final revision. There were still errors and changes to be made and they found them.

Thank you to Cindy Whitman, my first ever development editor, who said, "It's a good book, but I don't know the person writing it. Write yourself into the story." What a challenge that has been, but what a difference it made.

Manual Brower, my lovely Italian friend and teacher, corrected all my gross errors in the Italian language. And Stefano Tirani, friend and neighbor, also reviewed my less than accurate Italian before submission.

The Pat Conroy Literary Center has been a significant player in *Solo in Salento*.

Executive Director Jonathan Haupt understands and practices Pat Conroy's command to pay it forward. He is gracious with his time and knowledge. Also, a large thank you to the PCLC volunteers who welcomed me into their midst.

A royal thank-you goes to the larger-than-life Pat Conroy. I first met him at a book signing of Beach Music in 1995 in Cincinnati, Ohio. I didn't know I would move to his beloved Beaufort, South Carolina in 2014 and have the honor to meet him again. At that meeting, he shared with me his profound joy of life in the shake of his hand, in the tilt of his head as he listened intently to what I had to say. He embraced me as a long-lost friend. Without knowing me, he included me. His prose continues to sing musical notes in my head and heart. It's a song of joy.

Rebecca Bruff has been so generous in sharing her writing, publishing, social media, and book-launching experiences. Rebecca's book *Trouble the Water* is beautifully written. Rebecca also introduced me to David Larkin. His editorial encouragement propelled me to publish. And Rebecca introduced me to the main stars at Koehler Books, John Koehler and Joe Coccaro—two men and their staff who have changed my life forever.

Sandy and Carl are friends who endured much and still send sunshine into the world. Thank you special friends of my heart, particularly for allowing me to include parts of your story.

Thank you to new friends and supporters: Marly, Mihai, Cassandra, Cele and Lynn. Your generosity is humbling.

Grazie mille to Paolo Maragliulo, a generous man who welcomed me to his beloved Puglia and gave me the gift of passing through Salento.

To all the people of Otranto who offered me hospitality—Franco, Carlo, Giovanni, the owner of *Il Cantico dei Cantici*, the chef, and especially Francesco, who made every meal an event. To Fredrika, Mateo, and all who welcomed me to the table, *grazie mille*.

To all my sisters—the blood ones, the friend ones, the cyber ones and the sisterhood of the Old Commons neighborhood—thank you. A special thank you to Laine Andrew, a friend who now resides somewhere in the larger universe. She encouraged me to write *Solo in Salento* before the first word was written. Even in her last few days she unselfishly said, "You were born to write."

A special thank-you to Ray, who cooked every meal for months while I did my final rewrite. Thank you for being wise enough to stay out of my office, even when the papers, books, magazines, and goodness knows what else piled up on every available surface. You are my steadfast love.

To everyone who has listened *ad nauseam* to my endless ramblings about Solo in Salento.

Grazie mille a tutti.

And finally to YOU, the readers—the people who will determine the fate of *Solo in Salento*.

In *Shadow of the Wind*, Carlos Ruiz Zafon writes, "Every book ... has a soul. The soul of the person who wrote it and of those who read it and lived and dreamed with it. Every time a book changes hands, every time someone runs his eyes down its pages, its spirit grows and strengths."

YOU THE READERS—are the spirit of *Solo in Salento.*

Author's Notes

SOLO IN SALENTO: A Memoir is a work of creative nonfiction. My recollection of events, locales, and conversations are based on copious notes, travelogues, photographs, sketches, and memories collected during my stay in Otranto, Italy. Of course, all memory is flawed; and my grasp of Italian is minimal, making the dialogue with Italian speakers my best guess, based on circumstances and nuances. I tried to relate the conversations to evoke the feeling and meaning of what was said. Some names and identifying details have been changed to protect the privacy of individuals.

Solo in Salento: A Memoir is being launched is the midst of the 2020 COVID-19 pandemic. We are living in isolation, using terms like "shelter-in-place" and "social distancing." It's a time when humans suffer, yet the earth is renewed. As with all of life—the good versus the bad, the yang and yin, light and dark—we are challenged. We are wounded and face a brave new world as we seek to emerge from this crisis. It's a time for reflection and a chance to be better, kinder, gentler with each other and ourselves.

" . . . find out where joy resides, and give it a voice far beyond singing. For to miss the joy is to miss all." Robert Louis Stevenson.

Recommended Reading

Corona, Francesco. *The Mystery of Otranto's Mosaic.* 2004

Corti, Maria. *Otranto.* Translated by Bright, Jessie. New York: Italica Press, Inc. 1993

Estes, Clarissa Pinkola, PhD. *Women Who Run With the Wolves.* New York: Ballantine Books 1992

Hoffman, Daniel. *The Ottoman Empire & Early Modern Europe.* Cambridge University Press 2002

Gianfreda, Grazio. *Guide to Otranto.* Lecce: Edizioni Grifo 2011

William, Terry Tempest. *Finding Beauty in a Broken World* and *When Women Were Birds*